GW01607886

Blended Quilts II

From IN THE BEGINNING

MARSHA MCCLOSKEY

contents

Preface

Sharon Yenter and I met over 25 years ago when we both had small children to care for, and were working from our homes making patchwork items to sell at craft fairs. When Sharon opened her store, In the Beginning Fabrics, she hired me to teach basic quiltmaking classes. Over the years, there were times when our quilting paths diverged and we didn't spend much time together but, every year in December, Sharon would invite me to lunch for my birthday and we would go Christmas shopping.

We both looked forward to these outings as a chance to catch up and share new ideas. At our annual lunch in 2000, Sharon was bubbling with enthusiasm about a new project. She had just written and published "Floral Bouquet Quilts," a book that emphasized the use of large floral prints, and she wanted to do another that would put more emphasis on historical quilts and prints from our quilting history. Sharon knew of my love of old quilts and romantic, large-scale prints...would I be interested in collaborating on this new book? Well, of course! We happily blended our talents and our quilts and, in 2002, "Blended Quilts" was published. Sharon's "Blended Wall Quilts" followed in 2003, and I'm completing the "trilogy" with "Blended Quilts II."

The quilts in this book were created by an ensemble of quilters. At our organizational meeting, I challenged these talented ladies to create quilts within a certain framework. For the most part, we've planned quilts with large setting pieces and wide borders to showcase, not virtuoso patchwork, but the breath-taking designs and colors of the printed cloth. Each quilter rose to the challenge and created a uniquely beautiful quilt. As you sit down with this book, I hope you will savor and enjoy each one.

Introduction

Quilt Design Styles

When I first started quilting back in the late 1960s, the quilts that most attracted me were those made in the late 1800s. My favorites had intricate piecing, small prints, reserved colors, and high contrast. My favorite pieced design, the Feathered Star, was immensely popular around 1880.

Several years ago, I became interested in the pieced quilts of the early 1800s. These quilts have a different look. The dominant fabrics are large-scale chintz florals suitable for home furnishings, and the piecing is much simpler. The floral prints are flamboyant and colorful when compared to the darker, smaller prints popular later in the century. Not only were the early prints larger and brighter, they were used all together without much regard for color contrast or change in scale. Fabrics sewn next to each other sometimes blended visually one into the next, and pieced designs were lost in the exuberance of the printed cloth. They were the first Blended Quilts.

Pieced quilts from the late 1700s and early 1800s seem to fall into three general design groups: repeated block, strippy, and framed medallion. The quilt designs in this book all fit into one of these three groups, and there is a section devoted to each group. Introductions to each section tell about these quilt design styles and how to work with them.

What Does Blended Mean?

"Blended" refers to how the colors and designs on printed fabric interact. In these quilts, colors and motifs "blend" from one patch to the next, often "losing" the construction line where the prints meet. The edges of sewn patches become invisible and new figures or images emerge, created by the combinations of motifs printed on the cloth. There is a tension and built-in visual ambiguity created when the two strong visual images of geometric patchwork and printed floral motifs are used together. In Blended Quilts, by limiting the geometric element to simple patchwork designs and large pieces, we let the fabric win.

The root word for "blend" is blind. Synonyms for blend are: mix, mingle, blur, meet, merge, and marry. Another word to think about in this process is confuse: with the base words "found"— to establish, and "con" — to bring together; to confuse is to mix utterly. But these quilts should not go as far as disorder, disarray, jumble, muddle, or chaos.

Making a successful Blended Quilt is an exercise in a just-barely controlled mixing of colors, motifs, values, and shapes. The more orderly among quilters may find the process uncomfortable, as there is potential for the design to turn into a jumble of colors and prints that is difficult to look at, but with a little practice, quilters will soon develop complete control of their design. The results are well worth the effort.

Fabrics

You won't be able to duplicate our quilts exactly, but we can give you strategies for achieving their richly blended look. Many, but not all, of the fabrics we chose are reproductions of print styles popular in the late 1700s and early 1800s. Prints have personality, and the prints from that period had an elegant, romantic quality. We're also using some of the watercolor techniques developed by quilters during the 1990s to create a contemporary decorator look, somewhat like the warm, eclectic, and relaxed style of Shabby Chic.

The print styles that give the Blended look are described on pages 7-9. Collecting the fabrics is half the fun, but read this next section carefully before you go shopping.

Focus Prints: Chintz and Large-Scale Spaced-Florals

Chintz was considered the prestige fabric for quilts in the 1800s. Many beautiful reproduction prints are currently available and will give your Blended Quilt an equally lovely antique look. For your focus fabric, look for one or two large-scale spaced-floral or scenic prints with lots of colors. A spaced-floral is a print with fairly wide spaces between the large bouquets or flowers — perfect for wide borders, large alternate squares, and setting triangles. Large-scale "packed" florals with the motifs close together are not nearly as useful for focus prints. Large prints can be "selectively" cut (see pages 11-12) to feature particular motifs or they can be randomly cut, letting motifs fall where they may. Experiment and see which you like best.

Large-Scale Spaced-Floral

Packed Floral

Stripes and Border Prints

Some large-scale prints have a striped element in them and are fantastic for borders and the wide strips in strippy quilts. (See the pillar print in the Flying Geese strippy quilt on page 76.) Medium-scale striped motifs are useful for narrower borders. Shaded ombré-style stripes are especially wonderful blenders.

Look for simpler, smaller-scale stripes as well. These can provide a linear quality to patches, providing occasional visual relief from too many curves and flowers.

Small-Scale Stripe

Ombré Stripe

Flowing Stripe

Medium-Scale Spaced-Florals

To go with your focus prints, choose some floral prints of a slightly smaller scale and with fewer colors. Again, having motifs with spaces between them is important. Look for curves and vines as part of the overall design. These fabrics are used for creating a bridge across seam lines. Different floral prints blend together and create a flowing pattern from block to block.

Scenic Prints

Large-scale, multicolor pictorial prints depict scenes of animals, people, towns, plants, etc. Use a selectively cut scene for the center of a Medallion quilt, or cut the fabric randomly and surprise the viewer with tiny recognizable motifs in smaller patches.

Toiles

This style of copperplate printing reached its zenith in the 1770s in France. Pronounced "twal," these prints usually are finely etched, two-color prints perfect for block backgrounds, sashing, or pieces that need to read as quiet places. Toiles that are scenic and very directional call for careful selective cutting and arrangement (see pages 11-12).

Stash Prints

Blended Quilts are scrap quilts and you probably have many traditional prints in your collection that will work with the florals, stripes, scenics, and toiles described above. Not every print in a quilt can be a star; supporting players are needed as well. Pick many coordinating, go-with prints that are smaller in scale and have fewer colors than your focal prints.

Don't overmatch colors: the more fabrics you use in a composition, the less they need to match. For instance, as a color group, reds can range from pink to rust to red to brown.

Paisley. These designs have been popular since they originated in India in the 1600s. In Blended Quilts, their scale and visual movement make a flowing transition to other prints.

Small Prints. One- or two-color small floral prints work well in some places. Stay away from high contrast designs that appear spotty and busy.

Plaid. The most useful plaids seem to be low-contrast designs with only two or three colors that blend with the other fabrics. Straight lines introduce a rest from all the curves.

Geometrics. Like plaids, these are prints without flowers. Geometrics are linear designs often associated with men's ties, pajamas, and boxer shorts.

Quiet Prints. Look for two-color prints, or tone-on-tones, with low contrast and an all-over figure or linear design. Large-scale, flowing tone-on-tone prints are wonderful with the large-scale, multicolor florals. Visually neutral patterns can be used successfully with more busy and flamboyant prints.

Color Recipes

You will need a color recipe for your Blended Quilt. Decide which parts of the design will be dark and which light. Using colors from your focus print, assign a color definition for the light, medium, and dark. For example, the dark could be teal; the medium, rust; and the light, ecru with peach tones. Select a range of fabrics for each color in the recipe. If teal is one of the colors, pick several teal prints in differing intensities and visual textures. Pull every teal in your collection that even remotely fits the criteria. Not all of these will be used, but it is important to study the possibilities. Do the same with each color in the recipe.

Contrast and Value

In Blended Quilts, most of the fabrics you choose should have a fairly narrow range of value change, but some areas of higher contrast are needed — a few patches that are either lighter or darker than the rest. Contrast, both in color and visual texture, makes pieced designs visible.

Low-Contrast

Medium-Contrast

High-Contrast

Visual texture is the way a print looks. Is it spotty, smooth, plain, dappled, linear, rhythmical, or swirly? Are the figures spaced far apart or close together? Generally accepted quilt wisdom tells us that too many similar prints can create a dull surface or one that is visually confusing, and that we should mix large prints with small prints, and flowery allover designs with linear rhythmical prints.

Visual complexity is just what is needed in a Blended Quilt, and the old rules can be pushed. Using all small prints can be really boring, but mixing large prints can be exciting. Large prints work hard for you, making a quilt surface look more complex than just the pieced design. Small, regular prints, however, will often quiet down larger, more flamboyant ones and make them more usable. In the end, you, the quiltmaker, must be the judge of what is working in your quilt.

Tea Dying

You may discover fabrics in your collection that are too light. The old trick of tea-dyeing can work well here. You can achieve light or medium variations depending on the length of time you leave the fabric in the tea mixture.

The lighter toile is the original print. In the quilt, this toile was tea-dyed to tone down the background.

Tea-Dyeing Technique

1. Wash fabric using warm water and detergent.
2. Place 6 tea bags plus 2 teaspoons alum (used to set the color, it is available in drug stores) in a large glass bowl.
3. Bring 4 cups of water to a boil and pour into bowl. Stir with wooden spoon or chop sticks.
4. Cover bowl and allow tea to steep for 10 minutes. Remove tea bags.
5. Wet fabric completely and immerse it in tea solution in bowl.
6. Stir occasionally and check color every 10 minutes. You can get variations in color by dyeing multiple designs and removing some sooner than others. Your fabric will be much lighter dry than it appears when wet.
7. Remove when you are pleased with the color. Wash in warm, soapy water; rinse well, and hang to dry.

The Design Process

When you've chosen your quilt pattern and fabrics, it's time to do some cutting. You'll need a design wall — a piece of batting or flannel taped or pinned to the wall. Cut patches and place them on the design wall. One strategy is to cut the large setting pieces first, then cut the pieces for blocks. If you have chosen a border fabric, be sure to pin that to the design wall as well so you can keep it in view as you work.

In repeated block patterns, establish the pieced design with fairly high-contrast fabrics. Then as you progress, make succeeding blocks scrappier and more blended. As you place the sample patches next to each other, look at where the edges meet. Ideally, one fabric will blend into the next, and the seams will tend to disappear in some places. Shape and direct what the viewer sees by creating a few areas of higher contrast. Use darker, brighter, or lighter accent colors to add spice and interest. An example would be to accentuate directional rows of squares with high contrast, then break the row by continuing with much lower contrast patches.

Stand back often to get an overall view. You'll find that successive color and fabric choices will be determined by what is already on the design wall. The developing design will "tell" you what is needed next. If any one of your chosen fabrics falls short of expectations, remove it from the design wall, and audition a different fabric in its place. Try as many fabrics as necessary to get the desired effect.

A design wall allows you to arrange (and rearrange) your cut patches before sewing them together. In the Stepping Stones quilt, you can work with the small squares to relate one block to the next.

Random and Selective Cutting

The first large-scale cabbage rose fabric I ever tried was from Jeffrey Gutcheon's American Classic line. Up until then, I had believed that if you had a large motif in the fabric design, it had to be centered in each patch. Well, these flowers were larger than the patches I was cutting and I was at a complete loss. Then someone told me (sorry, I don't remember who) that if you just cut the fabric randomly, as it comes, without "fussy cutting," that it will work out fine — and it does! These random patches can be artfully arranged after they are cut. Sometimes a few will need to be cut over again if they don't quite have the right colors, but generally it's a very freeing concept that works for borders as well as blocks in Blended Quilts.

At some point, though, you will probably want to select an image (a figure or a specific part of a flower) for a particular patch. A clear ruler or "window" template can be used to locate just the part of the design you want to use. For a see-through "window" template, make a template of the desired size from translucent plastic. Mark the ¼" seam allowance on your template. Place the template on your fabric and move it around until you find a design you like. Draw around the template with a permanent pen or pencil, then cut on the marked line with fabric scissors, or with rotary cutter and acrylic ruler.

Some acrylic rulers, like the Precision Trimmer 3™, have appropriate markings for selective cutting of some sizes.

If you are making a quilt with blocks set "on point," make sure that you take this into account when selectively cutting squares from a pictorial print. Placing your template "on point" on the print will ensure that the buildings and/or figures will be right-side-up when sewn into your quilt.

Selective cutting can increase the impact of your borders. Study the pattern you are following, and the large-scale floral fabric you want to use, to decide just how you want to cut it. If you want a particular portion of the motif to show up regularly and evenly in all four borders, you will need to plan the border carefully. Pay special attention to the corners of the quilt. The width you cut the border strips is completely dependent on the design of the fabric. If the pattern says to cut 7" border strips and the portion of the design you have selected is 8", then adjust the directions to the new dimension. If your plan varies from the way the quilt in the photo was done, you may need extra yardage.

Random cutting. Start at one edge of fabric and cut border strips, letting floral motifs fall where they may.

Selective cutting. Center floral bouquets within each border strip.

Selective cutting. Center borders on "empty" vertical spaces of fabric, so that an equal amount of floral bouquet design falls at each edge of border strip.

Selective cutting. "Half and half" borders are planned so that floral bouquet motifs are on one side of the border strip, and background color is predominant on the other side of the strip.

Dense floral through border

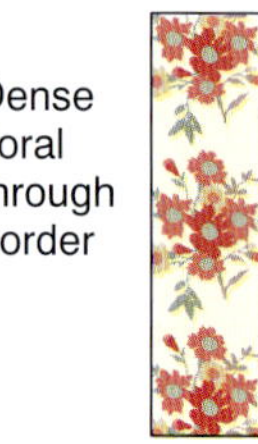

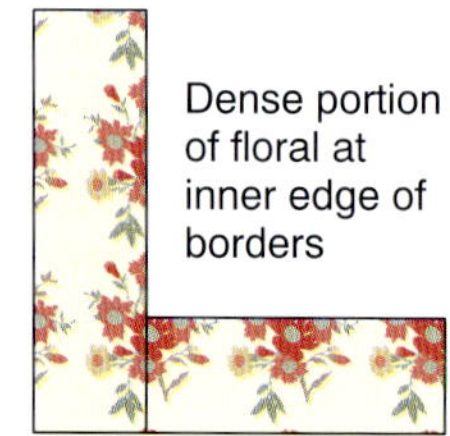

Dense portion of floral at inner edge of borders

Transitions

Close up, the fabrics you combine in your Blended Quilt will interact in different ways. Below are just some of the ways that prints can blend at the construction line between the patches. You can work for intentional transitions with selective cutting, or you can cut the prints randomly and wait for happy surprises as you place the patches side by side. Sometimes, just turning a patch or changing its placement creates better blending. As you play with the cut patches, remember that seam allowance will take away the outer ¼".

Motifs of the same color relate one fabric to the next, creating movement through the combined patches.

The background of one patch blends to the motif of another.

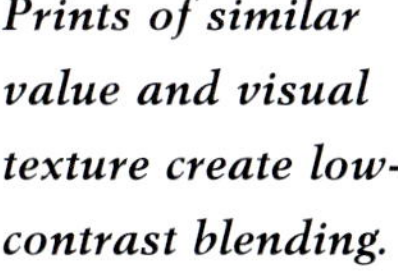

Prints of similar value and visual texture create low-contrast blending.

The figures of both patches blend at the seam line to form a new image.

Basic Quiltmaking

Supplies

- **Sewing machine.** A well-tuned machine with a good straight stitch is all that's needed for piecing your quilt top. If you plan to machine quilt your top, you'll need a walking foot (for straight-line quilting), or a darning foot (for free-motion quilting).
- **Iron and ironing board.** A shot of steam is useful.
- **Rotary cutter.** Pick one that fits your hand comfortably. The 45mm blade is a good size for most quilting applications.
- **Rotary mat.** You'll need one that's at least 18" x 24". If you have the space, a 24" x 36" mat is ideal.
- **Acrylic rulers** for rotary cutting. Handy ruler sizes for the quilts in this book are 6" x 24" and 6" x 12" for cutting strips and rectangles; 6½" x 6½" for cutting smaller pieces; and 12½" x 12½" for cutting larger pieces. The 3½" x 3½" and 6½" x 6½" Precision Trimmer™ rulers work beautifully for trimming your blocks.
- **Design wall.** Cut fabric patches can easily be arranged on this vertical surface to identify the color movement, value placement, and overall design. Look for flannel, thin batting, felt, or a product called Quilt Wall® available at many quilt shops. The advantage of Quilt Wall® is the 72" x 72" size and its holding power.
- **Scissors.** Three pairs are optimal: one for cutting fabric, one for cutting paper and plastic, and a small pair for snipping threads.
- **Sharp straight pins** for pinning seams. Have on hand rustproof safety pins if you plan to pin-baste prior to quilting.
- **Seam ripper.**
- **Tape measure.**
- **Marking tool, stencils, and yardstick** (optional) for marking quilting lines.

Fabric Tips

Buying Yardage

Blended Quilts have lots of fabrics in them. For best results, select lightweight, closely woven, 100% cotton fabrics. When a materials list calls for 1½ yards total assorted fabrics, it means that several different prints in the same color range should be chosen, and the actual combined amount needed will be 1½ yards. However, you may need to purchase more fabric to get the desired variety.

The materials list will often recommend "fat quarters." A fat quarter is a piece of fabric that measures approximately 18" x 21". Quilters like fat quarters because they provide more useable fabric than quarter yards measured off the bolt at 9". Quilt stores often sell precut fat quarters one at a time or in coordinated packets. It's a great way to get a wide variety of prints for your collection for not a lot of money. "Fat eighths" measure approximately 9" x 21".

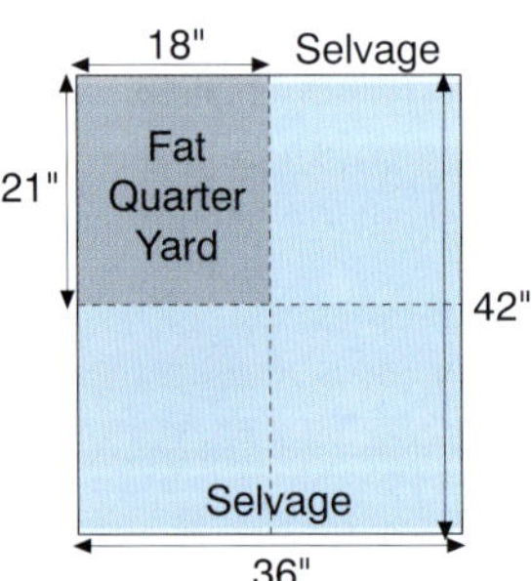

Your cutting decisions as well as the fabric design can affect yardage requirements. For the quilts in this book, yardage requirements for the floral large-scale fabrics are generous. In most cases, the borders are cut from the length of the fabric, rather than from the width, to avoid piecing seams that would create distracting breaks in printed designs. Consider cutting borders longer than needed, so you can work with the fabric to decide how you want the bouquets or other motifs to meet in the corners.

Usually there will be enough fabric leftover after cutting border strips to use in a few of the pieced blocks. This is desirable because it brings the colors of the border into the center of the quilt.

Prewashing

I preshrink my quilt fabrics before use. If you suspect a dark color will run, rinse it separately in warm water until the water remains clear. Tumble-dry fabric on warm cycle. Press gently with a hot iron on steam setting. You might find that a heavier-weight chintz print, intended for home decorating, is the perfect focal fabric for your quilt. Chintz for home decorating may have a glazed finish, which adds a shine or reflectiveness to the quilt's surface. Washing chintz removes much of the glazed finish, so if you want to maintain the polished look, don't prewash the chintz. Preshrink the other fabrics you will be using with the chintz, and dry clean your finished quilt if laundering becomes necessary.

Rotary Cutting Basics

Rotary cutting techniques are used for cutting pieces in our Blended Quilts. In the interest of accuracy, instructions for some pieced units call for pieces to be cut a little large, and then trimmed to the proper size after seams are sewn. Other units are constructed using a "sew and flip" method. Templates are provided (on pages 128-131) mainly for checking purposes, but you can use them for more traditional cutting methods if you choose.

Safety First

If you are new to rotary cutting, practice on scrap fabric first.

Always remember to:

- Keep your fingers and other body parts away from the blade (it's very sharp).
- Close the blade each time you finish cutting.
- Keep the cutter out of the reach of children.

Cutting Strips From Yardage

Fold the fabric selvage to selvage, aligning the widthwise and lengthwise grains as best you can. Place fabric on the rotary cutting mat with the folded edge closest to you. Align a square plastic cutting ruler with the fold of the fabric and place a cutting ruler to the left.

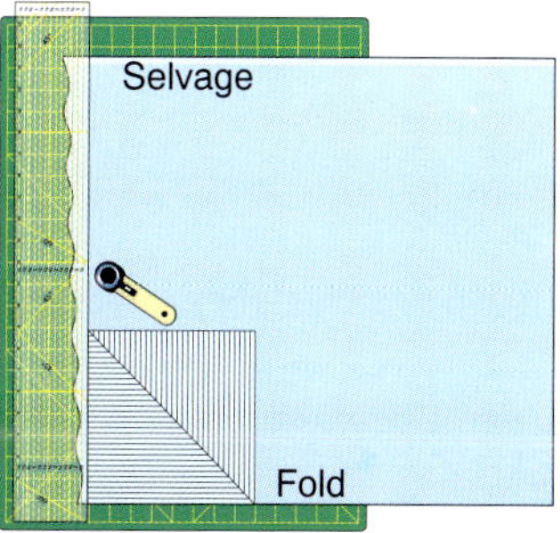

When making all cuts, fabric should be placed to your right. (If you are left handed, reverse the directions.) Remove the square plastic cutting ruler and make a rotary cut along the right side of the ruler to trim away the uneven raw edges of fabric. Be sure to hold the long ruler firmly in place, and roll the cutter away from you, cutting through all layers.

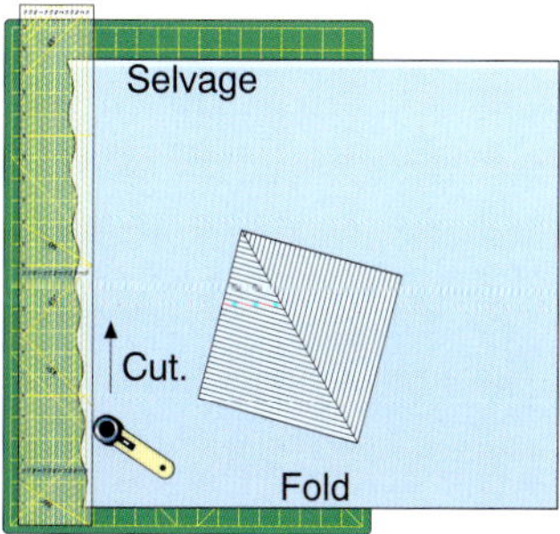

Make successive cuts measuring from the first cut. Refer to the quilt directions for the correct strip width. Position the ruler so that the strip width measurement (2" for example) is aligned with the cut edge of your fabric. Cut strip. To keep the ruler from slipping while cutting, pause occasionally and move your hand up on the ruler to maintain even pressure.

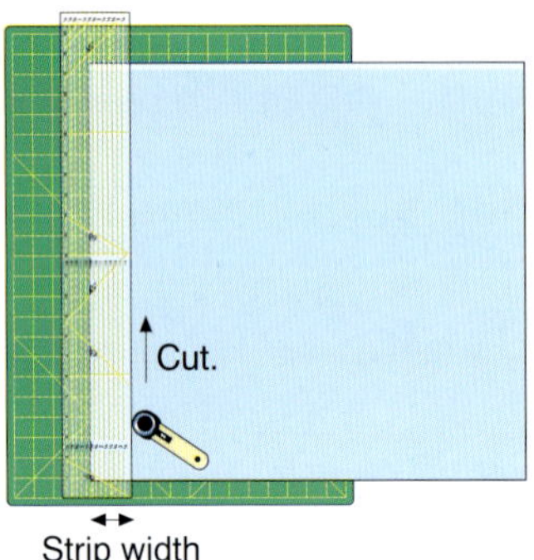

Most of the quilts in this book call for lengthwise border strips. To cut strips on the lengthwise grain, position the fabric so cuts will be parallel to the selvage. For your first cut, evenly trim away the selvage (approximately ¾"). Refer to quilt directions for correct strip width, then make successive cuts measuring from the first cut.

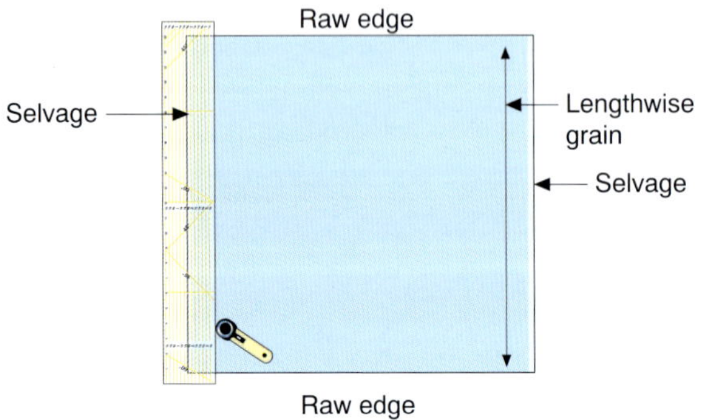

Squares and Rectangles

First cut fabric in strips the measurement of the finished square plus seam allowances. Using a square plastic cutting ruler, align the top and bottom edge of strip and cut fabric into squares the same width as the strip.

Cut rectangles in the same manner, first cutting strips the width of the finished rectangle plus seam allowances, then cutting to the proper length.

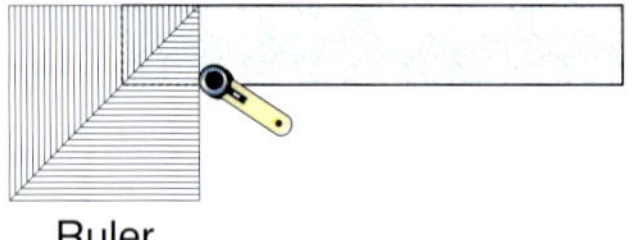

Triangles

Cut fabric in strips, then into squares the size specified in the instructions. The measurements given for half- and quarter-square triangles in the quilt directions include ¼" seam allowances. I trim points on triangles to make matching easier. See page 34 for how to trim points using the Precision Trimmer 3™ or 6™ ruler.

Half-Square Triangles

If you need a triangle with the straight grain on the short side, cut half-square triangles. Cut a square, then cut it in half diagonally once. The resulting two triangles will have short sides on the straight grain of the fabric and the long side on the bias.

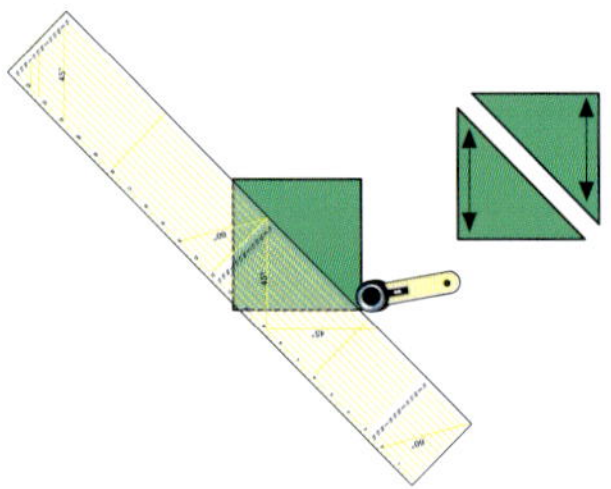

Quarter-Square Triangles

If you need a triangle with the straight grain on the long side, cut quarter-square triangles. Cut a square, then cut it in half diagonally twice. The resulting four triangles will have the long side on the straight grain and the short sides on the bias.

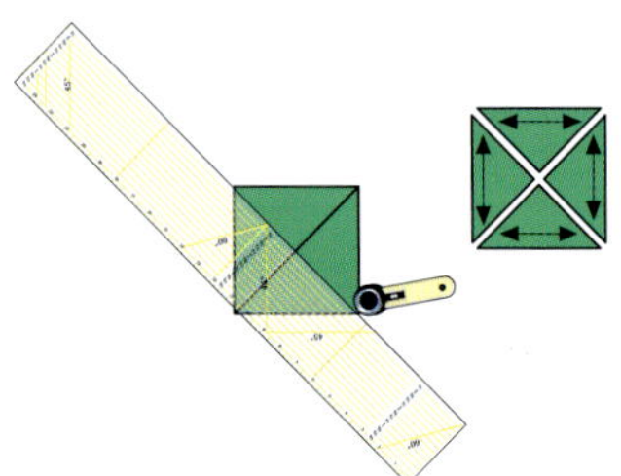

Machine Piecing

Use 100 percent cotton thread as light as the lightest fabric in the project. Most quilters choose one color of thread — usually white or a neutral color — and use it to piece the whole quilt regardless of color changes in the fabric. Sew exact ¼" seams. On some machines the width of the presser foot is ¼" and can be used as a guide. If you don't have such a foot, you'll need to establish the proper seam allowance on your sewing machine. Place a piece of quarter- or eighth-inch graph paper under the presser foot and gently lower the needle onto the line that is ¼" from the edge of the paper. Lay a piece of masking tape at the edge of the paper to act as the ¼" guide.

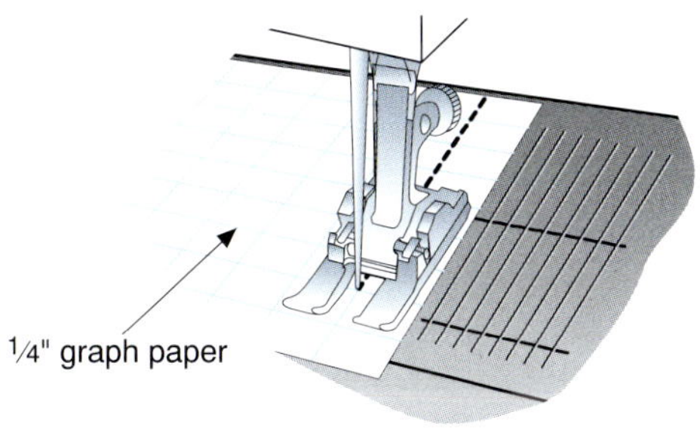

For the patterns in this book, sew from cut edge to cut edge. Backtacking is generally unnecessary.

Chain Piecing

Chain piecing is a great time-saver.

1. Sew the first set of pieces together and continue stitching off the edge for a few stitches, creating a "chain" of thread.
2. Without lifting the presser foot, arrange the next set of pieces and feed it under the foot while you sew. Continue in this manner until all of your sets have been stitched.
3. Remove the "chain" from the sewing machine and clip the threads between the stitched units.

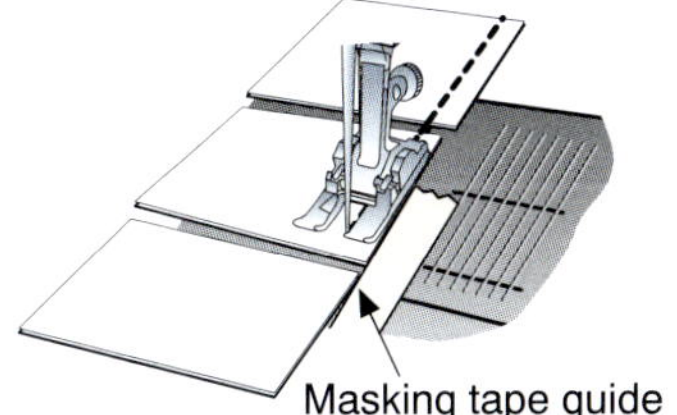

Pressing

In the quilts in this book, most seams are pressed to one side, toward the darker fabric whenever possible. Sometimes, for matching purposes, seams are pressed in opposite directions, regardless of which is the darker fabric. We sometimes press seams open to distribute bulk, as in the Pinwheel blocks on page 73.

Press with a dry iron that has a shot of steam when needed. Take care not to overpress. First, press the sewn seam flat to "set" it. Next, press the seam open or to the side as desired. Press from both the right and wrong sides to make the seam flat without little pleats at the ends.

Pinning

Pin seams before stitching if matching is involved, or if your seams are longer than 4". Pin points of matching (where seam lines or points meet) first. Once these important points are in place, pin the rest of the seam, easing if necessary.

Matching

1. Opposing seams. When stitching one seamed unit to another, press seam allowances on seams that need to match in opposite directions. The two "opposing" seams will hold each other in place and evenly distribute the bulk.

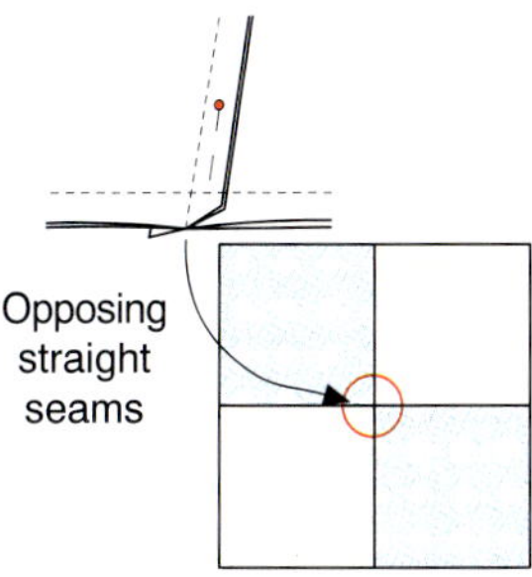

Often, the opposing seams are diagonal seams. Plan pressing to take advantage of opposing seams.

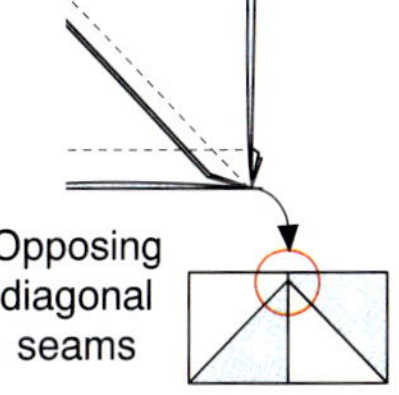

2. Positioning pin. Carefully push a pin straight through two points that need to match. Pull the pin tight to establish the proper point of matching. Pin the seam normally and remove the positioning pin before stitching.

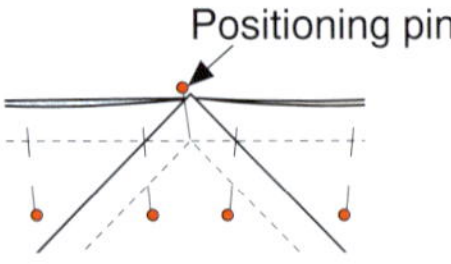

3. The X. When triangles are pieced, stitches will form an X at the next seam line. Stitch through the center of the X to make sure the points on the sewn triangles will not be chopped off.

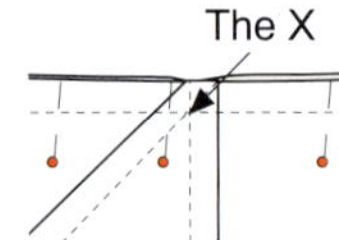

4. Easing. When two pieces to be sewn together are supposed to match but instead are slightly different lengths, pin the points of matching and lightly steam press the seam before stitching. Stitch with the shorter piece on top. The feed dog eases the fullness of the bottom piece.

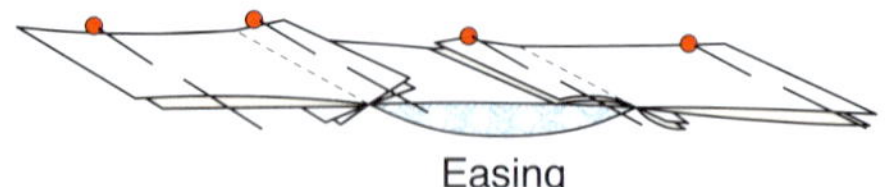

Check Your Work

Piecing a quilt top is always easier if you are accurate and check your work as you go along. Many of our quilts use pieced units (half- and quarter-square triangle units and fourpatches) that finish at 3". This means that before these units are sewn to other pieces, they should measure exactly 3½" from raw edge to raw edge.

Use the Precision Trimmer 6™ (or Precision Trimmer 3™) to check your work. Position the ruler on the pieced units as pictured and trim the edges to make perfect 3½" squares. In some patterns, this ruler is also used to trim down pieced units that have been intentionally made larger than needed.

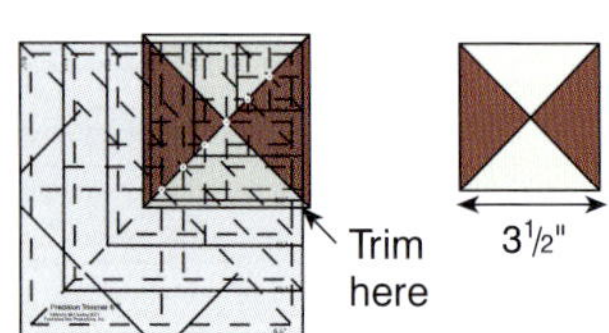

Setting the Quilt Blocks Together

Each quilt pattern has a Quilt Assembly Diagram showing how the parts will be sewn together. In repeated block patterns, pieced blocks and setting pieces are sewn together in rows. Sometimes the rows go across the quilt and sometimes on the diagonal. When sewing the rows together, press for opposing seams and pin all points of matching.

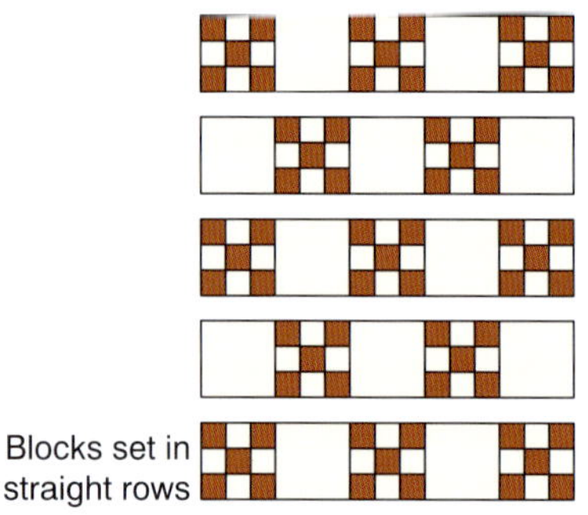

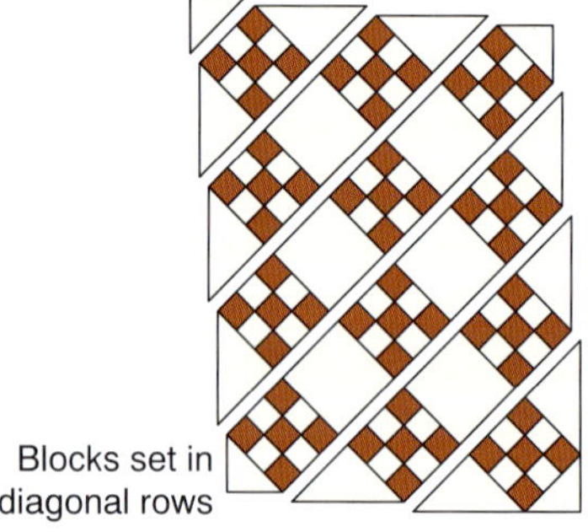

Borders

The borders for most of the quilts in this book are straight-sewn wide strips of fabric sewn to the sides and then to the top and bottom edges of the quilt top. If you prefer mitered corners for any of the quilts that have straight-sewn corners, you may need additional yardage to cut longer border strips.

Attaching Borders with Straight-Sewn Corners

1. To cut the two side borders to the correct length, measure the quilt top length through the center. (On large quilts, it's a good idea to measure the length along both outer edges as well and use an average of the three measurements.) Cut the two strips this length.

2. Mark the center and quarter points on both the quilt top and border strips.
3. Matching ends, centers, and quarter points, pin border strips to the quilt top. Pin generously, and press along the matched edges to set the seam before sewing. A shot of steam will help with any easing that might be required.
4. Using a ¼" seam allowance, stitch the border to the quilt top. Press the seam allowance to one side as directed in the quilt instructions.
5. Repeat steps 1-4 to measure the quilt width (including the borders just added), cut, and attach the top and bottom borders.

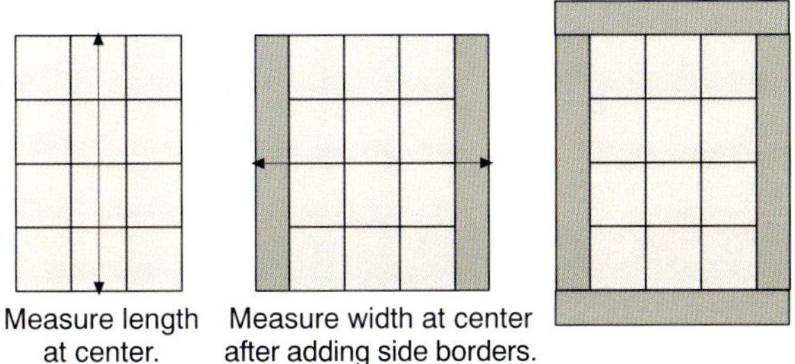

Attaching Borders with Mitered Corners

1. Estimate the finished outer dimensions of the quilt top after the borders have been added. For example, if your quilt top is 45" x 65" and the finished border width is 8", the quilt top will measure 61" x 81" (quilt dimensions plus two finished border widths). Cut border strips to these dimensions plus at least 2" extra for seam allowances and adjustments. It's always a good idea to play it safe and cut the strips a little longer than necessary.
2. Measure the quilt top through the center in both directions and note the measurements.
3. Mark the centers and quarter points on all four edges of the quilt top.
4. With pins, mark the length of the quilt top on the side border strips. Also mark the center and quarter points.

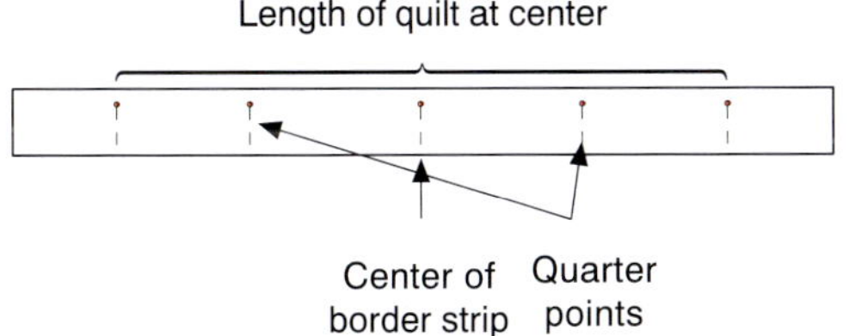

5. Pin the side borders to the quilt top, matching raw edges at the outer pins, centers, and quarter points.
6. Stitch, beginning and ending the stitching ¼" from the raw edges of the quilt top.

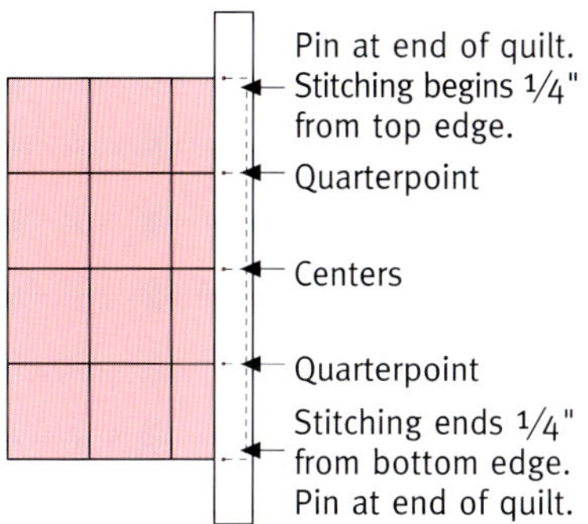

7. Repeat with the top and bottom borders.
8. Working on a large, flat, padded surface or the ironing board, fold the quilt so that the borders at one corner of the quilt are aligned with right sides together and raw edges even. Pin the borders together as shown. If possible, anchor the quilt top to the work surface with pins. Use a ruler and pencil to draw a 45° stitching line on the wrong side of the border. Begin at the end of the stitching and keep the edge of the ruler even with the folded edge of the quilt top.

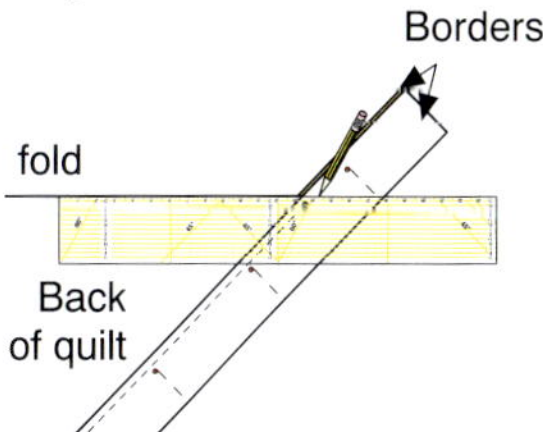

9. Machine baste on the drawn line. Open out the corner and check for accuracy. Adjust if necessary.
10. Stitch on the drawn line, beginning at the inner corner and ending at the border raw edges. Trim the excess, leaving a ¼"-wide seam allowance.

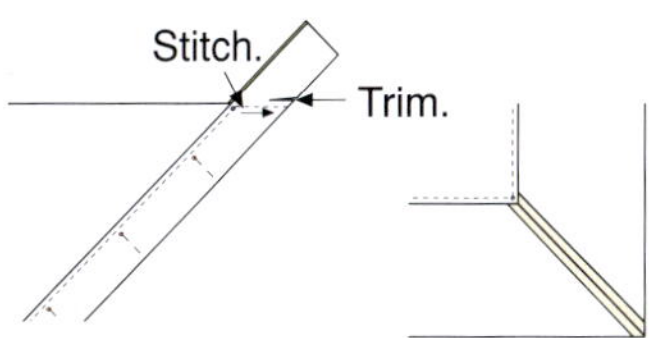

11. Press the seam open. Repeat with the remaining three corners.

Finishing Your Quilt

Backing and Batting

For all the quilts in this book, you will need to make the backing by cutting and sewing two or more lengths of fabric together.

1. Add 8" to the length and width of the completed quilt top for a working allowance (4" all the way around).
2. To make a backing that is large enough, cut lengths of fabric and sew them together on the long sides. Press the seams open. You can sew two lengths together with one center seam, or split the second length and sew the pieces to each side of the other length of fabric. Sometimes, to save fabric, it is best to cut and piece the backing so the seam runs across the width of the quilt.

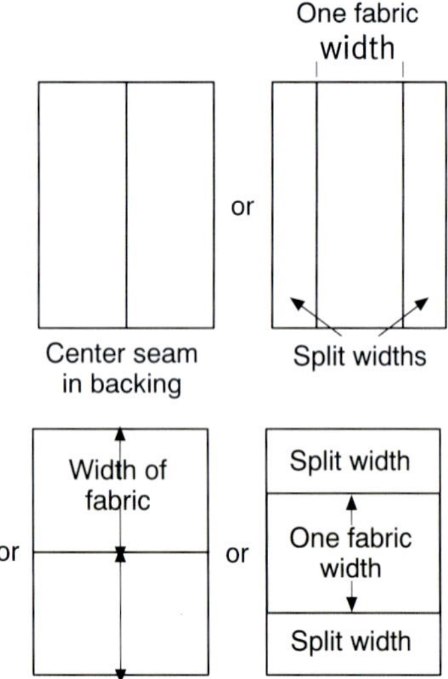

3. Choose a thin cotton or cotton-polyester blend batting in a size that is longer and wider than your quilt top. Trim batting to size of backing.

Layering the Quilt

1. Lay the backing face down on a large, clean, flat surface — the floor or a large table. With masking tape, tape the backing down to keep it smooth and flat while you are working with the other layers. If you are working on a table, part of the quilt will probably hang over the sides. Begin in the quilt center and work in sections toward the sides and ends.
2. Gently lay the batting on top of the backing, centering and smoothing it as you go.
3. Center the freshly ironed quilt top on top of the batting, right side up. Starting in the middle, gently smooth out fullness to the sides and corners. Take care not to distort the straight lines of the quilt design and the borders.
4. Use safety pins to hold the layers together, spacing them no more than a hand's width apart, or hand baste through all layers in the pattern shown, using light-colored thread. Start in the middle and make a line of long stitches to each corner to form a large X. Continue basting in a grid of parallel lines 6"-8" apart. Finish with a row of basting around the outside edges — ¼" away from the edge.

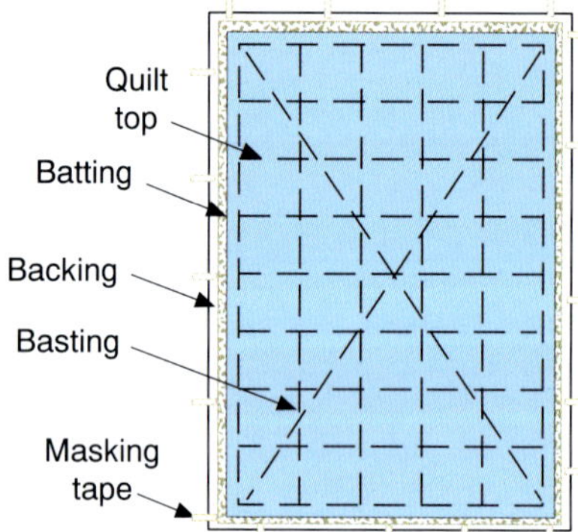

Quilting

The fabrics used in Blended Quilts make a quilt surface rich in design and color. Frankly, fancy quilting designs on some parts of these quilts simply won't show, so we try to plan simple designs to complement our simple piecing.

Quilting lines should be evenly distributed over the quilt surface. Directions that come with your batting will tell how close the quilting lines must be to keep the batting from coming apart when the quilt is washed. Avoid tight complicated designs that then require similar quilting over the whole quilt. Likewise avoid leaving large areas unquilted.

Some quilters prefer to mark their quilt top with quilting lines before it is assembled with the backing and batting. To do this, you will need marking pencils; a long ruler or yardstick; stencils or templates for quilting motifs; and a smooth, clean, hard surface on which to work. Thoroughly press the quilt top. Use a sharp marking pencil and lightly mark the quilting lines on the fabric. No matter what kind of marking tool you use, light lines will be easier to remove than heavy ones.

Quilt the layers together by hand or machine. This is a little sentence to cover a big subject. If this is your first quilt, be sure to check your quilt shop or library for some of the excellent books entirely devoted to hand quilting and machine quilting.

Binding

After quilting, machine-baste close to the quilt's edge, through all three layers. Trim excess batting and backing even with the edge of the quilt top. A rotary cutter and long acrylic ruler will ensure accurate straight edges before you apply the binding.

1. Cut binding strips 2½" wide, either with the straight grain of the fabric or on the bias. Join the strips together using diagonal seams as shown. Make enough continuous binding to go around the four sides of the quilt plus 6" - 10" for overlap.

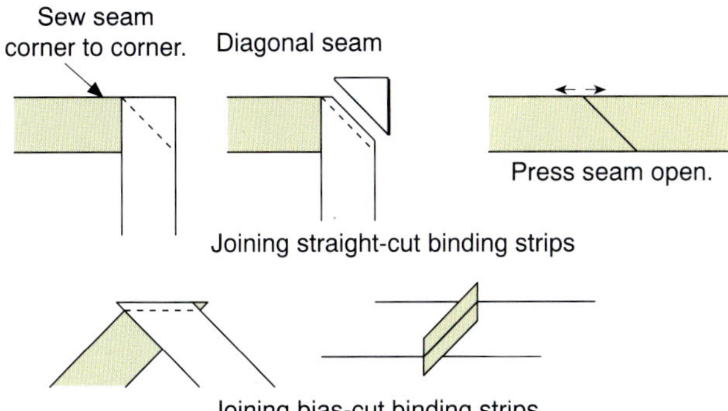

2. Fold the binding in half lengthwise with wrong sides together and press, taking care not to stretch it. At one end, open out the fold and turn the raw edge in at a 45° angle. Press. Trim, leaving a ¼" seam allowance.

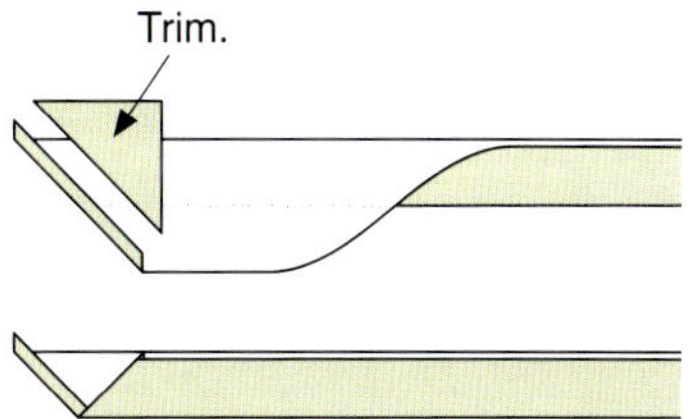

3. Beginning on one edge of the quilt a few inches from a corner, pin the binding to the quilt top. Beginning two inches from the folded end of the binding, stitch ⅜" from the raw edges and stop ⅜" from the raw edge at the corner. Backstitch and remove the quilt.

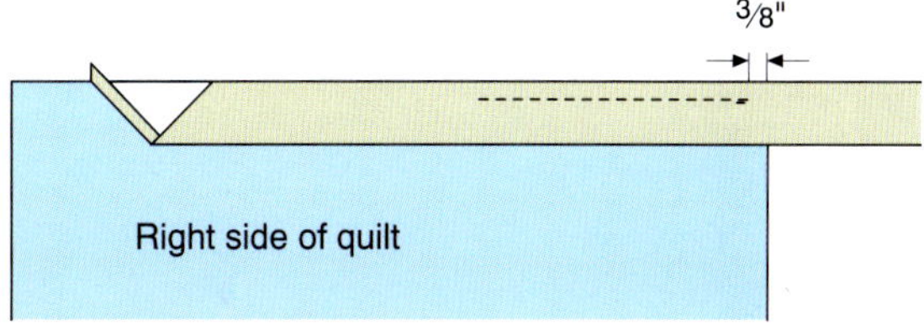

4. Fold the binding back on itself to create a 45° angle, then turn the binding down to make a fold in the binding that is in line with the upper raw edge of the quilt top. Pin. Stitch the binding to the quilt, ending ⅜" from the next corner. Backstitch and miter the corner as you did the previous one.

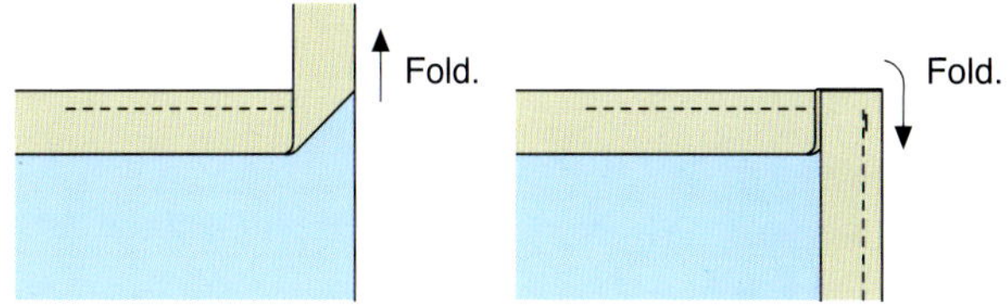

5. Continue in this manner until the binding has been stitched to all four edges of the quilt top. When you reach the beginning of the binding, trim away excess, leaving 1" to tuck into the folded binding. Complete the stitching.
6. Turn the binding to the back of the quilt and hand sew in place, mitering corners as shown.

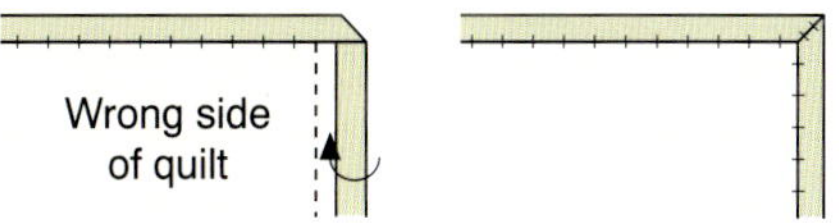

Burgundy Star

Cathedral of Roses

Gypsy Rondo

Robin's Nest

Stepping Stones

Repeated Block Quilts

In quiltmaking, when patchwork blocks are sewn together to make a quilt top, it is called the "set." Our first five quilt patterns are repeated block designs set in various ways. The repeated block style gained popularity in America during the early 1800s, and by 1850 became the dominant style.

In Gypsy Rondo, the star blocks are set straight and separated by set pieces called lattices or sashing strips. The Stepping Stones and Burgundy Star quilts contain diagonally set blocks, separated by alternating unpieced squares, with setting triangles filling in the outside edges. Cathedral of Roses and Robin's Nest have diagonally set blocks with alternate pieced blocks that create secondary designs.

The look of Blended Quilts depends mostly on the fabrics chosen. We let the fabric do the work and keep the piecing simple. Fabrics for borders and setting pieces are usually chosen first. These focus prints establish the color and style of the quilt. Look for gorgeous large-scale spaced-florals and border prints. Plan to use them mostly in the largest pieces of the design, but also in some of the piecing.

The directions for most of the quilts in this book instruct you to cut setting pieces and border strips first, and put them up on your design wall to form a framework. Blocks are then cut and pieced to fill in the blank spaces. This is the most successful way to approach the Blended process, but not the only way. You may want to piece blocks first and choose setting pieces and borders later. It is sometimes a good idea to put off actually cutting the large pieces until you are absolutely sure where you want them.

The patterns, as presented, are for only one size of quilt. This may or may not suit your needs. Will your quilt hang on the wall, be a throw, or cover a bed? Once you have decided how large you want the project to be, it is easy to add or subtract rows of blocks and setting pieces to reach your ideal quilt size. The illustrations on the next page show how to make Gypsy Rondo and Stepping Stones into bed-size quilts. You would, of course, need to purchase more fabric, make more blocks, and adjust the length of the borders.

Gypsy Rondo
Double to queen-size
Finished size: approximately $82\frac{1}{2}$" x 93"

- Make 30 pieced 9" blocks
- Cut twenty-five 2" x $9\frac{1}{2}$" rectangles for horizontal sashing
- Cut four 2" by 62" strips for vertical sashing
- Cut inner borders $2\frac{1}{2}$" wide
- Make 2 Ladder borders $6\frac{1}{2}$" x $55\frac{1}{2}$"*
- Make 2 Ladder borders $6\frac{1}{2}$" x 66"*
- Make 4 pieced 6" blocks
- Cut outer borders 8" wide

* *May need to trim to fit.*

Stepping Stones
Double to queen-size
Finished size: approximately 85" x 96"

- Make 30 pieced 8" blocks
- Cut 42 alternate blocks
- Cut 22 side-setting triangles
- Cut 4 corner-setting triangles
- Cut outer borders $8\frac{1}{2}$" wide

Setting Variations

Consider the color and value of setting pieces. Just because the pattern calls for a dark or medium value for a certain area, doesn't mean you have to do it that way. Illustrations ***A-D*** show four variations of the Burgundy Star quilt with different values in the alternate blocks, setting triangles, and borders. Illustrations ***E-F*** show simple variations that can be made using setting pieces provided with the pattern.

Feel free to experiment with different sets. Although I usually have a quilt plan in mind, I like to play a bit to see how the pieced blocks look in various arrangements before sewing them all together with the setting pieces. On your design wall, try diagonal and straight sets. Vary spatial arrangements and audition different prints for setting pieces and borders. Discovering a better quilt plan to suit the blocks after they are made is an exciting part of quiltmaking.

A
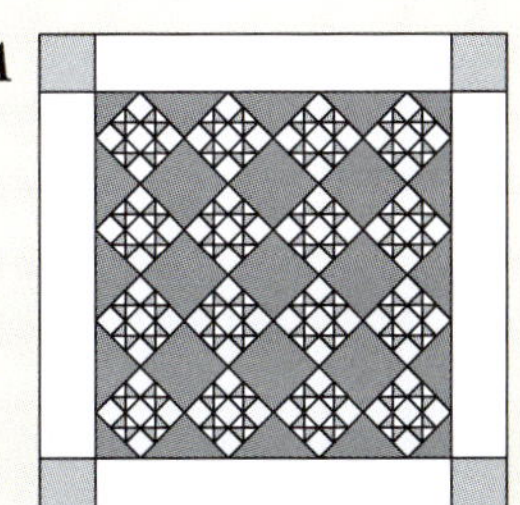

B
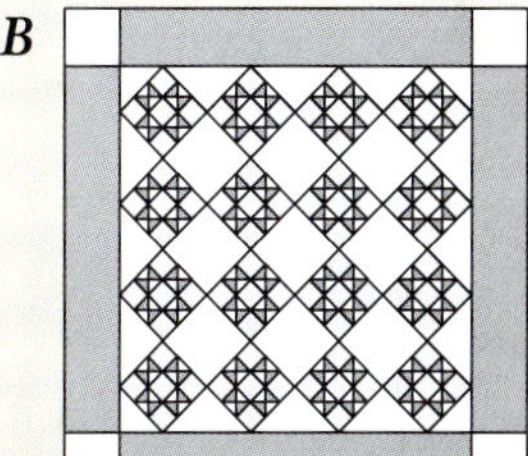

Try this! Change the value of alternate blocks and setting triangles.

C
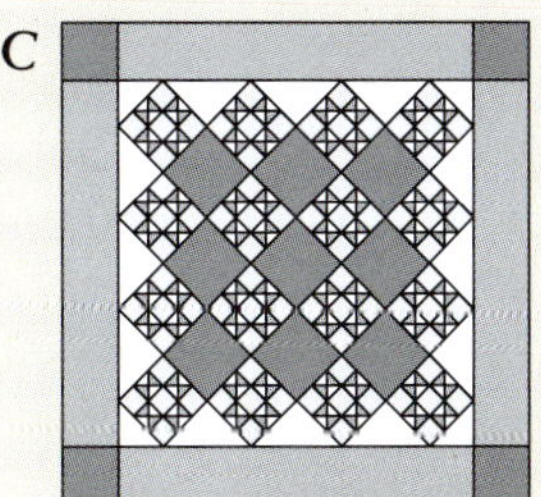

D
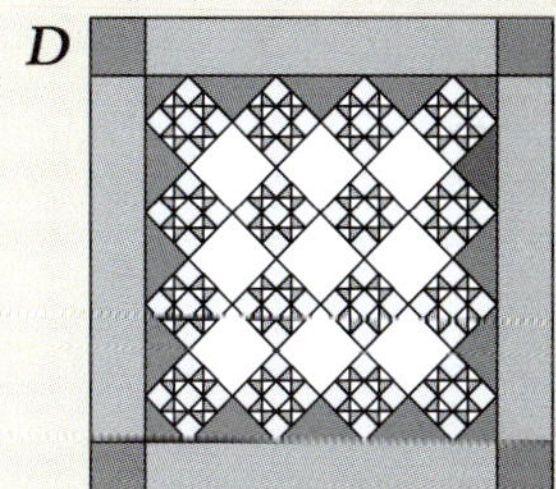

Try this! Use different fabrics for the alternate blocks and setting triangles.

E
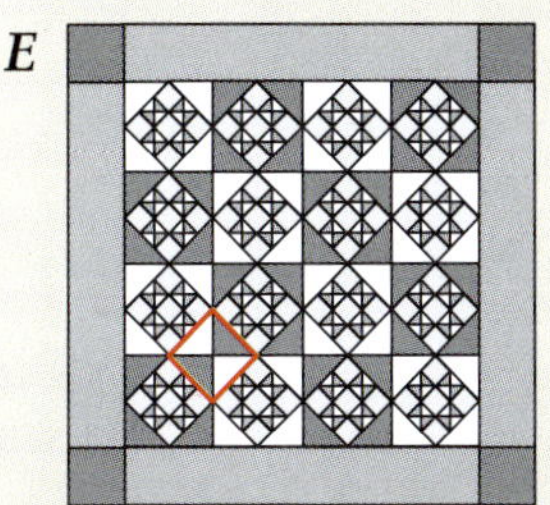

F
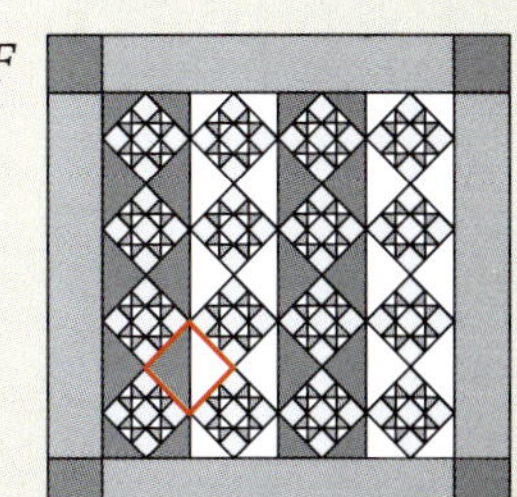

Try this! Use the setting triangles to create pieced alternate blocks.

G
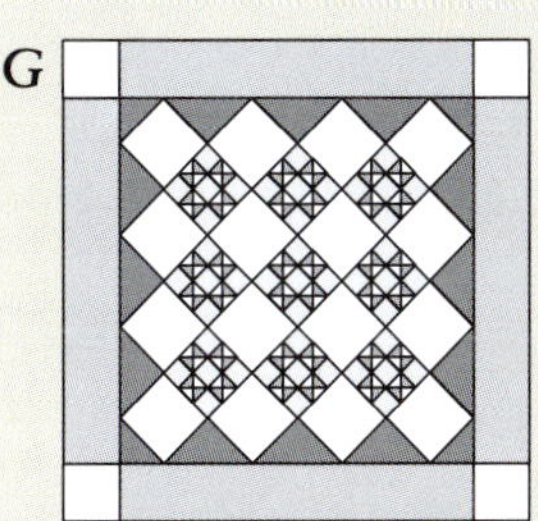

Try this! Put unpieced squares on the outside row of blocks to showcase a great print. If you make the quilt larger, you won't have to make as many pieced blocks.

H
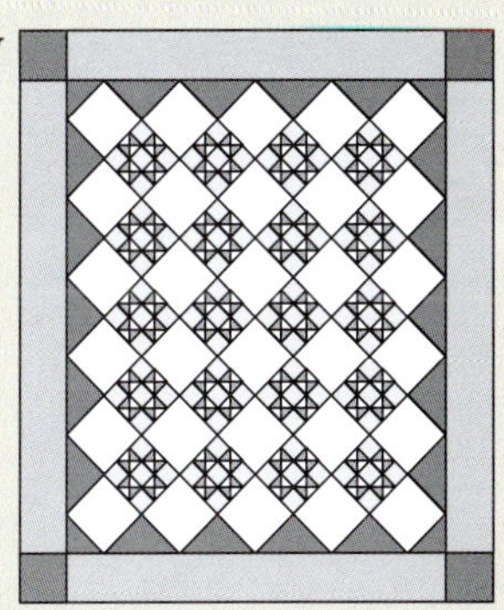

Gypsy Rondo

We can always count on Jackie Quinn to come up with fantastic color combinations. In Gypsy Rondo, orange, black, and lime-green predominate. I show Gypsy Rondo in Blended Quilts classes when students ask, "Can I use dark or bright fabrics in Blended Quilts?" This is a beautiful example of how to make a "blended" design with strong colors.

The border fabric is the focus print. All the other fabrics were chosen for color and scale to go with it. The second most important fabric is the fanciful stripe used for the lattices separating the Aunt Lottie's Star blocks. A good quilt-building strategy would be to cut the borders and lattice strips first, put them on your design wall, and "fill in" the blocks and pieced border sections.

Gypsy Rondo

DESIGNED BY: **Jackie Quinn** • QUILTED BY: **Kathy Staley**

FINISHED QUILT SIZE: **61½" x 72"** • FINISHED BLOCK SIZE: **9"**

Materials

Fabric requirements are based on 40" fabric width.

- Fabric A, large-scale dark spaced-floral, focus fabric for outer border and some piecing: 2 yds.
- Fabric B, floral stripe for lattices: 1½ yds.
- Fabric C, solid-looking black print for Ladder border and some piecing: 1 yd.
- Fabric D, medium-scale print for Ladder border: ½ yd.
- Fabric E, bright solid-looking print for edges of Ladder border: 1⅜ yds. (cutting strips on lengthwise grain) or ¾ yd. (cutting strips on widthwise grain)
- Fabric F, assorted light (beige or gold), medium, and dark coordinated prints for piecing: 6-10 fat quarters
- Binding: ⅔ yd.
- Backing: 4⅛ yds. (widthwise seam)
- Batting: 70" x 80"

Directions

Read these instructions thoroughly before you begin. See *Basic Quiltmaking,* beginning on page 14, for general quiltmaking directions. All cutting measurements include ¼"-wide seam allowance. Instructions are for rotary cutting. For traditional piecing, use templates R2, S3, S6, S7, S9, T7, and T9 in Template section beginning on page 128.

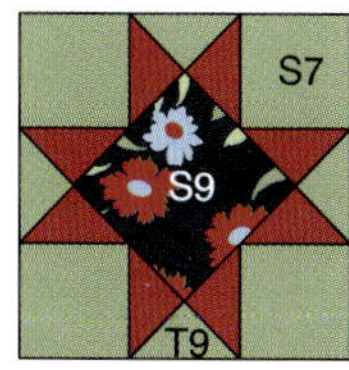

Aunt Lottie's Star
9" block

Aunt Lottie's Star
6" block

Quick Cutting Guide

For more detailed information, see complete cutting instructions given in each Step.

Fabric	Shape	Piece/ Template	Total Needed	Rotary Cutting		
				# to Cut	1st Cut	2nd Cut
Fabric A	▭	Outer border	4	4	8" x length of fabric*	
	□	S9	12§	12§	4¾" x 4¾"	
	□	S6	4	4	3 5/16" x 3 5/16"	
Fabric B	▭	Lattice border	2	2 lengthwise strips	2½" x 45"	
	▭	Lattice border	2	2 lengthwise strips	2½" x 30½"	
	▭	Lattice pieces	2	2 lengthwise strips	2" x 41"	
	▭	Lattice pieces	9	9	2" x 9½"	
Fabric C	△	T7	32	8	3¼" x 3¼"	⊠
	▭	R2	54	54	2" x 4½"	
Fabric D	▭	R2	52	52	2" x 4½"	
Fabric E	▭	Ladder border	4	4	1½" x 34½"	
	▭	Ladder border	4	4 lengthwise strips	1½" x 45"°	
Fabric F	□	S7	48	48	3½" x 3½"	
	△	T9	48	12	4¼" x 4¼"	⊠
	□	S3	16	16	2½" x 2½"	
	△	T7	16	4	3¼" x 3¼"	⊠
Fabric C or F	△	T9	96	24	4¼" x 4¼"	⊠

* Strips are cut longer than necessary, and will be trimmed to size later.
° If you are cutting on the widthwise grain, cut 5 strips, sew them together end-to-end, then trim to size.
§ If desired, cut some of these from scraps of other large-scale dark florals.

Step 1: Setting Pieces and Border Strips

Cut the border strips and lattices; then arrange them on your design wall.

From Fabric A, cut:

- 4 strips, the length of the fabric by 8" wide, for outer border. Strips are cut longer than necessary. They will be trimmed to size later. For now, pin them up on the design wall.

From Fabric B, cut:

- 2 lengthwise strips, 2½" x 45", for the Lattice border
- 2 lengthwise strips, 2½" x 30½", for the Lattice border
- 4 strips, the length of the fabric by 2" wide, for lattices between the blocks. Subcut 2 strips 41" long for the vertical lattices, and subcut the remaining 2 strips into 9 strips 9½" long for the horizontals.

Step 2: Blocks

Cut and piece Aunt Lottie's Star blocks. Make twelve 9" blocks for the quilt center and four 6" blocks for the border corners.

Cutting instructions are for one 9" Aunt Lottie's Star block. Repeat 12 times with different fabrics in each block.

From Fabric A or other large-scale dark floral, cut:

- 1 square, 4¾" x 4¾" (S9), for center

From assorted light and medium Fabrics F, cut:

- 4 squares, 3½" x 3½" (S7), for corners
- 1 square, 4¼" x 4¼"; cut square twice diagonally to make 4 quarter-square triangles (T9) for sides

From Fabric C or a medium to dark value Fabric F, cut:

- 2 squares, 4¼" x 4¼"; cut each square twice diagonally to make 8 quarter-square triangles (T9) for star points. Trim points for easy matching (see page 34).

Cutting instructions are for four 6" Aunt Lottie's Star blocks. In Jackie's quilt, these blocks each contain the same fabrics.

From Fabric A, cut:

- 4 squares, 3⁵⁄₁₆" x 3⁵⁄₁₆" (S6), for centers

From light Fabric F, cut:

- 16 squares, 2½" x 2½" (S3), for corners
- 4 squares, 3¼" x 3¼"; cut each square twice diagonally to make 16 quarter-square triangles (T7) for sides

From Fabric C, cut:

- 8 squares, 3¼" x 3¼"; cut each square twice diagonally to make 32 quarter-square triangles (T7) for star points. Trim points for easy matching.

Piecing

1. Arrange cut patches on design wall and when you are satisfied with the arrangement, piece the blocks together as shown. When sewn, the large blocks should measure 9½" x 9½", edge to edge, including seam allowances. The 4 smaller blocks should measure 6½" x 6½". Place each block back on the design wall as it is completed.

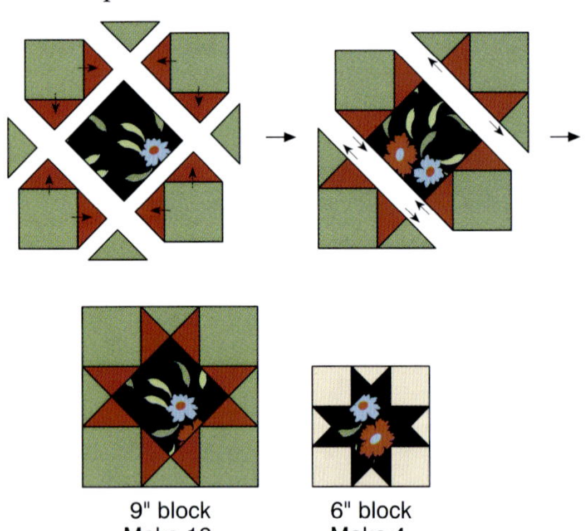

2. Join large Aunt Lottie's Star blocks with 2" x 9½" lattice strips in 3 vertical rows as shown in the Quilt Assembly Diagram on page 29.
3. Join rows of blocks together with 2" x 41" lattice strips.

4. Sew 2½" x 30½" Fabric B strips to top and bottom of quilt. Press seams toward border.
5. Sew 2½" x 45" Fabric B strips to sides of quilt. Press seams toward border.

Step 3: Borders

Cut and piece Ladder borders, and join all borders to quilt center.

From Fabric C, cut:
- 54 rectangles, 2" x 4½" (R2)

From Fabric D, cut:
- 52 rectangles, 2" x 4½" (R2)

From Fabric E, cut:
- 4 strips, 1½" x 34½"
- 4 strips, 1½" x 45" (If you are cutting on the widthwise grain, these strips will need to be pieced.)

Assembly

1. For top and bottom borders, join Fabric C and D rectangles as shown below. Each section contains 11 light and 12 dark rectangles. (If piecing is precise, this is ½" too long and you may need to trim to fit by shaving off ¼" at each end.) Join shorter Fabric E strips to either side of each section as shown.
2. For each side border section, join 15 light and 15 dark Fabric C and D rectangles as shown. (If piecing is precise, this is ½" too long and you may need to trim to fit by shaving off ¼" at each end.) Join longer Fabric E strips to either side of each section as shown.

Top and Bottom Border
Make 2.

Side Border
Make 2.

3. Measure width of the quilt top through center. The top and bottom Ladder border sections should be this measurement. Trim to fit if necessary. Join a small Aunt Lottie's Star block to either end of each Ladder border section. Press seams toward Ladder border.
4. Measure length of the quilt top through center. Trim the two long pieced Ladder border sections to this measurement if necessary, and sew to sides of quilt. Press seams toward border.
5. Join top and bottom Ladder border sections (with star blocks at each end) to quilt center. Press seams toward border.
6. For outer border, measure length of the quilt top through center. Trim two 8"-wide Fabric A strips to this measurement, and sew to sides of quilt. Press seams toward border.
7. Measure width of the quilt top, including borders just added, through center. Cut remaining two 8"-wide strips to this measurement and join to top and bottom of quilt. Press seams toward border.

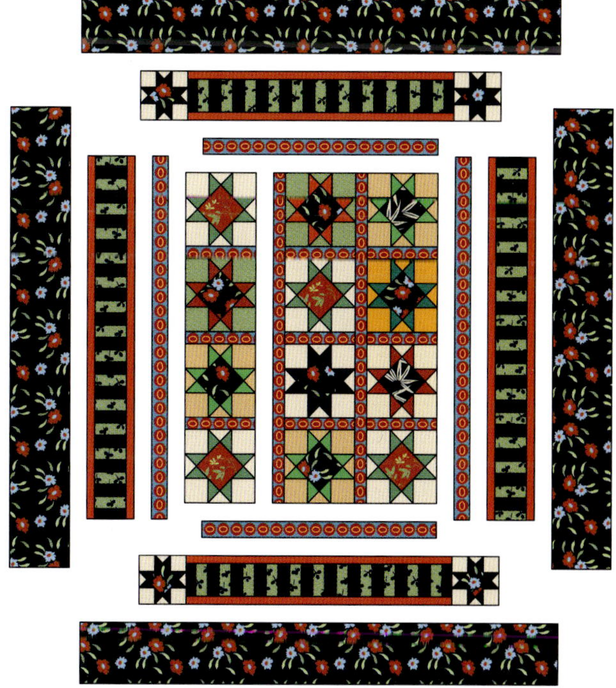

Quilt Assembly Diagram

See finishing instructions on pages 20-21.

Stepping Stones

Quilting tradition has it that during the 1700s, one yard of chintz was a valuable and welcome gift for a traveling husband to bring home to his wife. This quilt began with a meter of a glorious print given to me by a friend from Australia. Stepping Stones exists because of this gorgeous large-scale floral. To have maximum impact

as a focus fabric, it needed to be cut in the largest pieces possible.

I designed a simple quilt with unpieced alternate squares. I measured the fabric, did the math, and found that if I cut 8 ½" squares, I could get more squares than if I cut them 9 ½", and so settled on 8" finished blocks.

The quilt pictured has three different prints in the border, because I couldn't settle on just one print and decided to use all three. This "more-is-better" random use of gorgeous prints makes the quilt look richer and more interesting. The directions call for borders cut from two fabrics. You can choose to use more if you like.

Stepping Stones

DESIGNED BY: **Marsha McCloskey** • QUILTED BY: **Cindy Paulsgrove**

FINISHED QUILT SIZE: **62" x 73"** • FINISHED BLOCK SIZE: **8"**

Materials

Fabric requirements are based on 40" fabric width.

- Fabric A, large-scale light spaced-floral, for setting squares: 1⅜ yds.
- Fabric B, medium-scale print for setting triangles: ⅞ yd.
- Fabric C, assorted medium and dark prints for piecing: 5-6 fat eighths
- Fabric D, assorted light prints for piecing: 4-6 fat quarters
- Fabric E, large-scale dark floral for side borders: 1⅞ yds.
- Fabric F, a different large-scale dark floral for top and bottom borders: 1⅞ yds.
- Binding: ⅔ yd.
- Backing: 4⅛ yds. (widthwise seam)
- Batting: 70" x 81"

Directions

Read these instructions thoroughly before you begin. See *Basic Quiltmaking*, beginning on page 14, for general quiltmaking directions. All cutting measurements include ¼"-wide seam allowance. Instructions are for rotary cutting. For traditional piecing, use templates S3, S8, and R4 in Template section beginning on page 128.

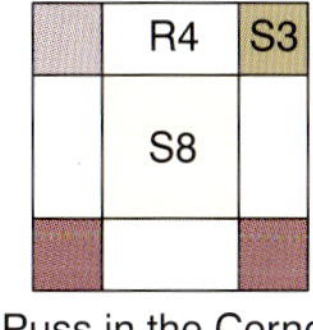

Puss in the Corner
8" block

S3
S3
R4
Stepping Stones
8" block

Quick Cutting Guide

For more detailed information, see complete cutting instructions given in each Step.

Fabric	Shape	Piece/ Template	Total Needed	Rotary Cutting		
				# to Cut	1st Cut	2nd Cut
Fabric A	□	Setting squares	20	20	8½" x 8½"	
Fabric B	△	Side-setting triangles	16 (2 extra)	4	12⅝" x 12⅝"	⊠
	◺	Corner-setting triangles	4	2	6⅝" x 6⅝"	⧄
Fabric C	□	S3	76	76	2½" x 2½"	
	□	S8	5	5	4½" x 4½"	
Fabric D	▭	R4	48	48	2½" x 4½"	
Fabric E	▭	Side borders	2	2	8½" x length of fabric*	
Fabric F	▭	Top & bottom borders	2	2	8½" x length of fabric*	

* Strips are cut longer than necessary, and will be trimmed to size later.

Trimming Points for Easy Matching

Using the Precision Trimmer 3™ or 6™

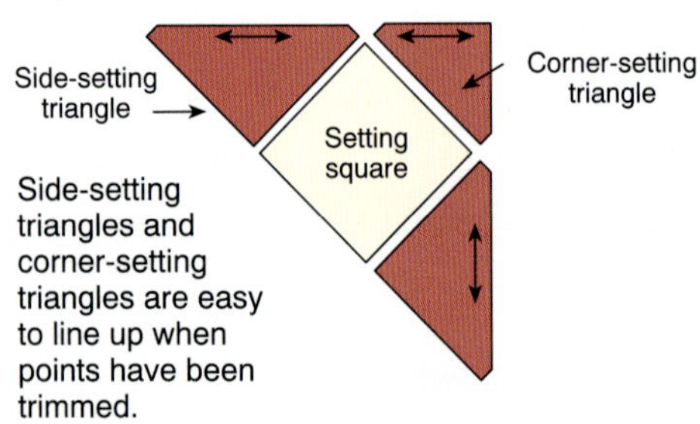

Trimming Side-Setting Triangles

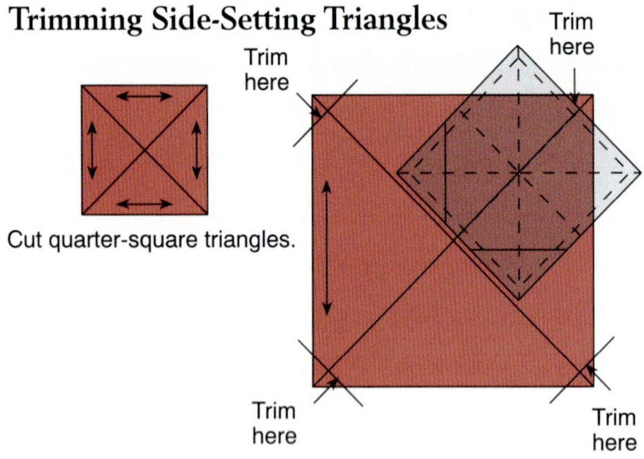

Cut quarter-square triangles.

Trimming Corner-Setting Triangles

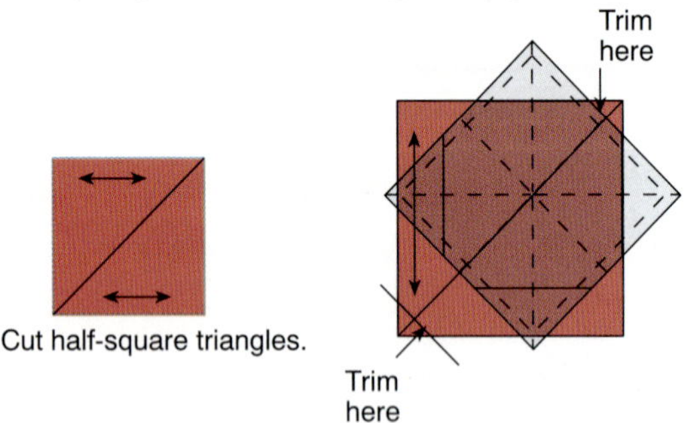

Cut half-square triangles.

Step 1: Setting Pieces and Border Strips

Cut the setting pieces and border strips; then arrange them on your design wall.

From Fabric A, cut:

- 20 squares, 8½" x 8½", for setting squares

From Fabric B, cut:

- 4 squares, 12⅞" x 12⅞"; cut each square twice diagonally to make 16 side-setting triangles (2 extra)*
- 2 squares, 6⅝" x 6⅝"; cut each square once diagonally to make 4 corner-setting triangles*

* *See sidebar for Trimming Points for Easy Matching.*

From Fabric E, cut:

- 2 strips, the length of the fabric x 8½" wide, for side borders. Strips are cut longer than necessary. They will be trimmed to size later. There will be enough leftover fabric to use in a few of the pieced blocks.

From Fabric F, cut:

- 2 strips, the length of the fabric x 8½" wide, for top and bottom borders. Strips are cut longer than necessary. They will be trimmed to size later. There will be enough leftover fabric to use in a few of the pieced blocks.

Step 2: Blocks

Make five 8" Puss in the Corner blocks and seven 8" Stepping Stones blocks.

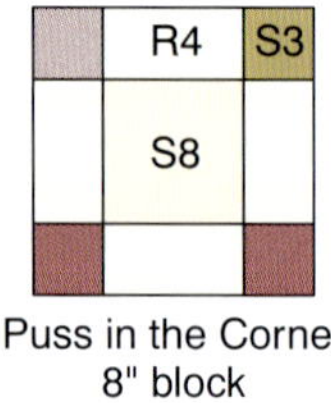

Puss in the Corner
8" block

Puss in the Corner

Cutting instructions are for 1 Puss in the Corner block. Repeat 5 times with different fabrics in each block.

From Fabrics C, cut:

- 4 squares, 2½" x 2½" (S3), for corners
- 1 square, 4½" x 4½" (S8), for center

From Fabrics D, cut:

- 4 rectangles, 2½" x 4½" (R4), for sides

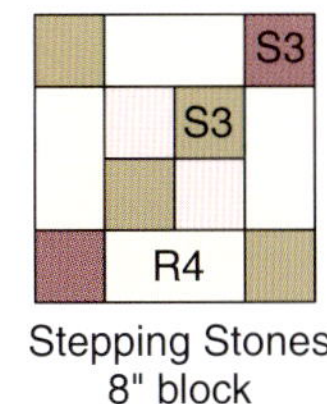

Stepping Stones
8" block

Stepping Stones

Cutting instructions are for 1 Stepping Stones block. Repeat 7 times with different fabrics in each block.

From Fabrics C, cut:

- 8 squares, 2½" x 2½" (S3), for center and corners (use at least 2 different prints)

From Fabrics D, cut:

- 4 rectangles, 2½" x 4½" (R4), for sides

Piecing

1. After arranging the patches on your design wall, piece the blocks. Join patches in rows, then stitch rows together. Edge-to-edge measurement of each block should be 8½" x 8½".

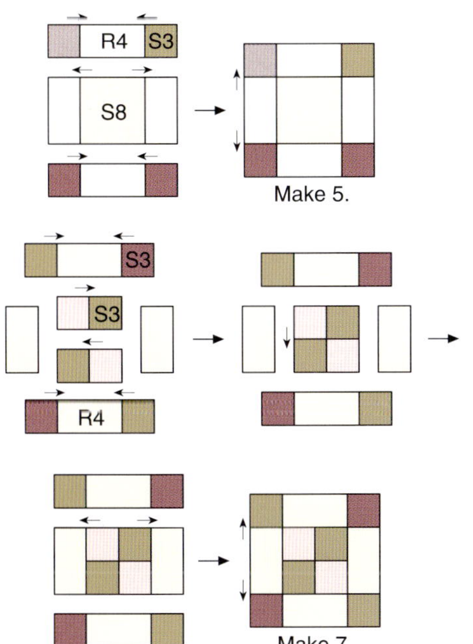

2. Join pieced blocks with setting pieces in diagonal rows as shown in the Quilt Assembly Diagram. Press for opposing seams from row to row. Sew diagonal rows together.

Step 3: Borders

Measure and trim the border strips cut in Step 1; then join them to the quilt center.

1. Measure length of the quilt top through center. Trim two 8½"-wide Fabric E strips to this measurement, and sew to sides of quilt. Press seams toward border.
2. Measure width of the quilt top, including borders just added, through center. Cut two 8½"-wide Fabric F strips to this measurement, and join to top and bottom of quilt. Press seams toward border.

Quilt Assembly Diagram

See finishing instructions on pages 20-21.

Burgundy Star

Barb Vose loves to make simple pieced designs with gorgeous prints. Here, her primary focus fabric is a large-scale light spaced-floral used for the large squares and triangles that are the setting pieces. Her second focus fabric is the border print: again a large-scale floral, but in a darker overall value. Prints and colors for the Variable Star blocks were chosen to go with the first two prints. These "go with" prints include large- and small-scale florals, dots, and stripes. Patches of the border print are also used in the Variable Star blocks to bring that color into the quilt center.

The look of this simple quilt design can be changed by making value changes in the setting pieces. See Setting Variations on page 23 for several examples.

Burgundy Star

DESIGNED BY: **Barbara Vose** • QUILTED BY: **Cindy Paulsgrove**

FINISHED QUILT SIZE: **67½" x 67½"** • FINISHED BLOCK SIZE: **9"**

Materials

Fabric requirements are based on 40" fabric width.

- Fabric A, large-scale light spaced-floral for setting squares and triangles, and border corners: 1⅞ yds.
- Fabric B, large-scale dark floral for border: 1¾ yds.
- Fabric C, assorted light-to-medium prints: 5-8 fat quarters
- Fabric D, assorted medium-to-dark prints: 5-8 fat quarters
- Binding: ⅔ yd.
- Backing: 4½ yds.
- Batting: 76" x 76"

Directions

Read these instructions thoroughly before you begin. See *Basic Quiltmaking*, beginning on page 14, for general quiltmaking directions. All cutting measurements include ¼"-wide seam allowance. Instructions are for rotary cutting. Some pieces are cut larger than needed and then trimmed to size. For traditional piecing, use templates S7 and T9 in Template section beginning on page 128.

Variable Star
9" block

Quick Cutting Guide

For more detailed information, see complete cutting instructions given in each Step.

Fabric	Shape	Piece/ Template	Total Needed	Rotary Cutting		
				# to Cut	1st Cut	2nd Cut
Fabric A	□	Setting squares	9	9	9½" x 9½"	
	△	Side-setting triangles	12	3	14" x 14"	⊠
	◺	Corner-setting triangles	4	2	7¼" x 7¼"	⧄
	□	Border corners	4	4	8½" x 8½"	
Fabric B	▭	Outer border	4	4	8½" x length of fabric*	
Fabric C	△	T9	128	32	4½" x 4½"°	
Fabric D	△	T9	128	32	4½" x 4½"°	
Fabric C *or* D	□	S7	80	80	3½" x 3½"	

* Strips are cut longer than necessary, and will be trimmed to size later.
° Leave as squares for now. These will be cut again during piecing process.

Step 1: Setting Pieces and Border Strips

Cut the setting pieces and border strips; then arrange them on your design wall.

From Fabric A, cut:

- 9 squares, 9½" x 9½", for setting squares
- 3 squares, 14" x 14"; cut each square twice diagonally to make 12 side-setting triangles*
- 2 squares, 7¼" x 7¼"; cut each square once diagonally to make 4 corner-setting triangles*
- 4 squares, 8½" x 8½", for border corners

* *See page 34 for Trimming Points for Easy Matching.*

From Fabric B, cut:

- 4 strips, the length of the fabric x 8½" wide, for outer border. Strips are cut longer than necessary. They will be trimmed to size later.

Block backgrounds blending with setting pieces adds to the "variability" of these easy-to-make stars.

Step 2: Blocks

Make sixteen 9" Variable Star blocks.

Cutting instructions are for 1 Variable Star block. Repeat 16 times with different fabrics in each block.

From Fabric C, cut:

- 2 squares, 4½" x 4½", for star point units (For traditional piecing, use T9 template for star-point triangles.)

From Fabric D, cut:

- 2 squares, 4½" x 4½", for star point units

From Fabric C or D, cut:

- 5 squares, 3½" x 3½" (S7), for star centers and corners

Piecing

1. Star points:

- For each block, choose 2 Fabric C and 2 Fabric D 4½" squares. Arrange the squares in pairs with right sides together. Working with one pair of squares at a time, make a cut diagonally, corner to corner, yielding 2 pairs of triangles. Stitching the long side, sew each triangle pair together with ¼" seams. Press seams to one side. Make 4 of these 2-triangle units for each block, 64 total.

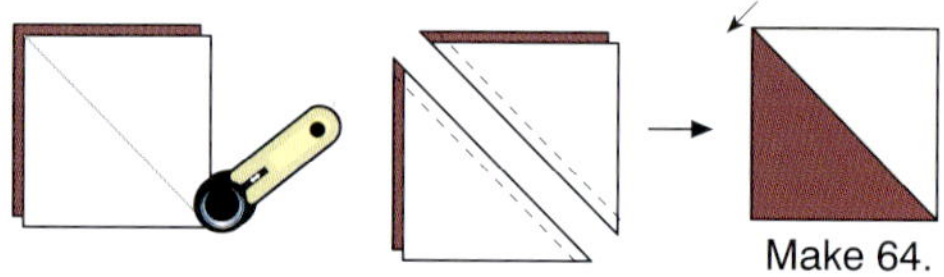

- To make the 4-triangle units, match pairs of 2-triangle units, right sides together, nesting opposing seams. Cut squares diagonally and sew resulting triangle pairs together with ¼" seams. Press seams to one side. Make 4 of these 4-triangle units for each block, 64 total.

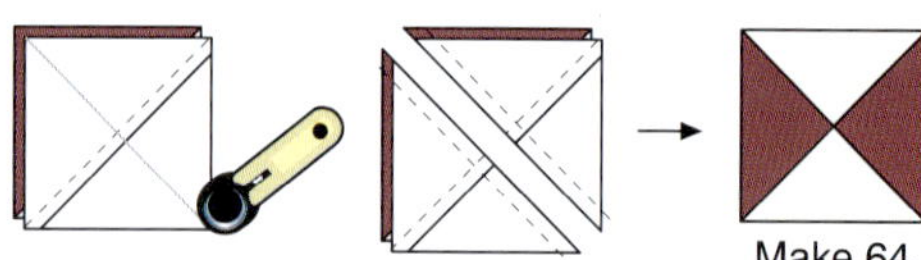

- Use the Precision Trimmer 6™ to trim each completed unit to 3½" x 3½", edge to edge.

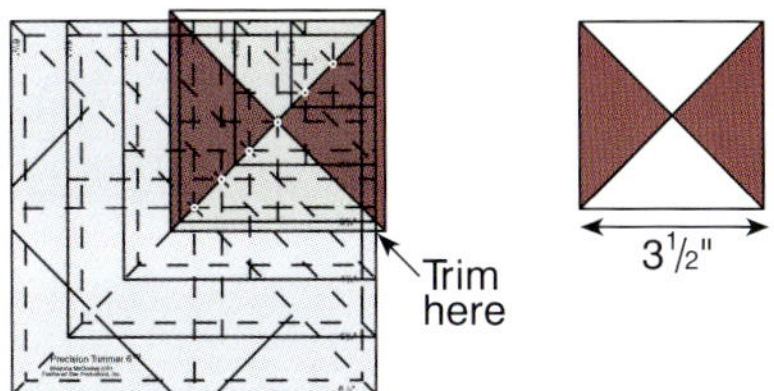

2. Piece 16 Variable Star blocks, joining 3½" squares with 4-triangle units in rows. Press seams toward 3½" squares. Join the rows. Press seams to one side.

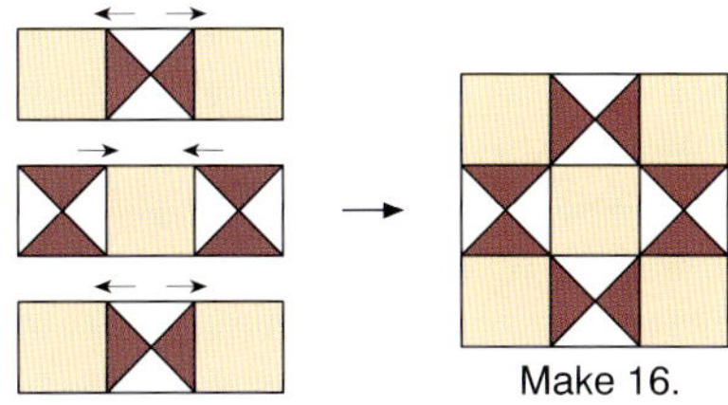

3. Join Variable Star blocks with setting pieces in diagonal rows as shown in the Quilt Assembly Diagram. Press for opposing seams from row to row. Sew rows together.

Step 3: Borders

Measure and trim the border strips cut in Step 1; then join them to the quilt center.

1. Measure the quilt top through center, edge to edge, in both directions. This is a square quilt, so the dimensions should be equal. Trim the four 8½"-wide strips to size, and sew two of them to sides of quilt. Press seams toward border.
2. To each end of the two remaining 8½"-wide strips, stitch one 8½" Fabric A square. Sew pieced strips to top and bottom of quilt as shown in the Quilt Assembly Diagram. Press seams toward border.

Quilt Assembly Diagram

See finishing instructions on pages 20-21.

Cathedral of Roses

Melissa McCulloch is a fabric designer, and has a strong color and design sense. She brings pieced design, subtle color, and luscious prints together in a quilt that invites you to linger and explore. The pieced block design, a Friendship block variation, is more complex than we find in other Blended Quilts, but the finished result is dazzling and well worth the effort.

In this quilt, the focus fabric and source of the color theme is the large-scale floral in the setting triangles and center squares of the Puss in the Corner blocks. The inner border looks like three separate strips, but is really one strip selectively cut from a printed border stripe. Melissa chose another border stripe for the outer border, and mitered the corners to make the design turn gracefully. "Quiet" prints in the center of the Friendship blocks are an important design element.

Cathedral of Roses

DESIGNED BY: **Melissa McCulloch** • QUILTED BY: **Sherry D. Rogers**

FINISHED QUILT SIZE: **73½" x 86"** • FINISHED BLOCK SIZE: **9"**

Materials

Fabric requirements are based on 40" fabric width.

- Fabric A, focus fabric, large-scale spaced-floral with dark background for setting triangles and centers of Puss in the Corner alternate blocks: 1¼ yds.
- Fabric B, striped print for inner border: 2¼ yds.
- Fabric C, large floral for outer border: 2¾ yds.
- Fabric D, 1-3 light finely-etched prints for center piecing in Friendship blocks: 1 yd. total
- Fabric E, assorted light, medium, and dark prints color-coordinated to focus fabric for piecing: 14-18 fat quarters or scraps
- Binding: ¾ yd.
- Backing: 5⅜ yds.
- Batting: 81" x 94"

Directions

Read these instructions thoroughly before you begin. See *Basic Quiltmaking*, beginning on page 14, for general quiltmaking directions. All cutting measurements include ¼"-wide seam allowance. Instructions are for rotary cutting. For traditional piecing, use templates R3, S2, S10, T1, T9, X1, and X2 in Template section beginning on page 128.

Puss in the Corner
9" block

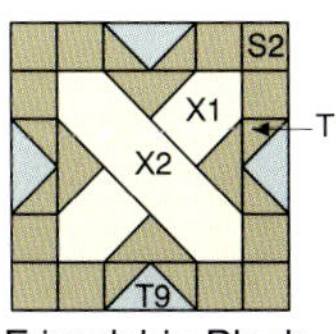

Friendship Block
9" block

Quick Cutting Guide

For more detailed information, see complete cutting instructions given in each Step.

Fabric	Shape	Piece/ Template	Total Needed	Rotary Cutting		
				# to Cut	1st Cut	2nd Cut
Fabric A	□	S10	12	12	6½" x 6½"	
	△	Side-setting triangles	16 (2 extra)	4	14" x 14"	⊠
	◺	Corner-setting triangles	4	2	7¼" x 7¼"	⧄
Fabric B	▭	Inner border	4	4	5¼" x length of fabric*	
Fabric C	▭	Outer border	4	4	6¾" x length of fabric*	
Fabric D	⬠	X1	40	40	(Template X1)°	
	⬡	X2	20	20	(Template X2)°	
Fabric E	□	S2	288	288	2" x 2"	
	▭	R3	48	48	2" x 6½"	
	◺	T1	160	80	2⅞" x 2⅞"	⧄
	△	T9	160	40	4¼" x 4¼"	⊠

* Strips are cut longer than necessary, and will be trimmed to size later.

° See page 46 for cutting tip.

Step 1: Setting Pieces and Border Strips

Cut the setting triangles, Puss in the Corner block centers, and border strips; arrange them on your design wall.

From Fabric A, cut:

- 12 squares, 6½" x 6½" (S10), for Puss in the Corner block centers
- 4 squares, 14" x 14"; cut each square twice diagonally to make 16 side-setting triangles (2 extra)*
- 2 squares, 7¼" x 7¼"; cut each square once diagonally to make 4 corner-setting triangles*

* *See page 34 for Trimming Points for Easy Matching.*

From Fabric B, cut:

- 4 strips, the length of the fabric x 5¼" wide, for inner border. Strips are cut longer than necessary. They will be trimmed to size later.

From Fabric C, cut:

- 4 strips, the length of the fabric x 6¾" wide, for outer border. Strips are cut longer than necessary. They will be trimmed to size later.

Step 2: Blocks

Make twelve 9" Puss in the Corner blocks and twenty 9" Friendship blocks.

Puss in the Corner
9" block

Puss in the Corner

Cutting instructions are for 1 Puss in the Corner Block. Repeat 12 times with different fabrics in each block. (6½" Fabric A S10 squares have already been cut.)

From Fabrics E, cut:

- 4 squares, 2" x 2" (S2), for corners
- 4 rectangles, 2" x 6½" (R3), for sides

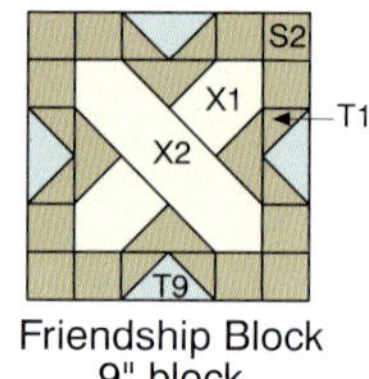

Friendship Block
9" block

Friendship

Cutting instructions are for 1 Friendship block. Repeat 20 times with different fabrics in each block.

From Fabrics D, cut:

- 1 strip, 2⅞" wide by about 18". Make Templates of X1 and X2 on page 131. Position the templates on the strip to cut 2 of X1 and 1 of X2.

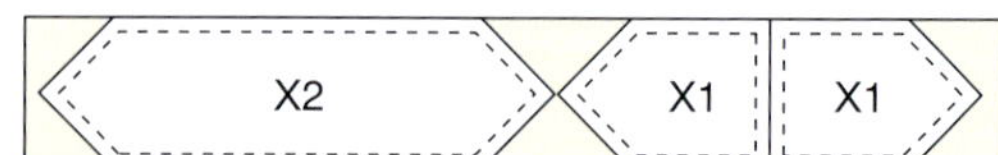

From one Fabric E, cut:

- 4 squares, 2⅞" x 2⅞"; cut each square once diagonally to make 8 half-square triangles (T1)
- 1 square, 4¼" x 4¼"; cut square twice diagonally to make 4 quarter-square triangles (T9)
- 12 squares, 2" x 2" (S2)

From a different Fabric E, cut:

- 1 square, 4¼" x 4¼"; cut square twice diagonally to make 4 quarter-square triangles (T9)

Piecing

1. After arranging the patches on your design wall, piece the blocks. Join patches in rows, then stitch rows together. Edge-to-edge measurement of each block should be 9½" x 9½".

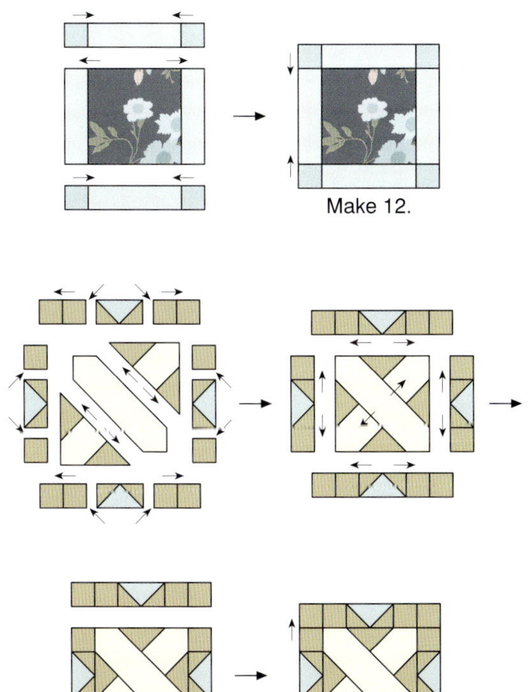

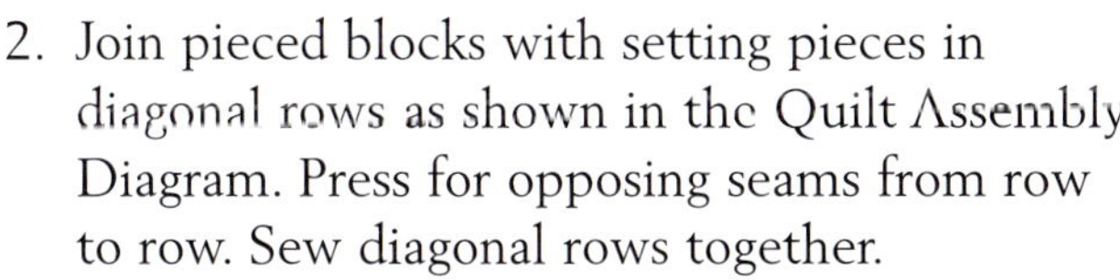

2. Join pieced blocks with setting pieces in diagonal rows as shown in the Quilt Assembly Diagram. Press for opposing seams from row to row. Sew diagonal rows together.

Step 3: Borders

To make the striped fabric motifs turn gracefully, Melissa mitered borders at the corners. Sufficient length has been allowed for this process. Sew border strips to quilt top using the Mitering Corners technique given on page 19.

Quilt Assembly Diagram

See finishing instructions on pages 20-21.

Robin's Nest

While browsing through her quilt books, Rachel Vanderlaan found an antique quilt from 1865 that caught her fancy. The simple pattern and muted colors set her to collecting chocolate brown and soft blue prints. The large-scale spaced-florals with blue and brown backgrounds blend beautifully, because the flowers in most of the prints share rosy hues in the petals and similar greens in the leaves and stems.

The coloring of the large triangles that make up the alternate blocks and setting triangles gives her quilt a vertical organization. It looks like a strippy quilt, but is actually made up of pieced squares in a diagonal repeated block set.

Robin's Nest

DESIGNED BY: **Rachel Vanderlaan** • QUILTED BY: **Kathryn Milburn**

FINISHED QUILT SIZE: **86½" x 86½"** • FINISHED BLOCK SIZE: **12"**

Materials

Fabric requirements are based on 40" fabric width.

- Fabric A, striped floral print for outer border: 2¼ yds.
- Fabric B, large-scale spaced-floral with medium background for side-setting triangles: ¾ yd.
- Fabric C, a 2nd large-scale spaced-floral with medium background for corner-setting triangles: ⅓ yd.
- Fabric D, a 3rd large-scale spaced-floral with medium background for alternate blocks: 1¼ yds.
- Fabric E, large-scale spaced-floral with dark background for alternate blocks: 1¼ yds.
- Fabric F, 1-2 large-scale spaced-florals with dark backgrounds for side-setting triangles: ⅔ yd. each
- Fabric G, assorted light, medium, and dark prints for piecing (include a toile): 10-12 fat quarters
- Binding: ¾ yd.
- Backing: 8 yds.
- Batting: 94" x 94"

Directions

Read these instructions thoroughly before you begin. See *Basic Quiltmaking*, beginning on page 14, for general quiltmaking directions. All cutting measurements include ¼"-wide seam allowance. Instructions are for rotary cutting. For traditional piecing, use templates R3, S2, S10, and T4 in Template section beginning on page 128.

Robin's Nest
12" block

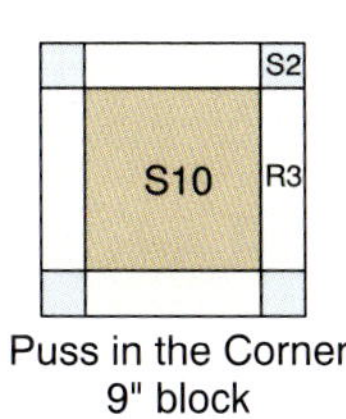

Puss in the Corner
9" block

Quick Cutting Guide

For more detailed information, see complete cutting instructions given in each Step.

Fabric	Shape	Piece/ Template	Total Needed	Rotary Cutting		
				# to Cut	1st Cut	2nd Cut
Fabric A		Border	4	4	9½" x length of fabric*	
Fabric B		Side-setting triangles	8	2	18¼" x 18¼"	
Fabric C		Corner-setting triangles	4	2	9⅜" x 9⅜"	
Fabric D		Alternate blocks	16	8	12⅞" x 12⅞"	
Fabric E		Alternate blocks	16	8	12⅞" x 12⅞"	
Fabric F		Side-setting triangles	4	1	18¼" x 18¼"	
Fabrics B-F		S10	9	9	6½" x 6½"	
Fabric G		T4	144	72	3⅞" x 3⅞"	
		S2	160	160	2" x 2"	
		S10	4	4	6½" x 6½"	
		R3	16	16	2" x 6½"	

* Strips are cut longer than necessary, and will be trimmed to size later.

Step 1: Setting Pieces and Alternate Blocks

Cut the large triangles and arrange them on your design wall. With the exception of the corners, all these triangles are the same size but have different grainlines. The setting triangles that fit along the outside edges, just inside the border, have straight grain on the long side and are cut as quarter-square triangles. Those that make up the 2-triangle alternate blocks have straight grain on the short side and are cut as half-square triangles.

From Fabric B, cut:

- 2 squares, 18¼" x 18¼"; cut each square twice diagonally to make 8 quarter-square triangles for side-setting triangles*

From Fabric C, cut:

- 2 squares, 9⅜" x 9⅜"; cut each square once diagonally to make 4 half-square triangles for corner-setting triangles*

From Fabric D, cut:

- 8 squares, 12⅞" x 12⅞"; cut each square once diagonally to make 16 half-square triangles for alternate blocks

From Fabric E, cut:

- 8 squares, 12⅞" x12⅞"; cut each square once diagonally to make 16 half-square triangles for alternate blocks

From Fabric F, cut:

- 1 square, 18¼" x 18¼"; cut square twice diagonally to make 4 quarter-square triangles for side-setting triangles* (For the scrappier look in Rachel's quilt, cut 2 squares from different fabrics, cut each square twice diagonally. You will have 4 triangles leftover.)

* *See page 34 for Trimming Points for Easy Matching.*

Step 2: Blocks

Robin's Nest
12" block

Make nine 12" Robin's Nest blocks, and 16 alternate blocks.

Cutting instructions are for 1 Robin's Nest block. Repeat 9 times with different fabrics in each block.

From leftover Fabrics B-F, cut:

- 1 square, 6½" x 6½" (S10), for center

From assorted Fabrics G, cut:

- 8 squares**, 3⅞" x 3⅞"; cut each square once diagonally to make 16 half-square triangles (T4)
- 16 squares**, 2" x 2" (S2)

** *Use at least 2 different prints.*

Piecing

1. After arranging the patches on your design wall, begin to piece the blocks. The fourpatches and 2-triangle squares should measure 3½" x 3½", edge to edge.

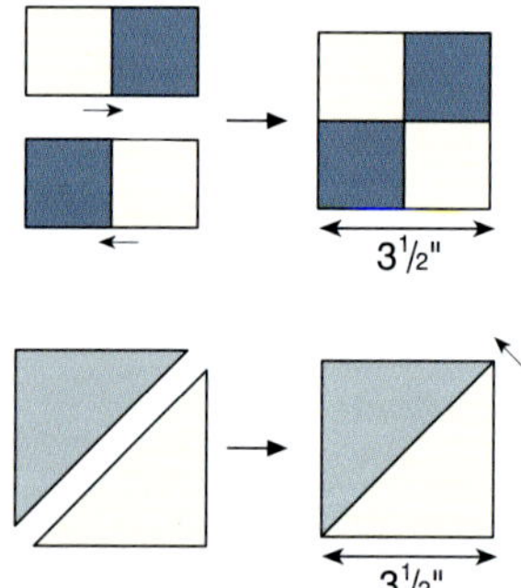

2. Join pieced units in rows, then stitch rows together. Edge-to-edge measurement of each block should be 12½" x 12½".

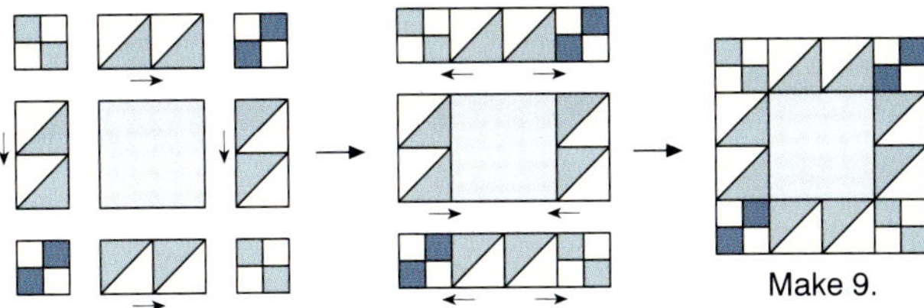
Make 9.

3. With large Fabric D and E half-square triangles, make sixteen 2-triangle alternate blocks. Edge-to-edge measurement of each block should be 12½" x 12½".

Make 16.

4. Join Robin's Nest blocks with alternate blocks and setting pieces in diagonal rows, as shown in the Quilt Assembly Diagram at right. Press for opposing seams from row to row. Sew diagonal rows together.

Step 3: Borders

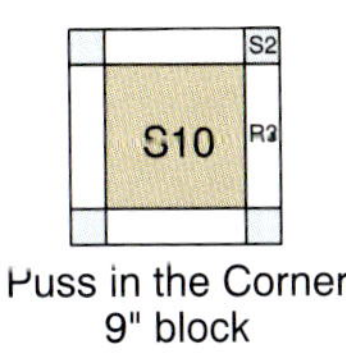

Puss in the Corner
9" block

Make four 9" Puss in the Corner blocks; cut borders strips and join them to quilt center.

From Fabric A border print, selectively cut:

- 4 strips, the length of the fabric by 9½" wide. Strips are cut longer than necessary. They will be trimmed to size later.

From Fabrics G, selectively cut:

- 4 squares, 6½" x 6½" (S10) (Rachel used a scenic toile here.)
- 16 squares, 2" x 2" (S2), for corners
- 16 rectangles, 2" x 6½" (R3)

Piecing

1. To make each Puss in the Corner block, stitch squares and rectangles together in rows as shown, then stitch rows together. Edge-to-edge measurement of each block should be 9½" x 9½".

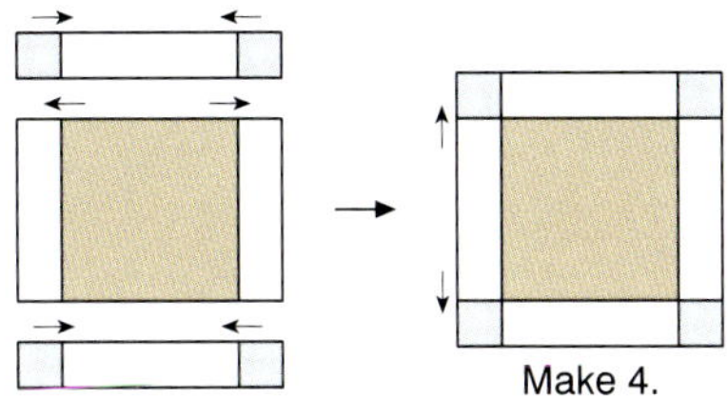
Make 4.

2. Measure the quilt top through center, edge to edge, in both directions. This is a square quilt, so the dimensions should be equal. Trim the four 9½"-wide strips to size, and sew two of them to sides of quilt. Press seams toward border.
3. To each end of the two remaining 9½"-wide strips, stitch one Puss in the Corner block; then sew to top and bottom of quilt as shown in the Quilt Assembly Diagram. Press seams toward border.

Quilt Assembly Diagram

See finishing instructions on pages 20-21.

Birds and Nines

Floral Cascade

Flying Geese

Black Forest

Morning Roses

Splendid Blended Olio

Strippy Quilts

Another quilt design style popular in the early 1800s was the Strippy or Bar quilt. In these quilts, patchwork was arranged in rows and usually separated by strips of unpieced fabric. Some quilts from the period were made entirely of alternating strips of chintz without any pieced blocks at all. Wide vertical strips, large setting triangles, and wide borders are all prime areas to showcase fabulous prints. Large-scale florals are the perfect choice for big triangles, and selectively-cut border prints work well for both dividing strips and borders.

There are six Strippy quilts in this section. Flying Geese, Black Forest, and Birds and Nines are all patterned after antique quilts. Morning Roses, Splendid Blended Olio, and Floral Cascade take the strip-quilt format and give it a slightly new twist. You can give a strippy look to a diagonal repeated-block design with careful placement of color and value in two-triangle alternate blocks (see Robin's Nest quilt page 50).

Nearly any pieced block design can be used in a strippy quilt. The blocks can be set straight or "on point" on the diagonal. If you choose to set blocks on point, fewer squares will be needed because the diagonal dimension of each block is 40% longer than that of its side. Diagonally set blocks require setting triangles to fill in the edges of the rows. See page 55 to learn how to draft setting triangles for any size design block.

The quilt diagrams on the next page show strippy quilts designed with 9" Double Ninepatch blocks. You could make the first quilt shown with large-scale floral setting triangles and striped floral dividing strips, selectively cut to the dimensions of the printed design. A second large-scale floral would be great for the wide border. Make your quilt larger or smaller by adding more blocks to the rows, adding more rows, or changing the width of the borders.

With only two alterations, you can turn the strippy set described above into a zigzag set. First, eliminate the long sashing strips between the rows of blocks. Second, offset the alternating block rows by half a block. Every other row will then include a half-block at the top and bottom. In this set, an odd number of rows actually works best because it creates a symmetrical design.

How to draft setting triangles to go with any size block.

1. On graph paper, draw two squares the finished size of your design block.
2. In the first square, draw one diagonal line to divide the square into two equal triangles (A). Each triangle is now the finished size of the side-setting triangle. This triangle needs to have straight grain on the long side. To get a cutting dimension, add a ¼" seam allowance around one of the triangles. Measure the long side of the triangle, including seam allowance, tip to tip. Using this measurement, cut a large square from your fabric. Cut the square twice diagonally to get four triangles. See page 34 for how to trim triangle points for easy matching.
3. In the second square, draw two diagonal lines to divide the square into four equal triangles (B). Each triangle is now the finished size of the corner-setting triangle. This triangle needs to have straight grain on the short side. To get a cutting dimension, add a ¼" seam allowance around one of the triangles. Measure the short side of the triangle, including seam allowances, corner to tip. Using this measurement, cut a large square from your fabric. Cut the square once diagonally to get two triangles. See page 34 for how to trim triangle points for easy matching.

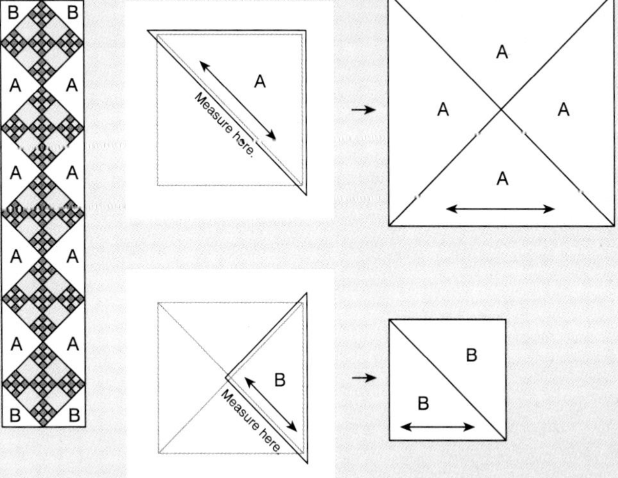

Morning Roses

In this quilt, the blocks are simple and the fabric fresh and pretty—like roses in the morning. When Margy Duncan was working on this quilt top, whenever she showed it to anyone they said, "The colors look so fresh!" The other fresh idea here is the way Margy combined an alternate repeated block design with the idea of a strippy. Again, the quilt design idea was fabric driven: she wanted to do the simple Churn Dash and Snowball combination, but one of her focus fabrics had a floral stripe. To have it all, she simply inserted the floral stripe between panels of repeated blocks.

Margy's color recipe for the Churn Dash blocks is blue motifs with pink backgrounds. She varied the value and density of the printed patterns to create the "now you see it, now you don't" look that is characteristic of Blended Quilts.

Morning Roses

DESIGNED AND QUILTED BY: **Margy Duncan**

FINISHED QUILT SIZE: **72½" x 76½"** • FINISHED BLOCK SIZE: **9"**

Materials

Fabric requirements are based on 40" fabric width.

- Fabric A, large-scale spaced-floral with light background focus fabric for outer border and Snowball block piecing: 3¾ yds.
- Fabric B, floral stripe for strips between pieced panels: 2 yds.
- Fabric C, assorted light, medium, and dark coordinated prints for piecing: 14-16 fat quarters or scraps (Margy used equal amounts of pinks and blues, and added a few yellow prints for variety.)
- Fabric D, tone-on-tone for inner border: ⅝ yd. for widthwise cuts or 2 yds. for lengthwise cuts
- Binding: ⅔ yd.
- Backing: 5⅛ yds.
- Batting: 81" x 85"

Directions

Read these instructions thoroughly before you begin. See *Basic Quiltmaking,* beginning on page 14, for general quiltmaking directions. All cutting measurements include ¼"-wide seam allowance. Instructions are for rotary cutting. Some pieces are cut larger than needed and then trimmed to size. For traditional piecing, use templates R1, S7, and T4 in Template section beginning on page 128.

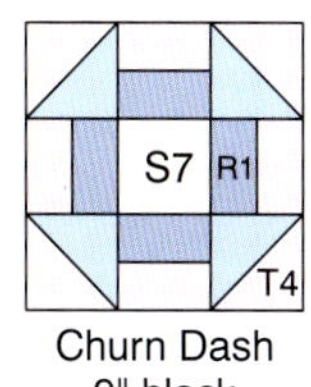

Churn Dash
9" block

Snowball
9" block

Quick Cutting Guide

For more detailed information, see complete cutting instructions given in each Step.

Fabric	Shape	Piece/ Template	Total Needed	Rotary Cutting		
				# to Cut	1st Cut	2nd Cut
Fabric A	▭	Outer border	4	4	5½" x 80"*	
	□	Snowball block	21	21	9½" x 9½"	
Fabric B	▭	Lattice strips	2	2	3" x length of fabric*	
Fabric C	□	S7	105°	105	3½" x 3½"	
	◺	T4	168	84	4" x 4"§	
	▭	R1	168	168	2" x 3½"	
Fabric D *Widthwise and lengthwise options given.*	▭	Inner border	4	8 strips —*OR*— 4 strips	2" x width of fabric* *(join strips end to-end in pairs)* 2" x length of fabric*	

* Strips are cut longer than necessary, and will be trimmed to size later.
° 84 of these will be used for corners of Snowball blocks.
§ Leave as squares for now. These will be cut again during piecing process.

Step 1: Borders, Snowball Block Centers, and Lattice Strips

Cut the borders, Snowball block centers, and Fabric B lattice strips; then arrange them on your design wall.

From Fabric A, cut:

- 4 strips, 5½" x 80", for outer borders. Strips are cut longer than necessary. They will be trimmed to size later. For now, pin them up on the design wall.
- 21 squares, 9½" x 9½", for Snowball blocks

From Fabric B, cut:

- 2 strips, the length of the fabric by 3" wide, for the vertical lattice strips dividing the panels of pieced blocks. Strips are cut longer than necessary. They will be trimmed to size later.

***From Fabric D, cut** (widthwise and lengthwise options given):*

- 8 strips, the width of the fabric x 2" wide, for inner border. Strips will need to be joined in pairs, end-to-end, to get enough length. Strips are longer than necessary. They will be trimmed to size later.

—OR—

- 4 strips, the length of the fabric by 2" wide, for inner border. Strips are cut longer than necessary. They will be trimmed to size later.

Step 2: Blocks

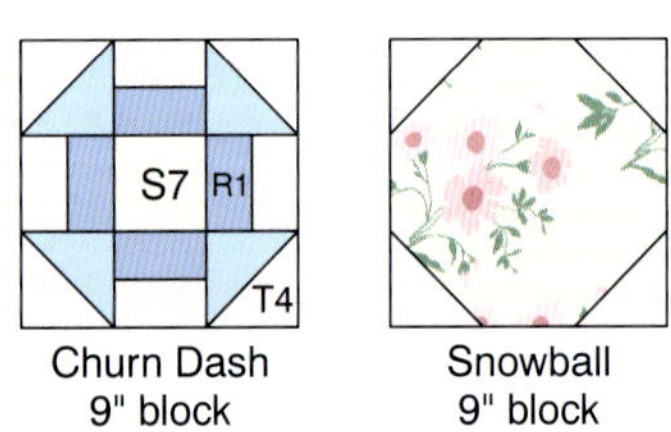

Churn Dash 9" block   Snowball 9" block

Cut and piece twenty-one 9" Churn Dash blocks and twenty-one 9" Snowball blocks. Sew them together to make quilt center.

Cutting instructions are for 1 Churn Dash block. Repeat 21 times with different fabrics in each block.

From Fabrics C, cut:

- 1 square, 3½" x 3½" (S7), for center
- 2 medium or dark squares, 4" x 4", for triangles
- 2 light squares, 4" x 4", for triangles
- 4 medium or dark rectangles, 2" x 3½" (R1)
- 4 light rectangles, 2" x 3½" (R1)

Cutting instructions are for 1 Snowball block. (9½" Fabric A squares have already been cut.) Repeat 21 times with different fabrics in each block.

From Fabrics C, cut:

- 4 squares, 3½" x 3½" (Margy cut all of her squares from pink prints.)

Piecing

1. Churn Dash Blocks

- Join light and medium (or dark) rectangles to make 4 squares, 3½" x 3½", for each block (84 total).

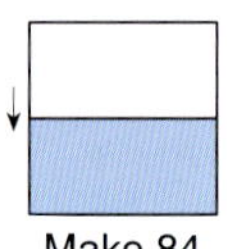
Make 84.

- Place 4" light and medium (or dark) squares right sides together. Cut diagonally and sew resulting triangle pairs together. Press seams towards the darker fabric. Make 4 for each block, 84 total.

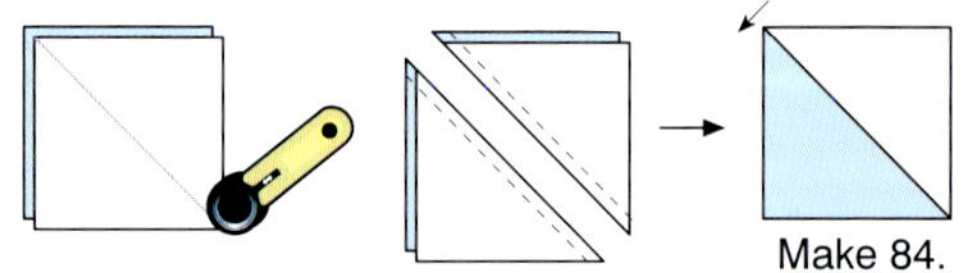
Make 84.

- Using the Precision Trimmer 6™ ruler, trim each completed square to 3½" x 3½", edge to edge.

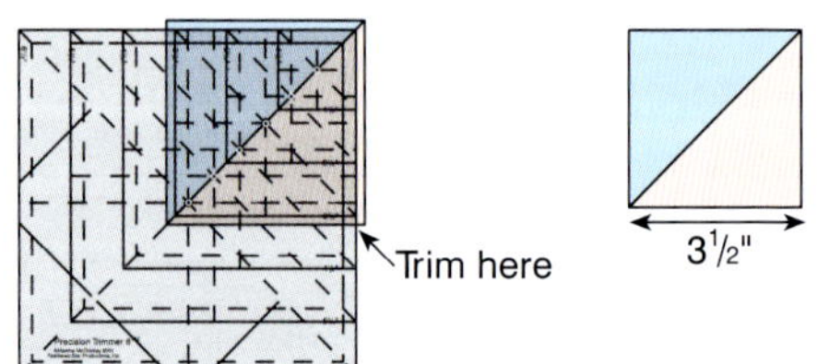

• Piece block, joining the 3½" units in rows. Join the rows. Edge-to-edge measurement should be 9½" x 9½".

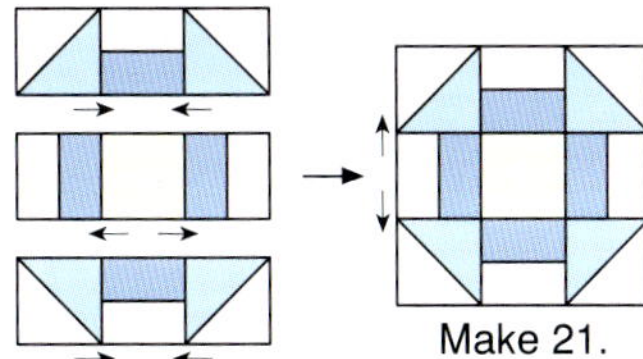
Make 21.

2. Snowball Blocks

• On the wrong side of four 3½" Fabric C squares, draw a diagonal line from corner to corner.

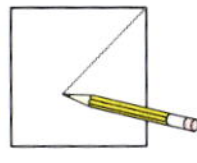

• With right sides together, place one 3½" Fabric C square on one corner of a 9½" Fabric A square. Stitch on the pencil line, then trim away the excess, leaving a ¼" seam allowance. Press seam toward the triangle. Repeat for remaining 3 corners. Edge-to-edge measurement should be 9½" x 9½".

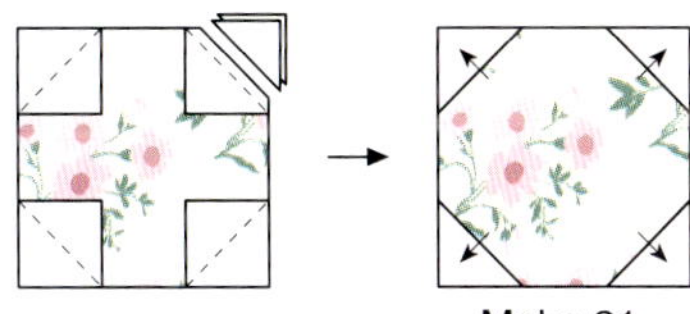
Make 21.

3. Arrange pieced blocks on design wall and when you are satisfied with the arrangement, piece the blocks together in 3 panels as shown.

Make 3.

4. Measure the length of each panel and trim the 3"-wide Fabric B strips to this length. Join panels and strips together as shown in the Quilt Assembly Diagram below. Press seams toward strips.

Step 3: Borders

Measure and trim borders strips; then join to quilt center.

1. For inner border, measure length of the quilt top through center. Trim two 2"-wide Fabric D strips to this measurement, and sew to sides of quilt. Press seams toward border. Measure width of the quilt top, including borders just added, through center. Cut remaining two 2"-wide strips to this measurement, and join to top and bottom of quilt. Press seams toward border.
2. For outer border, measure length of the quilt top through center. Trim two 5½"-wide Fabric A strips to this measurement, and sew to sides of quilt. Press seams toward border. Measure width of the quilt, including borders just added, through center. Cut remaining two 5½"-wide strips to this measurement, and join to top and bottom of quilt. Press seams toward border.

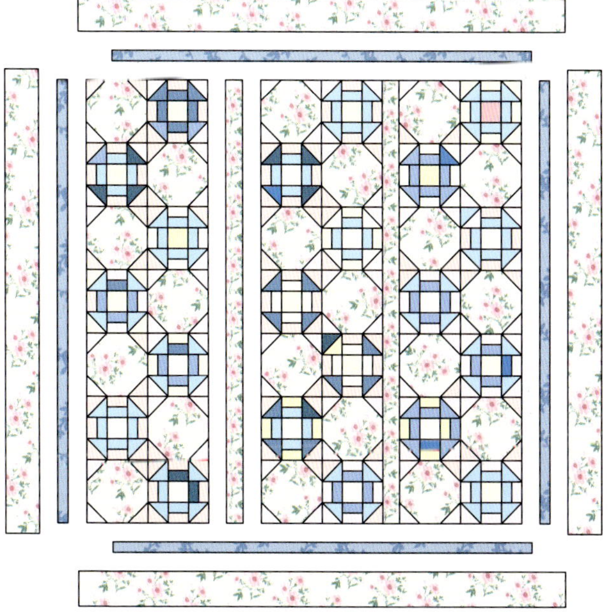
Quilt Assembly Diagram

See finishing instructions on pages 20-21.

Birds and Nines

Ann Stohl and her daughter Barbara Schroeder are a great team. Their quilts reflect the fun, creativity, and energy they put into their quiltmaking.

Ann writes, "The inspiration for the Birds and Nines (we originally called it Birds and Vines, but Marsha misread my handwriting!) quilt design was an antique Zigzag quilt top that I bought from Sharon Yenter in the 1980s. (See page 66.) Making it as a Blended quilt certainly changes the look!

"The first fabric we found was the honey-colored Mum floral. The second was another honey-colored print with roses. Third, was the butterscotch Birds and Vines fabric for the border. Then came a large variety of prints and coordinates. We tried to use reproduction fabrics: homespuns and prints that blended with the three main fabrics. The red became the constant in the body of the quilt and was repeated in the piped border and the binding to 'hold it all together.' The piping idea is from an antique Christmas quilt that I have—nothing new under the sun. These ladies of old thought of everything!"

Birds and Nines

DESIGNED BY: **Ann Stohl and Barbara Schroeder** • QUILTED BY: **Ann Stohl**

FINISHED QUILT SIZE: **68" x 76½"** • FINISHED BLOCK SIZE: **6"**

Materials

Fabric requirements are based on 40" fabric width.

- Fabric A, large-scale vine and bird print for outer border: 2¼ yds.
- Fabric B, medium-scale floral for inner border: 1 yd. for widthwise cuts or 1¾ yds. for lengthwise cuts
- Fabric C, large-scale spaced-floral with light background for zigzag setting triangles: 1 yd.
- Fabric D, a different large-scale spaced-floral with light background for zigzag setting triangles: ¾ yd.
- Fabric E, assorted light, medium, and dark coordinating prints for pieced blocks: 12-15 fat quarters or scraps
- Binding and piping for inner border: 1⅛ yds.
- Backing: 4⅞ yds. (widthwise seam)
- Batting: 76" x 85"

Directions

Read these instructions thoroughly before you begin. See *Basic Quiltmaking,* beginning on page 14, for general quiltmaking directions. All cutting measurements include ¼"-wide seam allowance. Instructions are for rotary cutting. For traditional piecing, use templates S1, S7, T4, and T6 in Template section beginning on page 128.

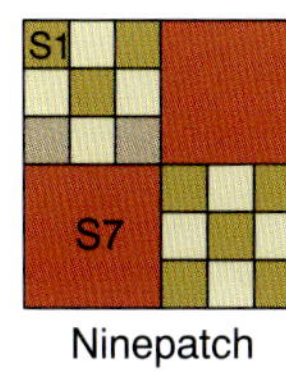

Ninepatch 6" block

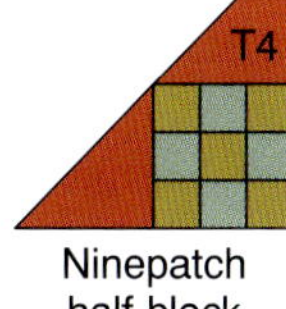

Ninepatch half-block

Quick Cutting Guide

For more detailed information, see complete cutting instructions given in each Step.

Fabric	Shape	Piece/ Template	Total Needed	Rotary Cutting		
				# to Cut	1st Cut	2nd Cut
Fabric A	▭	Outer border	4	4	10" x length of fabric*	
Fabric B *Widthwise and lengthwise options given.*	▭	Inner border	4	8 strips —*OR*— 4 strips	3½" x width of fabric* *(join strips end-to-end in pairs)* 3½" x length of fabric*	
Fabric C	◺	Corner-setting triangles T6	12	6	5⅛" x 5⅛"	⧄
	△	Side-setting triangles	32 *(2 extra)*	8	9¾" x 9¾"	⊠
Fabric D	△	Side-setting triangles	24	6	9¾" x 9¾"	⊠
Fabric E	□	S7	56	56	3½" x 3½"	
	□	S1	540	540	1½" x 1½"	
	△	T4	8	2	5½" x 5½"	⊠

* Strips are cut longer than necessary, and will be trimmed to size later.

Step 1: Borders and Setting Triangles

Cut the borders and setting triangles; then arrange them on your design wall. Ann determined the width of the border by the design of the fabric, and the way the vines would match at the corners.

From Fabric A, selectively cut:

- 4 strips, the length of the fabric x 10" wide, for outer border. Strips are cut longer than necessary. They will be trimmed to size later.

***From Fabric B, cut** (widthwise and lengthwise options given):*

- 8 strips, the width of the fabric x 3½" wide, for inner border. Strips will need to be joined in pairs, end-to-end, to get enough length. Strips are longer than necessary. They will be trimmed to size later.

—OR—

- 4 strips, the length of the fabric x 3½" wide, for inner border. Strips are cut longer than necessary. They will be trimmed to size later.

From Fabric C, cut:

- 6 squares, 5⅛" x 5⅛"; cut each square once diagonally to make 12 corner-setting triangles (T6) for panels #1, #3, and #5
- 8 squares, 9¾" x 9¾"; cut each square twice diagonally to make 32 side-setting triangles (2 extra) for panels #1, #3, and #5

From Fabric D, cut:

- 6 squares, 9¾" x 9¾"; cut each square twice diagonally to make 24 side-setting triangles for panels #2 and #4

Step 2: Blocks and Half-Blocks

Make twenty-eight 6" Ninepatch blocks and 4 half-blocks.

Cutting instructions are for 1 Ninepatch block. Repeat 28 times with different fabrics in each block.

From assorted Fabrics E, cut:

- 2 squares, 3½" x 3½" (S7)
- 8 light squares, 1½" x 1½" (S1), for Ninepatches
- 10 medium or dark squares, 1½" x 1½" (S1), for Ninepatches

Cutting instructions are for one Ninepatch half-block. Repeat 4 times with different fabrics in each block.

From assorted Fabrics E, cut:

- 1 square, 5½" x 5½"; cut square twice diagonally to make 4 triangles (T4) (only 2 are needed)
- 4 light squares, 1½" x 1½" (S1), for Ninepatch
- 5 medium or dark squares, 1½" x 1½" (S1), for Ninepatch

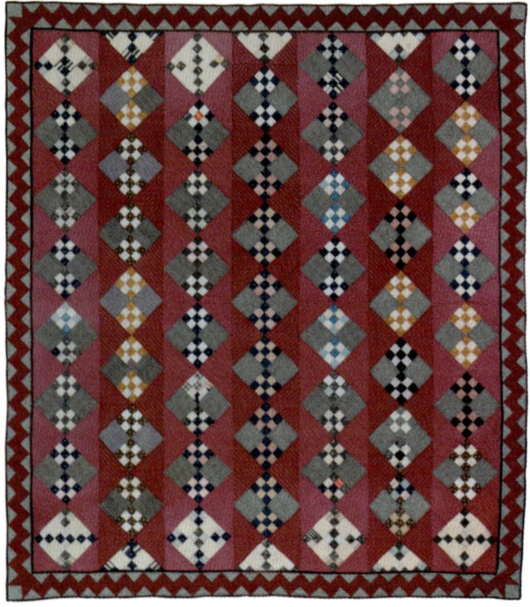

The prints chosen make a huge difference in a quilt's look. This antique Zigzag quilt was Ann Stohl's inspiration for Birds and Nines.

Piecing

1. Ninepatch blocks. For each block, make two small Ninepatches (edge-to-edge measurement should be 3½"), then join to 3½" plain squares to complete block. Edge-to-edge measurement should be 6½" x 6½".

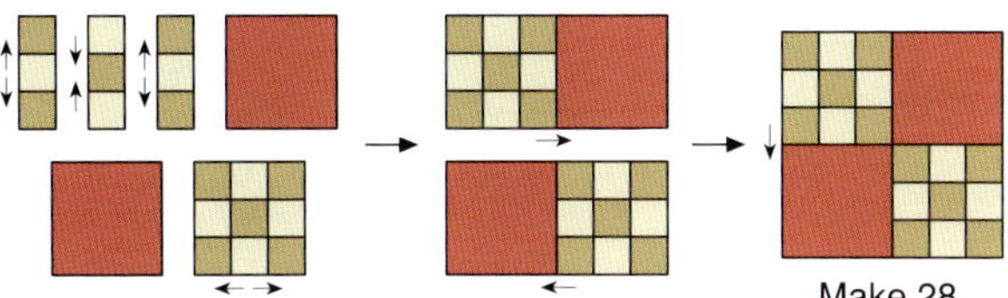

Make 28.

2. Ninepatch half-blocks. For each half-block, make one small Ninepatch and join with two triangles.

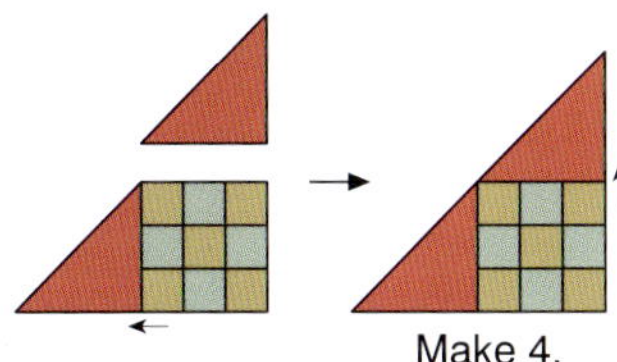

Make 4.

3. After playing with the blocks and setting triangles on the design wall, make the Strippy panels. Press seams toward triangles. Rows #1, #3, and #5 are the same and contain 6 blocks, 10 Fabric C side-setting triangles, and 4 Fabric C corner-setting triangles. Rows #2 and #4 contain 5 blocks, 2 half-blocks, and 12 Fabric D side-setting triangles. Join the rows as shown in the Quilt Assembly Diagram.

Make 3. Make 2.

Step 3: Borders

Measure and trim border strips, incorporate piping; then join to center of quilt.

1. Inner Border. Measure width of the quilt top through center and add 10". Trim two 3½"-wide Fabric B border strips to this measurement. Do the same for the length of the quilt.
2. Piping. From the binding fabric, cut eight strips the width of the fabric x 1½"-wide. Sew strips together in pairs, end-to-end, then trim to the same length as the Fabric B border strips. With the right side out, fold the narrow strips in half lengthwise and press. With right sides together and raw edges matching, machine baste piping (folded strip) to one edge of each Fabric B border strip. Join border strips with piping to quilt center and miter corners. (See page 19 for mitering instructions.)
3. Outer Border. Measure length of the quilt top through center. Trim two 10"-wide Fabric A border strips to this measurement, and sew to sides of quilt. Press seams toward border. Measure width of the quilt top, including borders just added, through the center. Cut remaining two border strips to this measurement, and join to top and bottom of quilt. Press seams toward border.

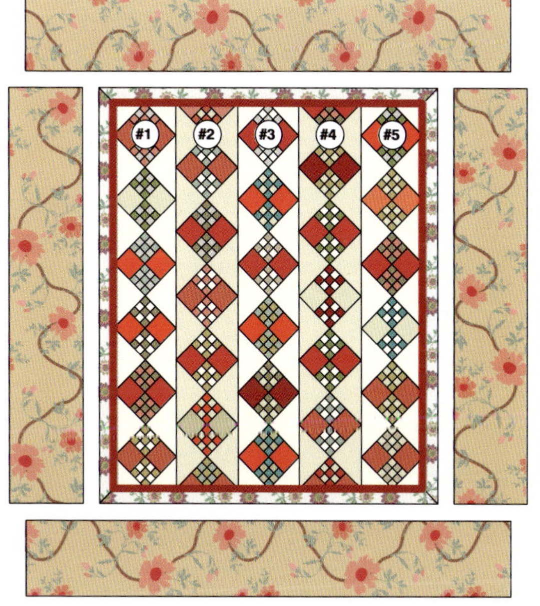

Quilt Assembly Diagram

See finishing instructions on pages 20-21.

Black Forest

Inspired by an 1800s quilt and a gorgeous border print, Barb Vose made this strippy design in only a few days. The piecing is so simple, the only thing that really took time was choosing the go-with fabrics from her scrap bag and arranging the patches on the design wall. The blocks are really scrappy and made with assorted prints. Most have similar colors and values. Be sure to use a few patches of lighter and darker prints so the shapes show clearly on some of the blocks. Piece the units, and place them on your design wall as you go. This way, you can rearrange for the best possible composition. To make this quilt even easier, consider using some unpieced 5½" squares cut from interesting fabrics to substitute for some pieced blocks.

Any pieced block design can be used for the vertical rows in a strippy quilt. Varying the block design here and there, like Barb did, adds interest. These rows of Fourpatch and Pinwheel blocks could also be considered for borders in a Medallion-style quilt.

BLACK FOREST

DESIGNED BY: **Barbara Vose** • QUILTED BY: **Cindy Paulsgrove**

FINISHED QUILT SIZE: **66½" x 79"** • FINISHED BLOCK SIZE: **5"**

Materials

Fabric requirements are based on 40" fabric width.

- Fabric A, border print, for top and bottom borders, and some piecing: 2⅛ yds.
- Fabric B, floral toile, for strips between rows and side borders, and some piecing: 2⅛ yds.
- Fabric C, large-scale floral for side triangles in pieced rows: 1½ yds.
- Fabric D, assorted prints for piecing Fourpatch and Pinwheel blocks: 6-8 fat quarters or scraps
- Binding: ¾ yd.
- Backing: 5⅛ yds.
- Batting: 75" x 87"

Directions

Read these instructions thoroughly before you begin. See *Basic Quiltmaking*, beginning on page 14, for general quiltmaking directions. All cutting measurements include ¼"-wide seam allowance. Instructions are for rotary cutting. Some pieces are cut larger than needed and then trimmed to size. For traditional piecing, use templates S5, T3, T5, and T10 in Template section beginning on page 128.

Fourpatch
5" block

Pinwheel
5" block

Quick Cutting Guide

For more detailed information, see complete cutting instructions given in each Step.

Fabric	Shape	Piece/ Template	Total Needed	Rotary Cutting		
				# to Cut	1st Cut	2nd Cut
Fabric A		Border *(top and bottom)*	2	2	8" x length of fabric*	
Fabric B		Side border and 3 vertical strips	5	5	8" x length of fabric*	
Fabric C		Side-setting triangles T10	64	16	8⁵⁄₁₆" x 8⁵⁄₁₆"	
		Corner-setting triangles T5	16	8	4⅜" x 4⅜"	
Fabrics A, B, and D		S5	124	124	3" x 3"	
		T3	40	20	3½" x 3½"°	

* Strips are cut longer than necessary, and will be trimmed to size later.
° Leave as squares for now. These will be cut again during piecing process.

Step 1: Borders, Strips, and Setting Triangles

Cut the borders, long strips, and setting triangles; then arrange them on your design wall.

From Fabric A, selectively cut:

- 2 strips, the length of the fabric x 8" wide, for top and bottom borders. Strips are cut longer than necessary. They will be trimmed to size later.

From Fabric B, cut:

- 5 strips, the length of the fabric x 8" wide, for strips in between pieced rows and side borders. Strips are cut longer than necessary. They will be trimmed to size later.

From Fabric C, cut:

- 16 squares, $8^{5}/_{16}$" x $8^{5}/_{16}$"; cut each square twice diagonally to make 64 quarter-square triangles (T10) for side triangles in pieced rows. Trim points as shown on page 34.
- 8 squares, $4^{3}/_{8}$" x $4^{3}/_{8}$"; cut each square once diagonally to make 16 half-square triangles (T5) for end triangles in pieced rows. Trim points as shown on page 34.

Step 2: Blocks

Make thirty-one 5" Fourpatch blocks and five 5" Pinwheel blocks.

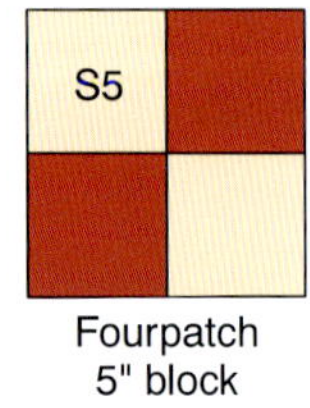

Fourpatch
5" block

Fourpatch

Cutting instructions are for 1 Fourpatch block. Repeat 31 times with different fabrics in each block.

From assorted Fabrics A, B, and D, cut:

- 4 squares, 3" x 3" (S5)

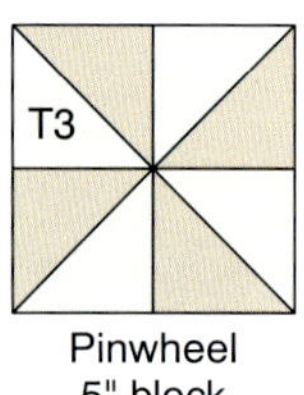

Pinwheel
5" block

Pinwheel

Cutting instructions are for 1 Pinwheel block. Repeat 5 times with different fabrics in each block.

From assorted Fabrics A, B, and D, cut:

- 4 squares, $3^{1}/_{2}$" x $3^{1}/_{2}$" (For traditional piecing, use T3 template to cut triangles.)

Piecing

1. Fourpatches. Place squares in a pleasing arrangement and stitch together as shown. Edge-to-edge measurement of each block should be $5^{1}/_{2}$".

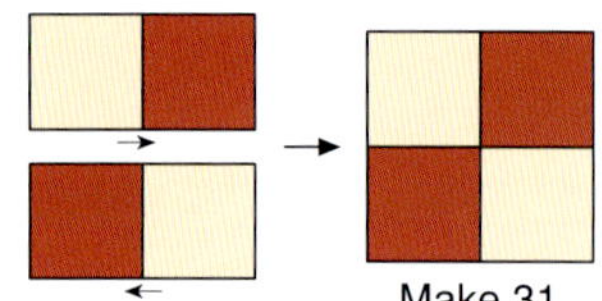

2. Pinwheels. For each block choose four $3^{1}/_{2}$" squares, using at least two different prints. Arrange the squares in pairs with right sides together. Working with one pair of squares at a time, make a cut diagonally, corner to corner, yielding 2 pairs of triangles. Stitching the long side, sew each triangle pair together. Make 4 for each block, 20 total.

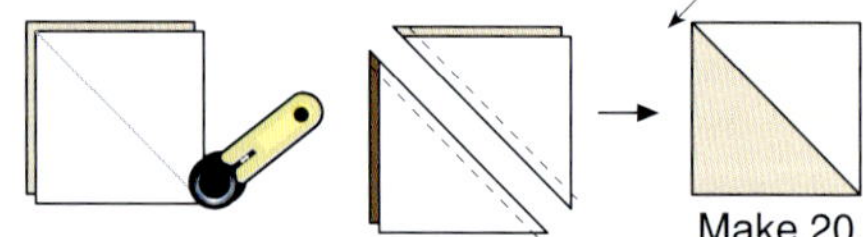

Using a square ruler with appropriate markings, trim the completed square to 3" x 3", edge to edge.

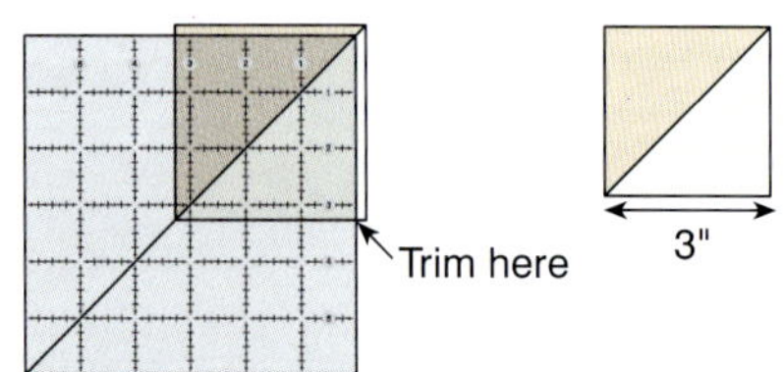

Piece block as shown. Edge-to-edge measurement of each block should be 5½". See the Tip at right for making perfect Pinwheels.

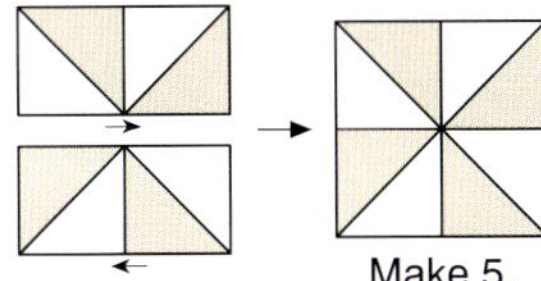

Make 5.

3. After playing with the units on your design wall, sew together 4 rows of 9 pieced blocks each, with appropriate setting triangles, as shown. Press seams toward triangles. When sewn, these rows should measure 7⅝" x 64⅛", edge to edge.

Make 4.

4. Step back and study the total look of the 8"-wide Fabric B strips, as placement of motifs may be important; then trim the strips to match the length of the pieced rows. Join strips and pieced rows as shown in the Quilt Assembly Diagram. Press seams toward strips.

Step 3: Borders

Measure width of the quilt top through center. Trim two 8"-wide Fabric A border strips to this measurement, and sew to top and bottom of quilt. Press seams toward border.

Quilt Assembly Diagram

See finishing instructions on pages 20-21.

Piecing Pinwheels

Here's a little trick for making the eight triangle points in the center of the Pinwheel block come together accurately.

1. Following assembly instructions, make 4 half-square triangle units.
2. Matching diagonal, opposing seams, chain piece 2 halves of the pinwheel. Make sure the triangles meet exactly at the ¼" seam line.

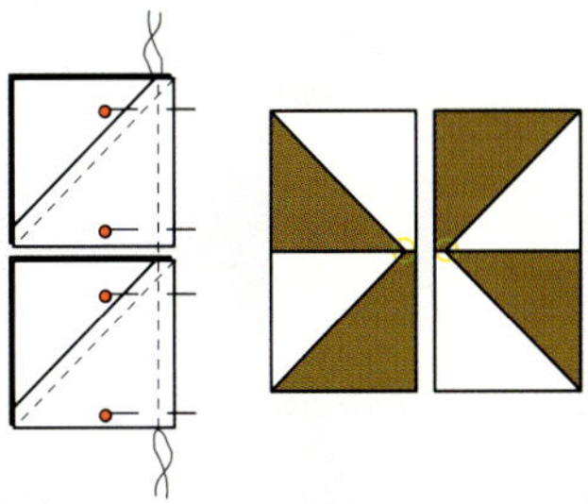

3. Press seams toward the darker fabric. With the right sides together, use a positioning pin to match the points of the triangles at the center seams. Opposing vertical and diagonal seams will "nest." Pin as shown. Stitch center seam through the X. Press center seam open.

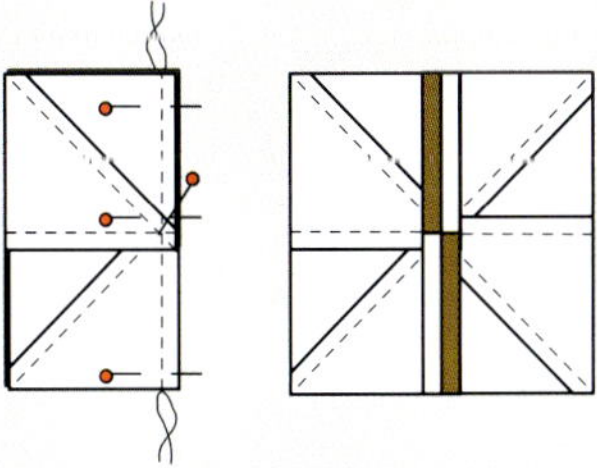

Flying Geese

Always on the lookout for unusual fabrics, Barb Vose gleefully snatched this pillar print from a sale table. It is the perfect focus fabric for the long strips that separate the rows of Flying Geese in her strippy quilt. Called pillar prints because they quite literally depict architectural pillars, these block or roller printed chintzes were popular during the early 1800s. Today, quilters can occasionally find pillar print reproductions. Because she wanted to selectively place the floral motifs, Barb bought extra fabric so lengthwise adjustments could be made.

The second important fabric here is the finely-etched light floral that is used for both the border print and the small background triangles in all the Flying Geese units. This print, when Barb found it, had a too-white background that she tea-dyed to take away the brightness. The rest of the prints, color-coordinated to the pillar print, are from her stash. Though the majority are reds and tans, the "sparkle" color is the light blue.

Flying Geese

DESIGNED BY: **Barbara Vose** • QUILTED BY: **Cindy Paulsgrove**
FINISHED QUILT SIZE: **69½" x 75½"** • FINISHED BLOCK SIZE: **3" x 6"**

Materials

Fabric requirements are based on 40" fabric width.

- Fabric A, pillar print for vertical strips: 2½ yds.
- Fabric B, large-scale, finely-etched light floral for border and Flying Geese background triangles: 4 yds.
- Fabric C, assorted prints for Flying Geese: 8-10 fat quarters or scraps
- Binding: ¾ yd.
- Backing: 5 yds.
- Batting: 78" x 84"

Directions

Read these instructions thoroughly before you begin. See *Basic Quiltmaking*, beginning on page 14, for general quiltmaking directions. All cutting measurements include ¼"-wide seam allowance. Instructions are for rotary cutting. These are "sew and flip" instructions. For traditional methods, use templates T4 and T6 in Template section beginning on page 128. For yet another way to make Flying Geese, see the sidebar on page 78.

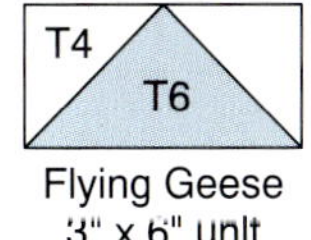

Flying Geese
3" x 6" unit

Quick Cutting Guide

For more detailed information, see complete cutting instructions given in each Step.

Fabric	Shape	Piece/ Template	Total Needed	Rotary Cutting		
				# to Cut	1st Cut	2nd Cut
Fabric A	▭	Vertical strips	5	5 lengthwise strips	6½" x 72"*	
Fabric B	▭	Outer border	4	4 lengthwise strips	8" x 78"*	
	◺	T4	160	160	3½" x 3½"°	
Fabric A and C	△	T6	80	80	3½" x 6½"°	

*Strips are cut longer than necessary, and will be trimmed to size later.
°Leave as squares or rectangles for now. These will be used in a "sew and flip" technique.

Step 1: Borders and Strips

Cut the long strips and borders; then arrange them on your design wall.

From Fabric A, selectively cut:

- 5 lengthwise strips, 6½" x 72", for the unpieced strips between the Flying Geese rows. To make better use of the print you have chosen, you may want to adjust the width of this strip. Strips are cut longer than necessary. They will be trimmed to size later.

From Fabric B, cut:

- 4 lengthwise strips, 8" x 78", for outer border. Strips are cut longer than necessary. They will be trimmed to size later.

Step 2: Flying Geese Units

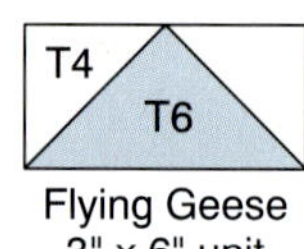

Flying Geese
3" x 6" unit

Make 80 Flying Geese units.

From Fabric B, cut:

- 160 squares, 3½" x 3½", for background triangles (T4)

From assorted Fabric C prints and Fabric A, cut:

- 80 rectangles, 3½" x 6½", for large triangles (T6)

Piecing

1. On the wrong side of 160 3½" Fabric B squares, draw a diagonal line from corner to corner.

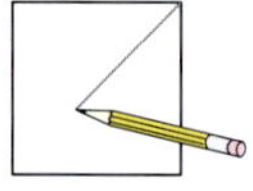

Use the Precision Trimmer 6™

Another way to make an accurate Flying Geese unit! In this method, triangles are overcut (larger than in traditional piecing) and sewn together. Then, the Flying Geese unit is trimmed to the proper size. Barb uses this method and so do I. It is right-on accurate and seems to use less fabric than the "sew and flip" method.

Flying Geese Unit: 3" x 6" finished

1. Cut 1 square, 7½" x 7½". Cut twice diagonally to make 4 quarter-square Triangles C. (This adds 1½" to the finished long side of the triangle.)

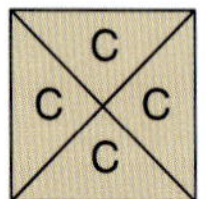

2. Cut 4 squares, 4¼" x 4¼". Cut once diagonally to make 8 half-square Triangles D. (This adds 1¼" to the finished short side of the triangle.)

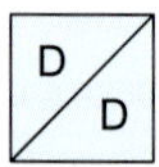

3. To make Flying Geese unit, stitch 2 Triangles D to each Triangle C. Trim pieced unit to 3½" x 6½" using the Precision Trimmer 6™ ruler.

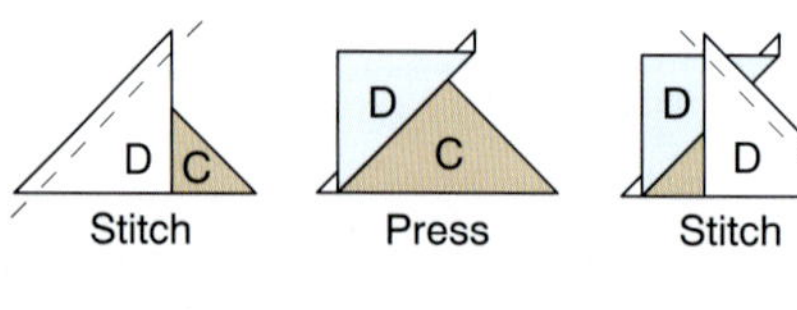

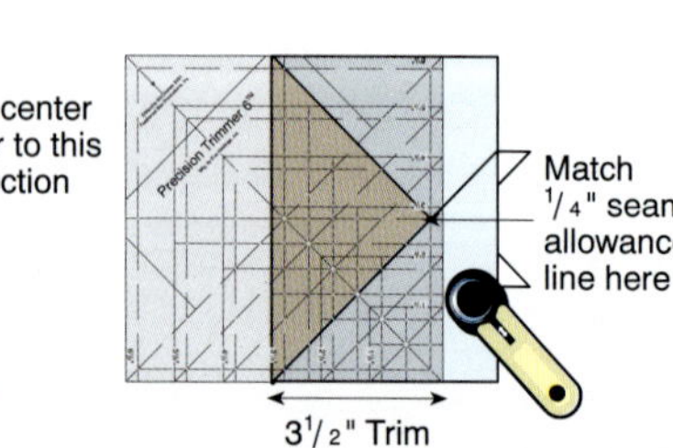

2. With right sides together, place one 3½" Fabric B square on one corner of a 3½" x 6½" Fabric C or A rectangle. Stitch on the pencil line, then trim away the excess, leaving a ¼" seam allowance. Press seam toward the triangle. Repeat for other end of rectangle to make a Flying Geese unit that measures 3½" x 6½", edge to edge. Repeat to make 80 units.

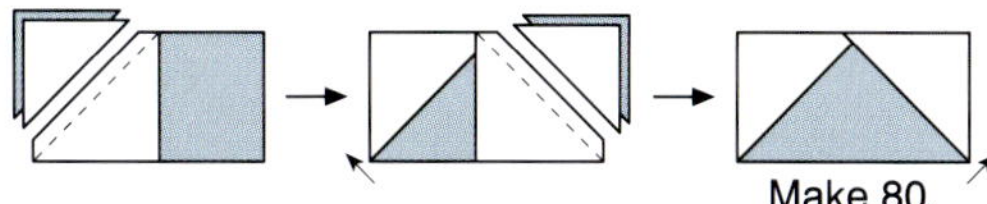

3. After playing with the units on your design wall, join the Flying Geese together in 4 rows of 20 each as shown in the Quilt Assembly Diagram at right. Press seams in one direction. When sewn, each row should measure 6½" x 60½".
4. Step back and see the total look of the 6½"-wide Fabric A strips, as placement of motifs may be important; then trim the strips to match the length of the pieced rows of Flying Geese. Join strips and pieced rows as shown in the Quilt Assembly Diagram. Press seams toward strips.

Notice how the blue triangle patches pick up the blue in the focus fabric, adding just the right amount of sparkle to the color arrangement.

Step 3: Borders

Trim border strips and join to quilt center.

1. Measure length of the quilt top through center. Trim two 8"-wide border strips to this measurement, and sew to sides of quilt. Press seams toward border.
2. Measure width of the quilt top, including borders just added, through the center. Cut remaining two border strips to this measurement and join to top and bottom of quilt. Press seams toward border.

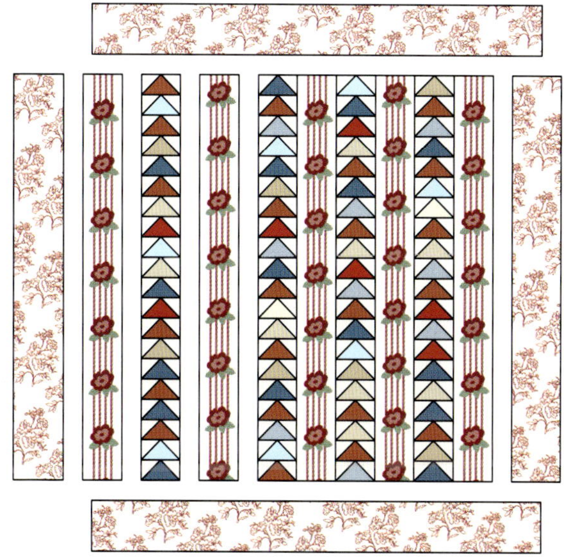

Quilt Assembly Diagram

See finishing instructions on pages 20-21.

Splendid Blended Olio

The dictionary gives two definitions of the word "Olio":

1. a highly spiced stew of meat and vegetables;

2. a collection, miscellany, as of musical numbers.

Looking at this quilt, I think either definition fits. Ann Stohl and Barbara Schroeder's focus fabric, the French floral montage used in the border, is a rich and colorful reproduction print that Sharon Yenter licensed from Le Musée de l'Impression sur Etoffes in Mulhouse, France.

Ann says, "We were attempting to stay within the guidelines set by Marsha: use simple shapes and let the fabric do the work. Each simple 6" block is a small blended version of one of the color schemes found in the border fabric motifs.

The fabrics we used taught us about blending; they always 'looked wrong when they weren't right.' The key is to work around a central color and value scheme. We tried to achieve a balance of lights and darks, placing stars and squares on the design wall and rearranging them until we were pleased. We always used a reducing glass to help make our decisions. Sometimes we looked so much, we lost our sense of balance. I helped and sewed, but Barbara had the ability to stick with it and make the design work."

Splendid Blended Olio

DESIGNED BY: **Ann Stohl and Barbara Schroeder** • QUILTED BY: **Debie Brown**

FINISHED QUILT SIZE: **65½" x 56½"** • FINISHED BLOCK SIZE: **6"**

Materials

Fabric requirements are based on 40" fabric width.

- Fabric A, large-scale floral print for border: 2¼ yds.
- Fabric B, assorted prints (mostly stripes) for vertical strips that separate the pieced panels, and top and bottom inner borders: 6 pieces, ¼ - ⅜ yd. each
- Fabric C, assorted light, medium, and dark coordinating prints for pieced blocks: 12-15 fat quarters or scraps
- Binding: ⅔ yd.
- Backing: 3⅞ yds.
- Batting: 65" x 74"

Directions

Read these instructions thoroughly before you begin. See *Basic Quiltmaking*, beginning on page 14, for general quiltmaking directions. All cutting measurements include ¼"-wide seam allowance. Instructions are for rotary cutting and some "sew and flip" construction. Some pieces are cut larger than needed and then trimmed to size. For traditional piecing, use templates S2, S7, T1, and T9 in Template section beginning on page 128.

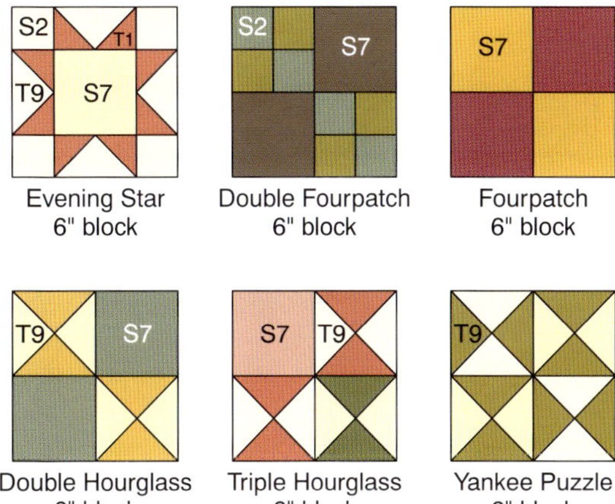

Evening Star 6" block | Double Fourpatch 6" block | Fourpatch 6" block | Double Hourglass 6" block | Triple Hourglass 6" block | Yankee Puzzle 6" block

Quick Cutting Guide

For more detailed information, see complete cutting instructions given in each Step.

Fabric	Shape	Piece/ Template	Total Needed	Rotary Cutting		
				# to Cut	1st Cut	2nd Cut
Fabric A	rectangle	Outer border	4	4	8½" x length of fabric*	
Fabric B	rectangle	Vertical strips	7	7	*(See Step 3 on page 85.)*	
	rectangle	Horizontal strips	3	3	*(See Step 4 on page 85.)*	
Fabric C *Evening Star (15 blocks)*	square	S7	15	15	3½" x 3½"	
	square	S2	60	60	2" x 2"	
	triangle	T9	60	60	2" x 3½"°	
	right triangle	T1	120	120	2" x 2"°	
Fourpatch (5 blocks)	square	S7	20	20	3½" x 3½"	
Double Fourpatch (5 blocks)	square	S7	10	10	3½" x 3½"	
	square	S2	40	40	2" x 2"	
Double Hourglass (12 blocks)	triangle	T9	96	24	4½" x 4½"§	
	square	S7	24	24	3½" x 3½"	
Triple Hourglass (1 block)	triangle	T9	12	4	4½" x 4½"§	
	square	S7	1	1	3½" x 3½"	
Yankee Puzzle (4 blocks)	triangle	T9	64	16	4½" x 4½"§	

* Strips are cut longer than necessary, and will be trimmed to size later.
° Leave as squares or rectangles for now. These will be used in a "sew and flip" technique.
§ Leave as squares for now. These will be cut again during piecing process.

Step 1: Border Strips

Cut the outer border strips and arrange them on your design wall.

From Fabric A, cut:

- 4 strips, the length of the fabric x 8½" wide, for outer borders. Strips are cut longer than necessary. They will be trimmed to size later. Ann and Barbara decided at the end to make the top and bottom borders narrower, but you can decide that later.

Step 2: Blocks

Make forty-two 6" pieced blocks. This quilt has 15 Evening Star, 5 Fourpatch, 5 Double Fourpatch, 12 Double Hourglass, 1 Triple Hourglass, and 4 Yankee Puzzle blocks. Instructions for each block design are given here. (Cutting instructions are for one block. You can decide how many of each to make.) Edge-to-edge measurements should be 6½" x 6½".

Evening Star

From Fabrics C, cut:

- 1 square, 3½" x 3½" (S7), for center
- 4 squares, 2" x 2" (S2), for corners
- 4 rectangles, 2" x 3½", for star point units
- 8 squares, 2" x 2", for star point units

Piecing

1. Make 4 star point units for each block.

- On the wrong side of eight 2" squares, draw a diagonal line from corner to corner.

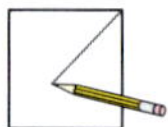

- With right sides together, place one 2" square on one corner of a 2" x 3½" rectangle. Stitch on the pencil line, then trim away the excess, leaving a ¼" seam allowance. Press seam toward the small triangle. Repeat for other end of rectangle to make a star point unit that measures 2" x 3½", edge to edge. Repeat to make 4 units.

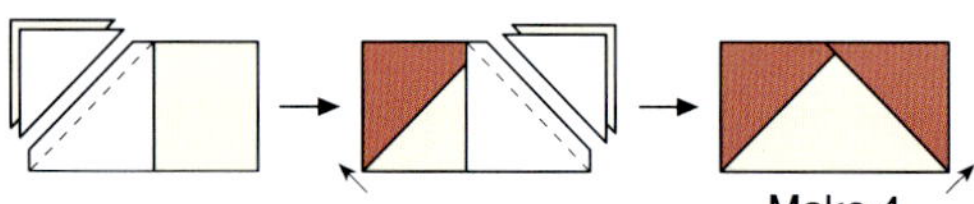

2. Join star point units together in rows with 3½" and 2" squares. Join rows together.

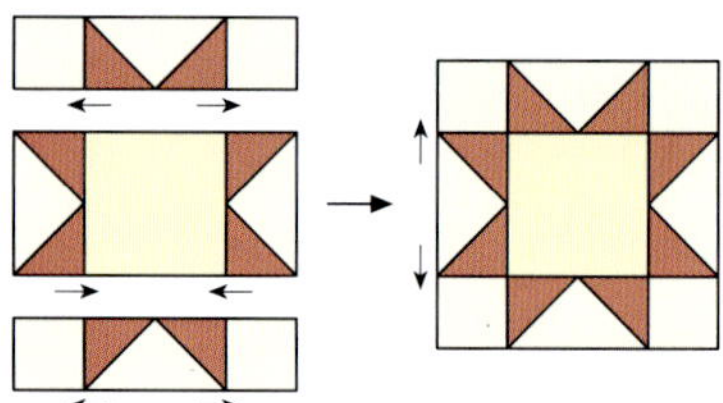

Fourpatch and Double Fourpatch

From Fabrics C, cut:

- 8 squares (at least 2 different fabrics), 2" x 2" (S2)
- 6 squares (at least 3 different fabrics), 3½" x 3½" (S7)

Piecing

To make Fourpatch and Double Fourpatch blocks, place squares in a pleasing arrangement and stitch together as shown. Each small Fourpatch should measure 3½" x 3½", edge to edge. The larger blocks should measure 6½" x 6½".

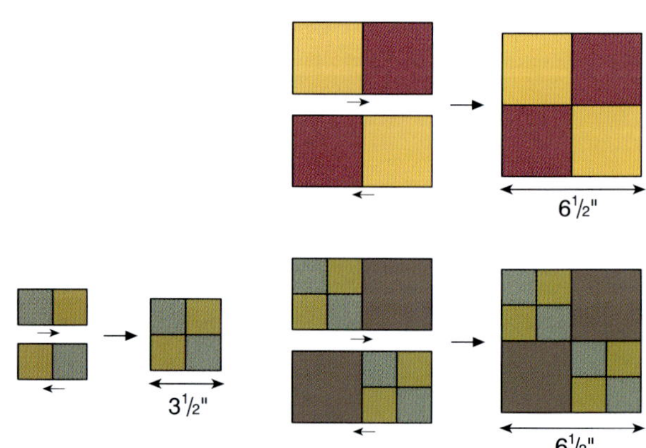

Double Hourglass, Triple Hourglass, and Yankee Puzzle

All of these designs contain pieced 3" Hourglass units. Cutting instructions are for two units.

From Fabrics C, cut:

- 1 light square, 4½" x 4½"
- 1 dark square, 4½" x 4½"

1. Place squares together with right sides facing. Cut diagonally, from corner to corner, yielding 2 pairs of triangles. Stitching the long side, sew each triangle pair together. Press seams to one side.

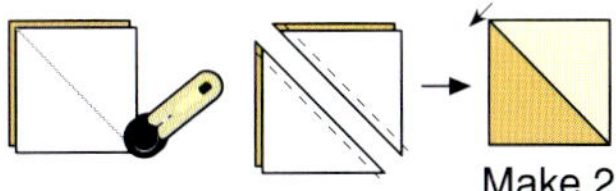

2. To make the Hourglass, match pairs of 2-triangle units, right sides together, nesting opposing seams. Cut diagonally and sew resulting triangle pairs together. Press seams to one side.

3. Use the Precision Trimmer 6™ to trim the completed unit to 3½" x 3½", edge to edge.

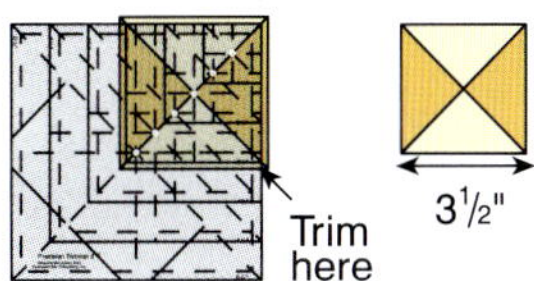

4. For the Double Hourglass block, make two 3½" Hourglass units and cut 2 squares, 3½" x 3½". Piece as shown.

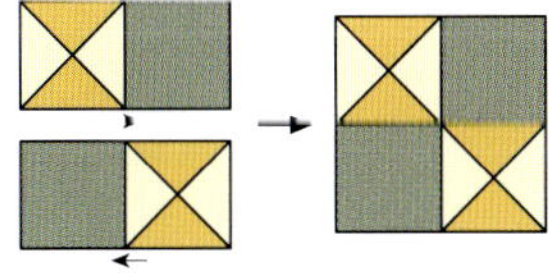

5. For the Triple Hourglass block, make three 3½" Hourglass units and cut 1 square, 3½" x 3½". Piece as shown.

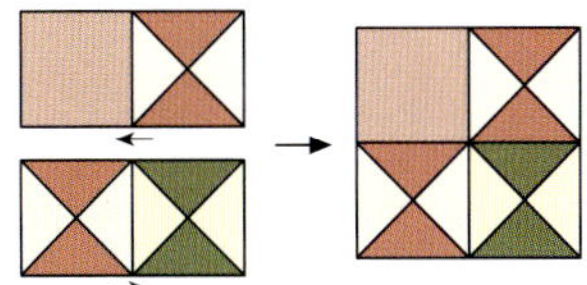

6. For the Yankee Puzzle block, make four 3½" Hourglass units and piece as shown.

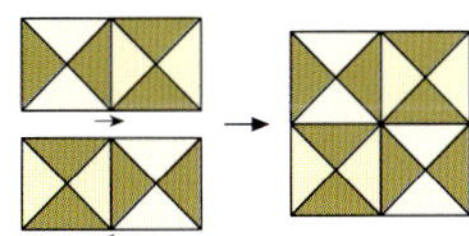

Step 3: Quilt Top Assembly

1. After playing with the blocks on the design wall, join the 6" blocks in 6 rows of 7 blocks each as shown in the Quilt Assembly Diagram.
2. Cut Fabric B strips to go between the rows at various widths (1½" to 3"). This is a visual decision you will make when you see the blocks and fabrics on the design wall. Trim the length of the strips to match the pieced rows of blocks. (You may need to piece strips, end-to-end, to get the length needed.) Join the rows and strips as shown in the Quilt Assembly Diagram.

Step 4: Borders

1. Cut three strips, 1½"-wide x width of fabric, from a Fabric B print. Join three strips end-to-end. Cut long strip in half, and trim to fit the width of the quilt. Join strips to top and bottom. Press seams toward border.
2. Measure length of the quilt top through center (the way this quilt is oriented, the length is less than the width). Trim two 10"-wide Fabric A border strips to this measurement, and sew to sides of quilt. Press seams toward border.
3. Measure width of the quilt top, including borders just added, through center. Cut remaining two border strips to this measurement, and join to top and bottom of quilt. Press seams toward border.

Quilt Assembly Diagram

See finishing instructions on pages 20-21.

Floral Cascade

Marsha asked each quilter to write something about her quilt. Here are Vicki Hurst's comments: "The focal fabric of this quilt is obviously the large floral print in the three main panels. I knew I had to use the fabric in strips somehow. My original idea was to use all three elements of older-style quilts: medallion, strippy, and repeat blocks. I think I was only somewhat successful, but without a predetermined quilt pattern, the design wants to create itself once you get started. At first, I was going to use only two strips of the large-scale floral (my strippy element) with a wider pieced panel in between (medallion). It just didn't work. After consultations with Marsha and others, a third strip was added, which in effect eliminated the medallion, but it worked. I felt the outer border needed a lot of piecing as the panel area was so simple. The design came to me out of the blue while lying in bed. I was worried I wouldn't remember it in the morning, but not worried enough to get up and sketch a reminder."

FLORAL CASCADE

DESIGNED BY: **Victoria Hurst** • QUILTED BY: **Sherry D. Rogers**

FINISHED QUILT SIZE: **69½" x 87½"**

Materials

Fabric requirements are based on 40" fabric width.

- Fabric A, large-scale floral for 3 vertical strips and Border #2 piecing: 2¾ yds. (yardage is generous to allow for selective cutting)
- Fabric B, large-scale spaced-floral with light pink background for piecing: 1½ yds.
- Fabric C, assorted light green prints for piecing and inner border strip: ⅓ yd. piece plus 6 fat quarters
- Fabric D, assorted beige prints for piecing: 3-4 fat quarters
- Fabric E, assorted red prints for piecing and inner border strip: ½ yd. piece plus 6 fat quarters
- Fabric F, assorted lavender prints for piecing and inner border strip: ⅓ yd. piece plus 2-3 fat quarters
- Binding: ¾ yd.
- Backing: 5⅝ yds.
- Batting: 78" x 96"

Quick Cutting Guide

For more detailed information, see complete cutting instructions given in each Step.

Fabric	Shape	Piece/ Template	Total Needed	Rotary Cutting		
				# to Cut	1st Cut	2nd Cut
Fabric A		Vertical strips	3	3 lengthwise strips	9½" x 57½"	
		S7	46	46	3½" x 3½"	
		S10	4	4	6½" x 6½"	
		S2	8	8	2" x 2"	
Fabric B		S10	10	10	6½" x 6½"	
		R3	88	88	2" x 6½"	
Fabric C-F *From fat quarters:*		R5	24	24	2¾" x 6½"	
Fabric C *From ⅓ yd. piece:*		Border #1	4	6	1¼" x width of fabric*	
From fat quarters:		R3	46	46	2" x 6½"	
		S7	38	38	3½" x 3½"	
Fabric D		S2	144	144	2" x 2"	
Fabric E *From ½ yd. piece:*		Border #1	4	6	2" x width of fabric*	
From fat quarters:		S2	84	84	2" x 2"	
		R3	42	42	2" x 6½"	
Fabric F *From ⅓ yd. piece:*		Border #1	4	6	1¼" x width of fabric*	
From fat quarters:		S2	68	68	2" x 2"	

* Set 2 strips aside. Join remaining 4 strips together, end-to-end, in pairs to make 2 long strips.

Directions

Read these instructions thoroughly before you begin. See *Basic Quiltmaking*, beginning on page 14, for general quiltmaking directions. All cutting measurements include ¼"-wide seam allowance. Instructions are for rotary cutting. For traditional piecing, use templates S2, S7, S10, R3, and R5 in Template section beginning on page 128.

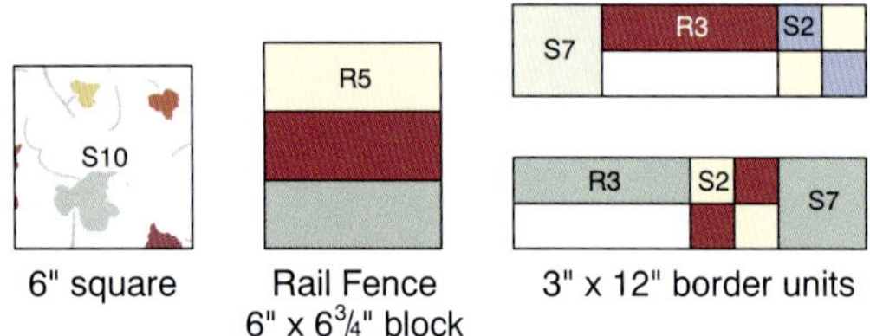

6" square
Rail Fence 6" x 6¾" block
3" x 12" border units

Step 1: Center Panel

Cut all the center panel pieces; then place them on design wall to evaluate before sewing.

From Fabric A, selectively cut:
- 3 panels, 9½" x 57½"

From Fabric B, cut:
- 10 squares, 6½" x 6½" (S10), for pieced panels

From assorted Fabrics C, D, E, and F fat quarters, cut:
- 24 rectangles, 2¾" x 6½" (R5), for the Rail Fence blocks in pieced panels

Piecing

1. With assorted rectangles, make 8 Rail Fence blocks. These are not square, but measure 6½" x 7¼", edge to edge.

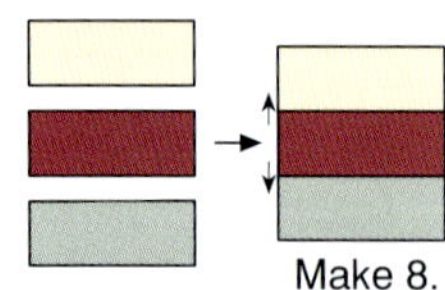
Make 8.

2. Join Rail Fence blocks with Fabric B squares to make 2 panels as shown. These should measure 6½" x 57½", edge to edge.

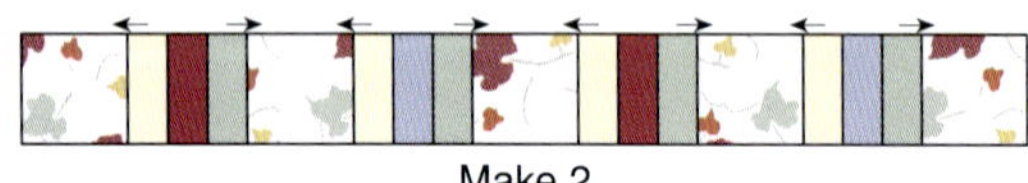
Make 2.

3. Join pieced panels with 3 Fabric A panels as shown in the Quilt Assembly Diagram on page 91. These 5 panels, when sewn together, should measure 39½" x 57½", edge to edge.

Step 2: Border #1

Cut borders strips and join to quilt center.

From ⅓-yd. piece of Fabric C, cut:
- 6 strips, the width of the fabric x 1¼" wide; set 2 strips aside, join remaining 4 strips end-to-end in pairs to make 2 long strips

From ½-yd. piece of Fabric E, cut:
- 6 strips, the width of the fabric x 2" wide; set 2 strips aside, join remaining 4 strips end-to-end in pairs to make 2 long strips

From ⅓-yd. piece of Fabric F, cut:
- 6 strips, the width of the fabric x 1¼" wide; set 2 strips aside, join remaining 4 strips end-to-end in pairs to make 2 long strips

Piecing

1. Matching strip lengths, make the border units by sewing a narrow Fabric C and F strip on either side of the wider Fabric E strip as shown. From shorter strips, trim top and bottom borders to 3½" x 39½" to match quilt width. From longer strips, trim side borders to 3½" x 63½" to match quilt length including top and bottom borders.

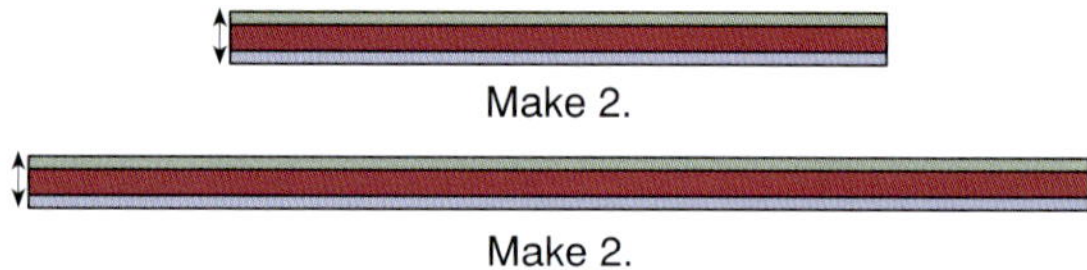
Make 2.
Make 2.

2. Join the shorter strips to the top and bottom of the quilt center. Join the longer strips to sides. Press seams toward borders.

Step 3: Border #2

Cut and sew the pieced border, and join to quilt center.

From Fabric A, cut:
- 46 squares, 3½" x 3½" (S7)
- 4 squares, 6½" x 6½" (S10)
- 8 squares, 2" x 2" (S2)

From Fabric B, cut:
- 88 rectangles, 2" x 6½" (R3)

From assorted Fabric C prints, cut:

- 46 rectangles, 2" x 6½" (R3)
- 38 squares, 3½" x 3½" (S7)

From assorted Fabric D prints, cut:

- 144 squares, 2" x 2" (S2)

From assorted Fabric E prints, cut:

- 84 squares, 2" x 2" (S2)
- 42 rectangles, 2" x 6½" (R3)

From assorted Fabric F prints, cut:

- 68 squares, 2" x 2" (S2)

Piecing

1. For Corner Units, make:

- 4 Fourpatches with Fabric A and E 2" squares.

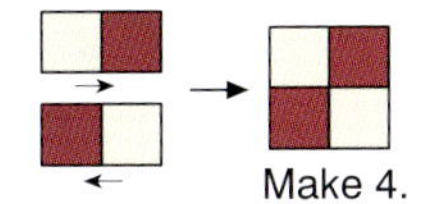
Make 4.

- 8 rectangles with Fabric B and E 2" x 6½" patches.

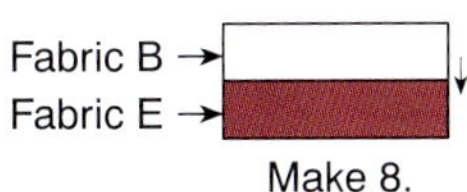

Make 8.

- 8 rectangles with Fabric B and C 2" x 6½" patches.

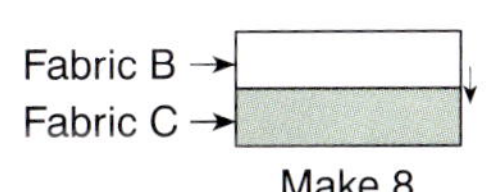

Make 8.

2. Join pieced units and Fabric A squares (3½" and 6½") to make 4 corner units as shown. (Pay careful attention to color placement.)

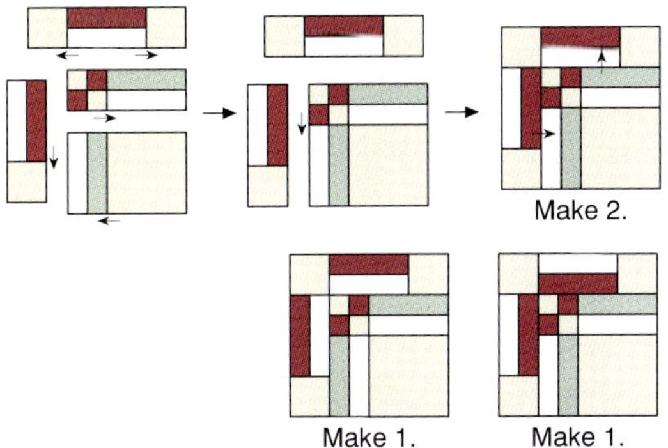

3. For top, bottom, and side borders, make:

- 38 Fourpatches with Fabric D and E 2" squares.

Make 38.

- 34 Fourpatches with Fabric D and F 2" squares.

Make 34.

- 34 rectangles with Fabric B and E 2" x 6½" patches.

Make 34.

- 38 rectangles with Fabric B and C 2" x 6½" patches.

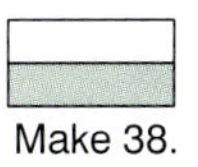
Make 38.

4. Join pieced units and 3½" Fabric A and C squares to make 34 of Border Unit 1 and 38 of Border Unit 2 as shown. (Pay careful attention to color placement.)

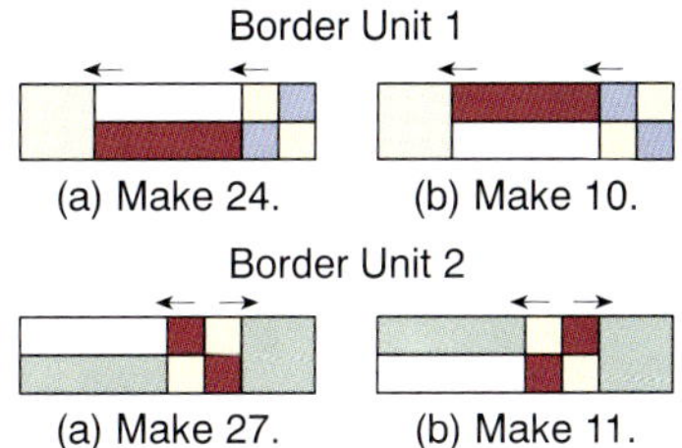

5. Arrange these units in alternating format, and join to make border sections as shown in Quilt Assembly Diagram.

- For top, use 7 Border Units 1a and 8 Border Units 2a.
- For bottom, use 7 Border Units 1a and 8 Border Units 2a.
- For left side, use 10 Border Units 1b and 11 Border Units 2b.
- For right side, use 10 Border Units 1a and 11 Border Units 2a.

6. Join side border sections to sides of quilt.
7. Join a corner unit to each end of the top and bottom border sections, and join to quilt center as shown in the Quilt Assembly Diagram.

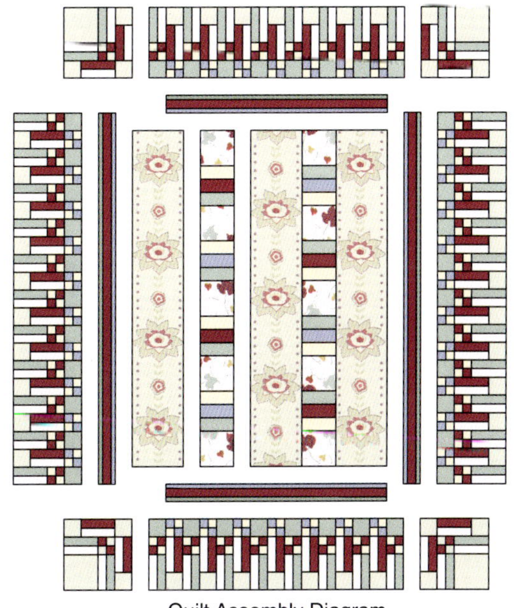
Quilt Assembly Diagram

See finishing instructions on pages 20-21.

Garden Dance

Memories of Versailles

Blue Meadow

Garden View

Medallion Quilts

The framed medallion quilt style is one of the oldest. This style features a printed panel or patchwork block in the quilt center, surrounded by rows and rows of pieced and plain borders. Traditional English framed medallion quilts were very large, made to cover large beds. They often look like the pieced borders were added until the size was right. The quiltmakers were much more relaxed about exact fit than we are today. Sometimes, strips of simple patchwork were pieced and trimmed to fit the center, or narrow plain borders were placed between pieced areas as spacers. Sometimes adjustments were made by placing lengths of fabric strips between the piecing in the border design.

Three of our four framed medallion quilts are small — suitable for throws and wall hangings. Make them larger by adding as many plain or pieced borders as you wish.

The Center

In the spirit of "letting the fabric do the work," the designers of the medallion quilts in this pattern section chose to selectively cut prints for their quilt centers. The first three quilts (Memories of Versailles, Blue Meadow, and Garden Dance) have square centers, and the last quilt (Garden View) has a rectangular center. In each case, the size of the motif on the printed fabric determined the size of the center panel.

Measure the desired motif to find the best dimensions. If your center is to be square, it can be cut straight or on the diagonal. If the motif looks best in a diagonal square, consider spray starching the fabric before it is cut so the bias edges will not stretch. When cutting a rectangle, try to use finished dimensions for the width and length that are divisible by the same numbers, i.e. 12" x 15" (both divisible by 3). This will make planning repeats for pieced borders a lot easier.

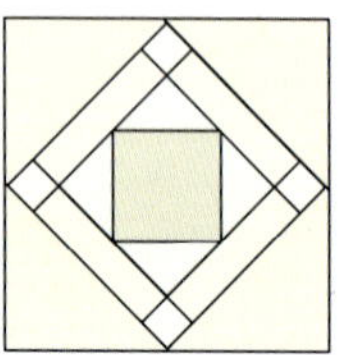

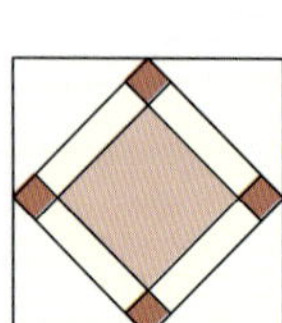

Squaring Out

Many medallion quilts have large triangles surrounding the center square or panel to form a new larger square. Instructions on page 55 tell how to draft setting triangles for any size block. If your medallion center square isn't too large, use the example given for cutting the B (corner-setting) triangles.

Sometimes the triangles you need will be too large to draw, so here's another way to figure cutting measurements. Measure the finished side of the center square. Divide this measurement by 1.414. This dimension will be the finished short side of your large triangle. Add ⅞" (.875) for seam allowances. This will be the size of the squares to cut to get half-square triangles (straight grain on the short side) to fit around the center square. Cut two squares; then cut each square once diagonally to make four triangles. Trim points for matching as described on page 34.

To calculate the size of corner-setting triangles:

1. Measure the finished size of center square. Example: 9".
2. Divide by 1.414. Example: 9" ÷ 1.414 = 6.35" (round up to 6⅜")
3. Add ⅞" seam allowance. Example: 6⅜" + ⅞" = 7¼"
4. Cut two 7¼" squares. Cut each square once diagonally to make 4 corner-setting triangles.

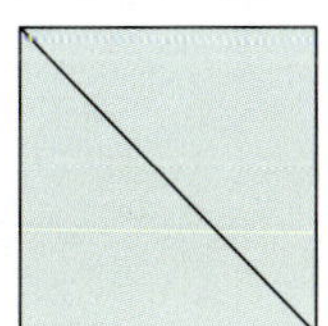

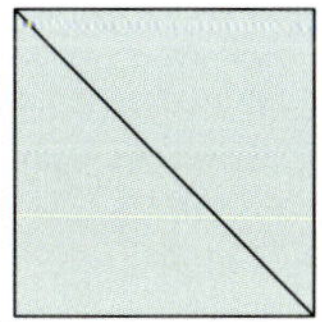

If the print you're using is directional, be sure to cut each square in opposite directions so the triangles can be added to the center with printed motifs aligned.

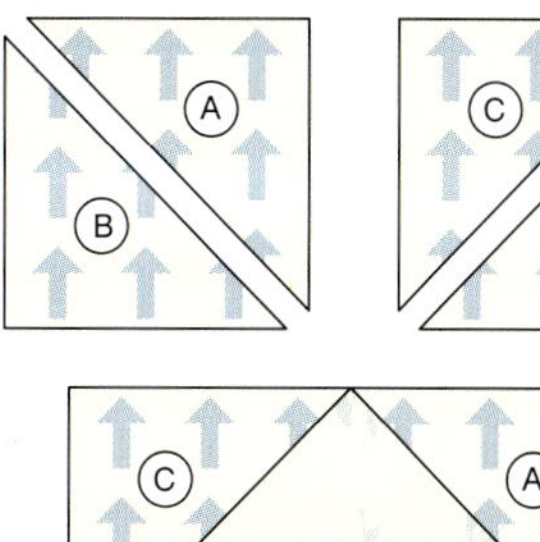

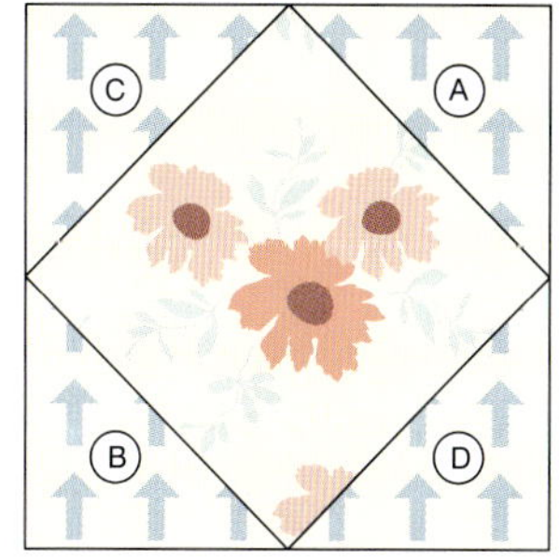

Easy Pieced Borders

Following are a number of approaches to creating a border to complete your medallion quilt.

• **Plan it mathematically.** Pieced border designs are basically unit blocks or portions of unit blocks strung together in rows. Each design unit within a border design is called a repeat. For these quilts, keep the piecing simple. For a pieced border to fit evenly, the finished dimensions of the central patchwork design need to be equally divisible by the border repeat measurement. To use 2" repeats, for instance, the space in which the border is to fit needs to have a finished dimension divisible by 2". A 4" border repeat fits only measurements evenly divisible by 4" and so on.

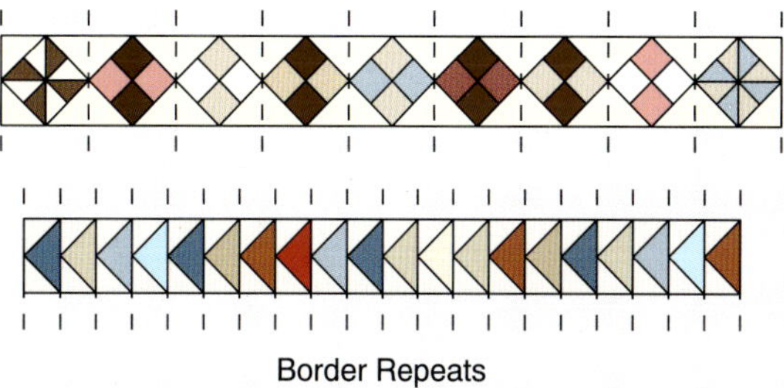

Border Repeats

• **Add a spacer strip.** If the repeat dimensions don't fit the quilt center, add a narrow plain border to the center to bring it out to a dimension that will work. A spacer strip can fill in whatever space you need. Wait to cut it until the center and border sections are complete. To arrive at a dimension for the spacer strip, measure the pieced sections. Do not include seam allowances in these calculations. Subtract the size of the quilt center from the length of the pieced border. Divide the resulting dimension by two and you'll have the finished width of the spacer strip. Add ½" to the length and width for seam allowances before cutting strips.

Add spacer strips to quilt center, as needed, to fit pieced borders.

• **Use pieced corner squares**. Piece only the corner squares and use unpieced border strips in between. It will still have the effect of a pieced border. And if you repeat it with two or three borders the corner blocks will begin to "chain." Take advantage of printed stripes to make the plain borders more interesting.

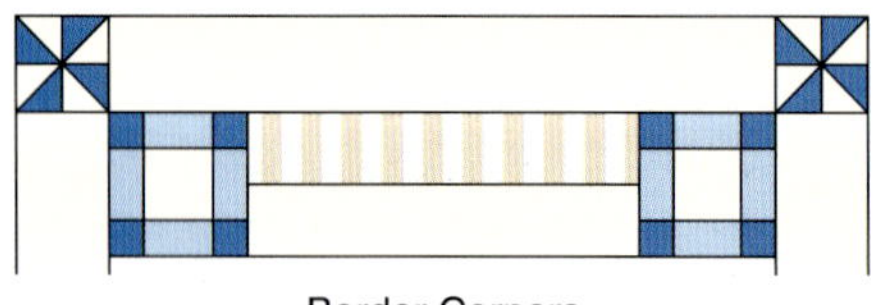

Border Corners

• **Use spacer strips between the blocks.** Piece the corner squares and one or two pieced squares for each side of the quilt — fill in the rest of the border space with strips of fabric to make the border long enough.

Spacer Strips Between the Blocks

• **Make a random pieced border.** Measure the border space and fill it with random bits of patchwork, plain squares, and strips of fabric. See Garden View on page 122.

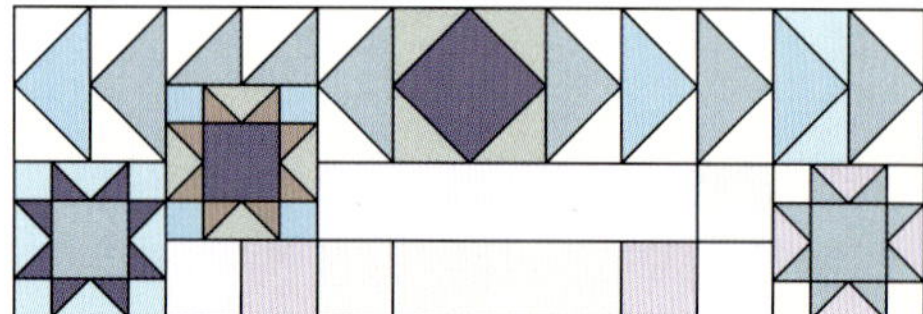

Random Pieced Border

• **Trim to fit.** Piece a border strip longer than the side of the quilt center and trim it to fit disregarding where the pattern ends or how it turns the corner. (I've never been able to do this!)

A Trimmed-to-Fit fourth border, and an unpieced fifth border, is added to the Blue Meadow design to make the quilt larger.

Border Designs

Examples of typical border designs/repeats used in Framed Medallions include these simple pieced designs: Fourpatch, Ninepatch, Puss in the Corner, Stars, Chain of Squares, Flying Geese, and Sawtooth.

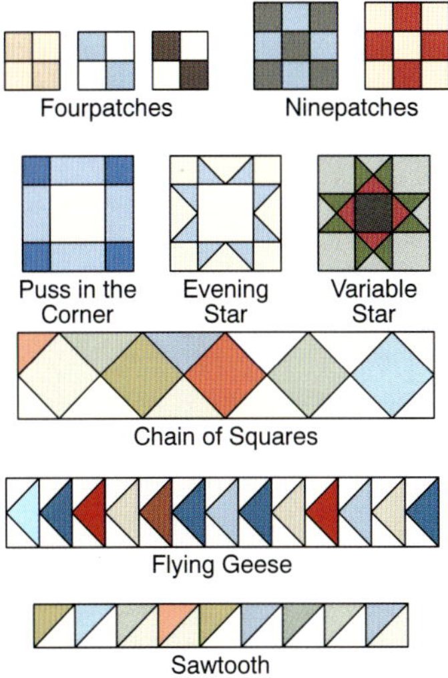

Sewing Tip

When pinning borders in place for sewing, I like to work at the ironing board. Pin the quilt to the board to keep it from slipping. Position the border on the quilt by matching centers, ends, and important points of matching. Ease and generously pin everything in between. Pressing the border to the quilt top with a steam iron at this point helps the two fit together and makes the sewing go more smoothly. Steam both shrinks and stretches fabric, allowing you to adjust the fit where it is needed.

Blue Meadow with Flying Geese Borders

Finished size: approximately 78½" x 78½"

In this example, a spacer strip and two borders have been added to the Blue Meadow design to make the quilt larger.

- Make 72 flying Geese Units (3" x 6" finished size, see instructions on pages 78-70).
- Cut four 6½" squares for corners.
- Cut and add spacer strips to bring center measurement out to dimensions of pieced border strips.
- Add 6"-wide (6½" cut) unpieced outer border with 6" stars at corners.

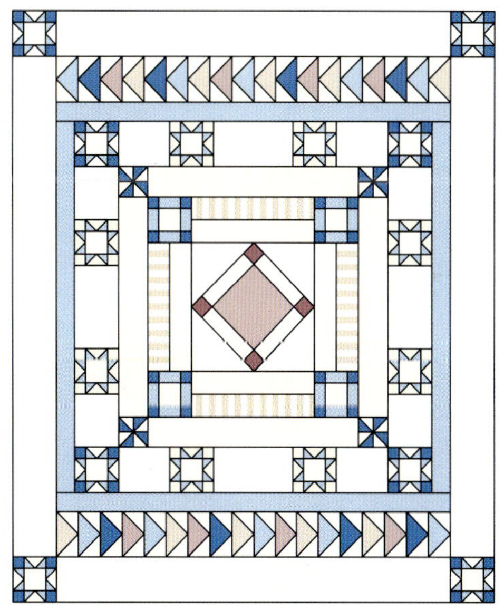

Rectangular Blue Meadow

Finished size: approximately 66½" x 78½"

To change a square quilt to a rectangle, add borders to the top and bottom, but not the sides.

Memories of Versailles

Cathy Mathes writes, "This quilt was inspired by my trip to Provence and Paris in the summer of 2002. At Versailles, there is a depth of color, shadows, and richness that I wanted to capture in this quilt. We were there on a late summer evening when the sun slanted low over the formal gardens and into the windows of the Hall of Mirrors — absolutely beautiful!

"The Toile is from L'Isle sur la Sorgue, a small village in Provence. I bought the fabric at an outdoor market and was taken by the butter yellow and true red. The other fabrics are from my stash. I wanted to play the green prints against one another—pushing the color limits — almost like eating too much chocolate!"

Memories of Versailles

DESIGNED BY: **Cathy Mathes** • QUILTED BY: **Kathy Staley**

FINISHED QUILT SIZE: **82" x 82"**

Materials

Fabric requirements are based on 40" fabric width.

- Fabric A, large-scale floral with green background for center square: 1 fat quarter
- Fabric B, medium-scale red print for triangles around the center square: 1 fat quarter
- Fabric C, medium-scale yellow and green stripe for Borders #1 and #5: 2½ yds.
- Fabric D, assorted green prints for Border #2 and some piecing: ½ yd. each of 4 different prints
- Fabric E, assorted beige-to-gold prints for piecing: 4-6 fat eighths or scraps
- Fabric F, large-scale red and yellow scenic toile for largest triangles: 1¾ yds.
- Fabric G, medium-scale light floral for Border #3: ¾ yd. (cut widthwise) or 1⅝ yds. (cut lengthwise)
- Fabric H, assorted red prints for piecing: 2-3 fat quarters or scraps
- Fabric I, large-scale floral with brown background for Border #4: 1⅞ yds.
- Binding: ¾ yd.
- Backing: 8 yds.
- Batting: 90" x 90"

Quick Cutting Guide

For more detailed information, see complete cutting instructions given in each Step.

Fabric	Shape	Piece/ Template	Total Needed	Rotary Cutting		
				# to Cut	1st Cut	2nd Cut
Fabric A	□	Center square	1	1	12½" x 12½"	
Fabric B	◺	Triangles	4	2	9⅜" x 9⅜"	⧄
Fabric C	▭	Border #1	4	4 lengthwise strips	4½" x 30"*	
	▭	Border #5	4	4	4½" x length of fabric*	
Fabric D	▭	Border #2	16	4 each from 4 different prints	2" x 25½"	
	□	S2	16	16	2" x 2"	
Fabric E	□	S3	16	16	2½" x 2½"	
	△	T7	16	4	3¼" x 3¼"	⊠
	□	S5	16	16	3" x 3"	
	△	T8	16	4	3¾" x 3¾"	⊠
Fabric F	◺	Triangles	4	2	27" x 27"	⧄
Fabric G	▭	Border #3	4	4 lengthwise strips§	3½" x 52¾"	
Fabric D or H	□	S3	4	4	2½" x 2½"	
	△	T7	48	12	3¼" x 3¼"	⊠
	□	S5	4	4	3" x 3"	
	△	T8	48	12	3¾" x 3¾"	⊠
Fabric I	▭	Border #4	4	4 lengthwise strips	8" x 58¾"	

* These are cut long to allow for mitering.

§ If cutting on widthwise grain, cut six 3½"-wide strips. Join, end-to-end, to make one long strip. From long strip, trim 4 strips to proper size.

Directions

Read these instructions thoroughly before you begin. See *Basic Quiltmaking*, beginning on page 14, for general quiltmaking directions. All cutting measurements include ¼"-wide seam allowance. Instructions are for rotary cutting. For traditional piecing, refer to templates S2, S3, S5, T7, and T8 in Template section beginning on page 128.

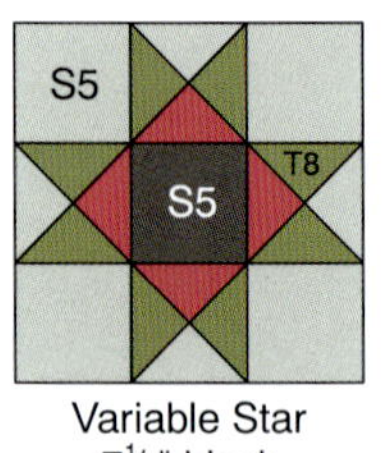

Variable Star
7½" block

Variable Star
6" block

Fourpatch
3" block

Step 1: Center Panel

Audition and cut all the center panel pieces; then arrange them on your design wall before stitching.

From Fabric A, selectively cut:

- 1 square, 12½" x 12½"

From Fabric B, cut:

- 2 squares, 9⅞" x 9⅞"; cut each square once diagonally to make 4 half-square triangles. For a perfect fit, trim triangle points with the Precision Trimmer 6™ ruler as shown.

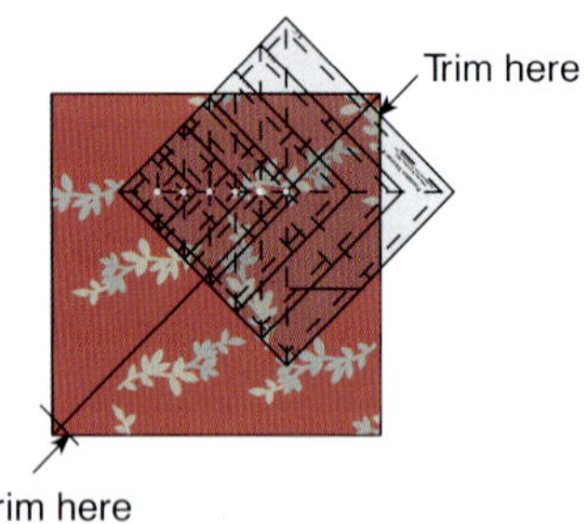

Piecing

Sew Fabric B triangles to Fabric A center square as shown, opposite sides first, then the other two.

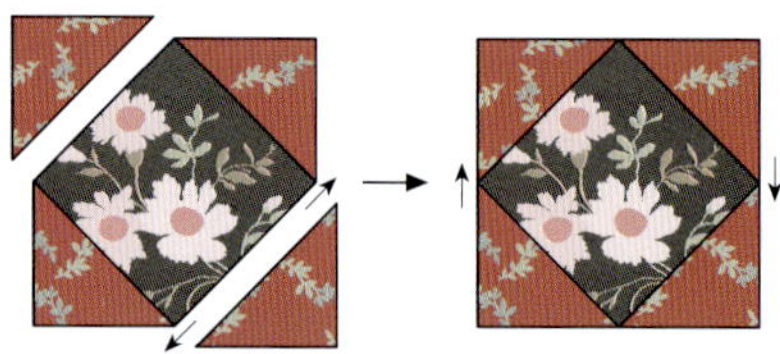

Step 2: Border #1

From Fabric C, cut:

- 4 lengthwise strips, 4½" x 30"

Piecing

Sew strips to center square using the Mitering Corners technique given on page 19. The quilt center so far should measure 25½", edge to edge.

Step 3: Border #2

Make four 6" Variable Star blocks and 4 striped border units; join to quilt center.

Variable Star Blocks

Cutting instructions are for one 6" Variable Star block. Each star has 4 different fabrics: choose from assorted Fabrics D, E, and H. Repeat 4 times with different fabrics in each block. Cathy used her reds and green interchangeably.

From Fabrics D or H, cut:

- 1 square, 2½" x 2½" (S3), for center
- 2 squares, 3¼" x 3¼" (T7); cut each square twice diagonally to make 8 quarter-square triangles for star points
- 1 square, 3¼" x 3¼" (T7); cut square twice diagonally to make 4 quarter-square triangles to fit around the center square

From Fabrics E, cut:

- 4 squares, 2½" x 2½" (S3), for corners
- 1 square, 3¼" x 3¼" (T7); cut square twice diagonally to make 4 quarter-square triangles for background

Striped Border Units

From each of 4 different Fabrics D, cut:

- 4 strips, 2" x 25½", for striped units (sixteen strips total)

Piecing

Make four 6" Variable Star blocks.

1. Arrange the triangles in 4-triangle star point units. Stitch together as shown. Each unit should measure 2½" x 2½", edge to edge. Make 4 for each block, 16 total.

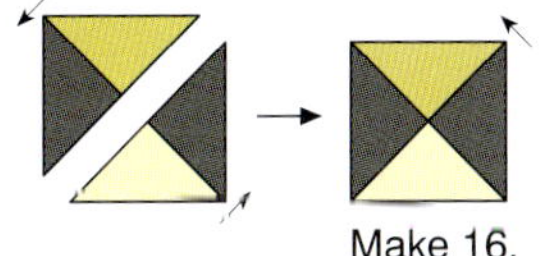

Make 16.

2. Using pieced units and 2½" squares, piece blocks as shown. Sewn blocks should measure 6½" x 6½", edge to edge.

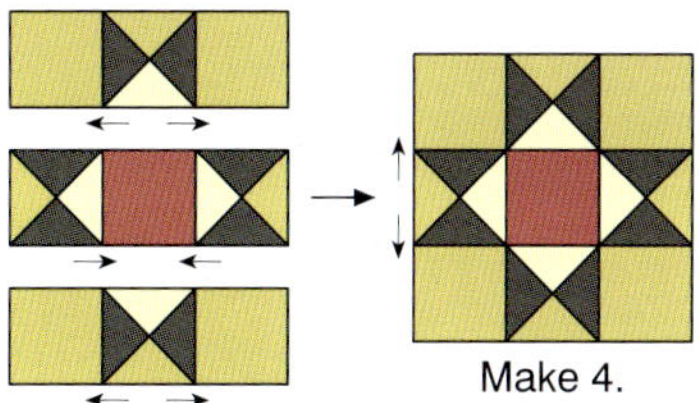

Make 4.

3. Make 4 striped units. Sew Fabric D strips together in sets of 4 as shown. Press seams in one direction. Sewn units should measure 6½" wide.

Make 4.

4. Join 2 striped units to sides of quilt center. Join a 6" Variable Star block to each end of 2 remaining striped units. Join to top and bottom. Quilt center should now measure 37½" x 37½", edge to edge.

Step 4: Large Toile Triangles

From Fabric F, cut:

- 2 squares, 27" x 27"; cut each square once diagonally to make 4 half-square triangles For a perfect fit, trim triangle points as shown on page 100.

Piecing

Sew Fabric F triangles to quilt center square as shown, opposite sides first, then the other two. Press seams toward triangles. Quilt center should now measure 52¾" x 52¾", edge to edge.

Step 5: Border #3

Cut border strips; make 3" Fourpatch blocks and join to quilt center.

From Fabric G, cut:

- 4 lengthwise strips, 3½" x 52¾". (If cutting widthwise grain, cut six 3½"-wide strips. Join end-to-end, to make one long strip; from long strip, trim 4 strips to proper size.)

From Fabrics D, cut:

- 16 squares, 2" x 2" (S2), for Fourpatch blocks

Piecing

1. Make 4 Fourpatch blocks. Place squares in a pleasing arrangement and stitch together as shown. Each should measure 3½" x 3½", edge to edge.

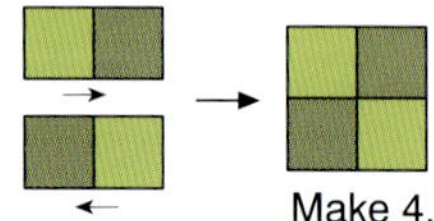

2. Add 2 Fabric G border strips to sides of quilt center. Join a Fourpatch to each end of 2 remaining strips. Join to top and bottom. Quilt center should now measure 58¾" x 58¾", edge to edge.

Step 6: Border #4

Make four 7½" Variable Star blocks; cut border strips and join to quilt center.

From Fabric I, cut:

- 4 lengthwise strips, 8" x 58¾"

Cutting instructions are for 1 Variable Star block. Repeat 4 times with different fabrics in each block.

From Fabrics D or H, cut:

- 1 square, 3" x 3" (S5), for center
- 2 squares, 3¾" x 3¾" (T8); cut each square twice diagonally to make 8 quarter-square triangles for star points
- 1 square, 3¾" x 3¾" (T8); cut square twice diagonally to make 4 quarter-square triangles to fit around the center square

From Fabric E, cut:

- 4 squares, 3" x 3" (S5), for corners
- 1 square, 3¾" x 3¾" (T8); cut square twice diagonally to make 4 quarter-square triangles for background

Piecing

1. Make 4 Variable Star blocks. Arrange triangles in 4-triangle star point units. Stitch together as shown. Each unit should measure 3" x 3", edge to edge. Make 4 for each block, 16 total.

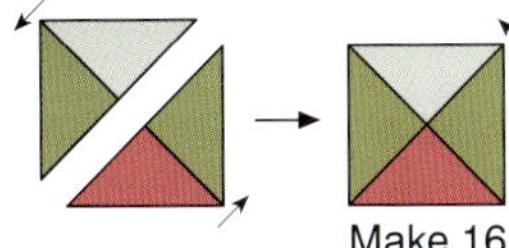

2. Using pieced units and 3" squares, piece blocks as shown. Sewn blocks should measure 8" x 8", edge to edge.

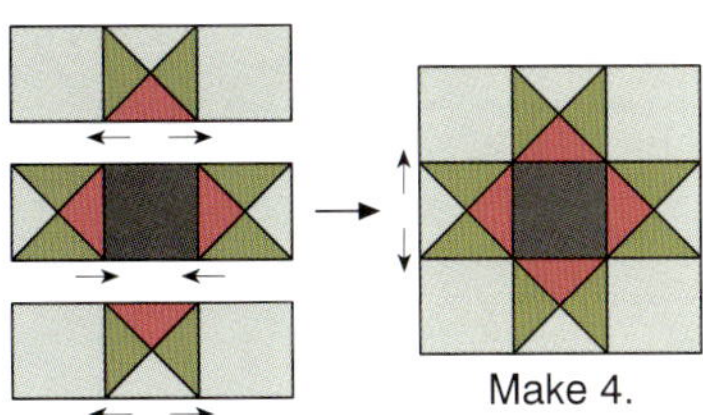

3. Join two Fabric I strips to sides of quilt center. Join a Variable Star block to each end of the 2 remaining border strips. Join to top and bottom.

Step 7: Border #5

From Fabric C, cut 4 strips, $4\frac{1}{2}$" x length of fabric. Join strips to all 4 sides of quilt and miter corners (see page 19).

Quilt Assembly Diagram

See finishing instructions on pages 20-21.

Blue Meadow

The focus print for Barb Vose's medallion wall quilt is a large-scale spaced-floral with a striped background. This fabric inspired the color recipe of "yellow and blue, with a touch of red." Notice how the

background stripe is selectively cut for the second border to draw your eye to the center of the quilt. The quilt is soft and fresh, just the right size for a welcoming wallhanging. To make it larger, consider more pieced borders or a wide floral print border.

See pages 93-95 for more border suggestions. Use the Flying Geese from the strippy quilt on page 76 to make a smashing pieced border.

BLUE MEADOW

DESIGNED BY: **Barbara Vose** • QUILTED BY: **Cindy Paulsgrove**

FINISHED QUILT SIZE: **49½" x 49½"**

MATERIALS

Fabric requirements are based on 40" fabric width.

- Fabric A, large-scale floral with striped background: ¾ yd.
- Fabric B, medium-scale yellow spaced-floral for piecing and binding: 1½ yds.
- Fabric C, large-scale yellow spaced-floral for piecing: ½ yd.
- Fabric D, large-scale medium-dark blue spaced-floral for piecing: 1 fat quarter
- Fabric E, red floral: 1 fat eighth or scraps
- Fabric F, blue/tan toile: ⅔ yd.
- Fabric G, blue on yellow small-scale light print for block backgrounds: ½ yd.
- Fabric H, 2 different large-scale prints with light background: ½ yd. each
- Binding: included in Fabric B
- Backing: 3½ yds.
- Batting: 58" x 58"

QUICK CUTTING GUIDE

For more detailed information, see commplete cutting instructions given in each Step.

Fabric	Shape	Piece/ Template	Total Needed	Rotary Cutting		
				# to Cut	1st Cut	2nd Cut
Fabric A	□	Center square	1	1	8½" x 8½"	
	▭	Border #1	4	4	3½" x 17½"	
	□	S7	4	4	3½" x 3½"	
Fabric B	▭	Center block	4	4	2½" x 8½"	
	▭	Border #1	4	4	3½" x 17½"	
	▭	Border #2	4	4	4½" x 29½"	
Fabric C	◺	T2	16	8	3" x 3"*	
	△	T9	16	16	2" x 3½"°	
	□	S7	8	8	3½" x 3½"	
Fabric D	□	S2	16	16	2" x 2"	
	◺	T2	16	8	3" x 3"*	
	□	S2	16	16	2" x 2"	
Fabric E	□	S3	4	4	2½" x 2½"	
Fabric F	▭	R1	16	16	2" x 3½"	
	◺	T1	96	96	2" x 2"°	
Fabric G	□	S2	32	32	2" x 2"	
	△	T9	32	32	2" x 3½"°	
Fabric H	◺	Triangles	4	2	9⅜" x 9⅜"	⧄
	▭	Border #3	4	4	6½" x 11½"	
	▭	Border #3	8	8	6½" x 7½"	
Fabric A *and/or* C	□	S7	4	4	3½" x 3½"	

* Leave as squares for now. These will be cut again during piecing process.

° Leave as squares or rectangles for now. These will be used in a "sew and flip" technique.

Directions

Read these instructions thoroughly before you begin. See *Basic Quiltmaking*, beginning on page 14, for general quiltmaking directions. All cutting measurements include ¼"-wide seam allowance. Instructions are for rotary cutting. Some pieced units are made larger than needed and then trimmed to size. For traditional piecing, use templates R1, S2, S3, S7, T1, T2, and T9 in Template section beginning on page 128.

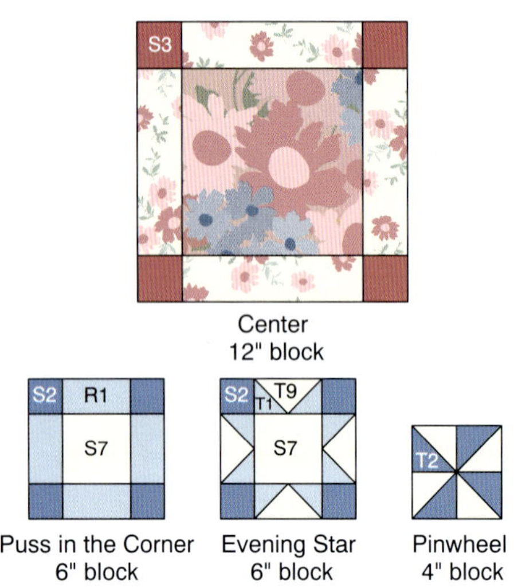

Center
12" block

Puss in the Corner
6" block

Evening Star
6" block

Pinwheel
4" block

Step 1: Center Panel

Audition and cut all the center panel pieces; then arrange them on your design wall before stitching.

From Fabric A, selectively cut:

- 1 square, 8½" x 8½"

From Fabric B, cut:

- 4 rectangles, 2½" x 8½"

From Fabric E, cut:

- 4 squares, 2½" x 2½" (S3)

From Fabrics H, cut:

- 2 squares, 9⅜" x 9⅜"; cut each square once diagonally to make 4 half-square triangles. For a perfect fit, trim triangle points with the Precision Trimmer 6™ ruler as shown.

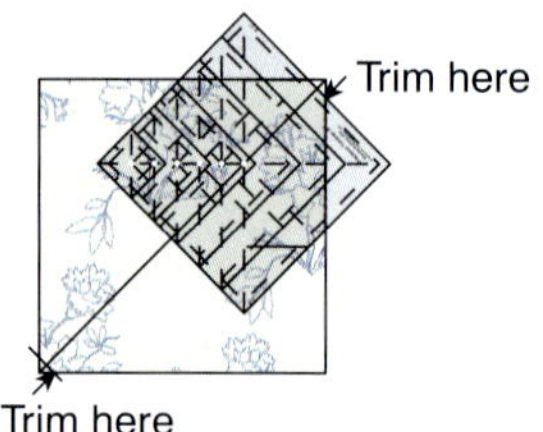

Piecing

1. Join a Fabric B rectangle to each side of the Fabric A square. Join a 2½" Fabric E square to each end of the 2 remaining rectangles. Join to top and bottom. Quilt center should now measure 12½" x 12½", edge to edge.

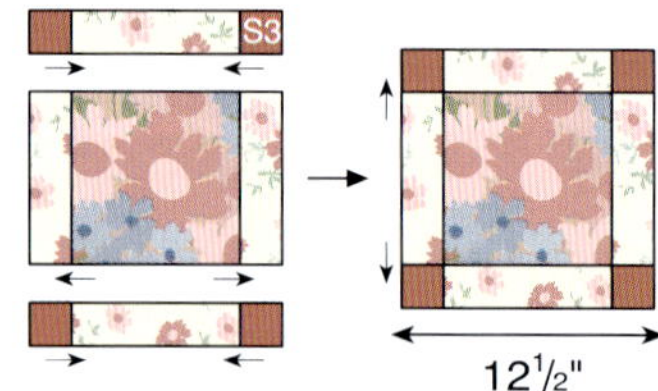

2. Sew Fabric H triangles to pieced center square as shown, opposite sides first, then the other two. Center panel should now measure 17½" x 17½", edge to edge.

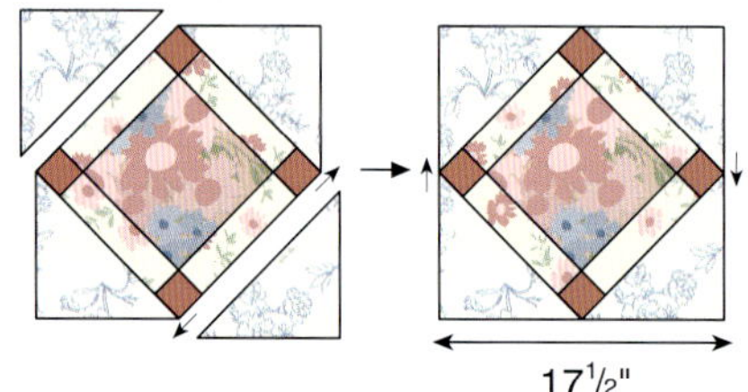

Step 2: Border #1

Make four side sections and four 6" Puss in the Corner blocks.

From Fabric A, cut:
- 4 strips, 3½" x 17½"

From Fabric B, cut:
- 4 strips, 3½" x 17½"

From Fabrics A and/or C, selectively cut:
- 4 squares, 3½" x 3½" (S7), for centers

From Fabric F, cut:
- 16 rectangles, 2" x 3½" (R1), for sides

From Fabric D, cut:
- 16 squares, 2" x 2" (S2), for corners

Piecing

1. Sew Fabric A and Fabric B strips together as shown to make 4 side sections. Sewn side section should measure 6½" x 17½", edge to edge.

Make 4.

2. Piece 4 Puss in the Corner blocks as shown. Sewn block should measure 6½" x 6½", edge to edge.

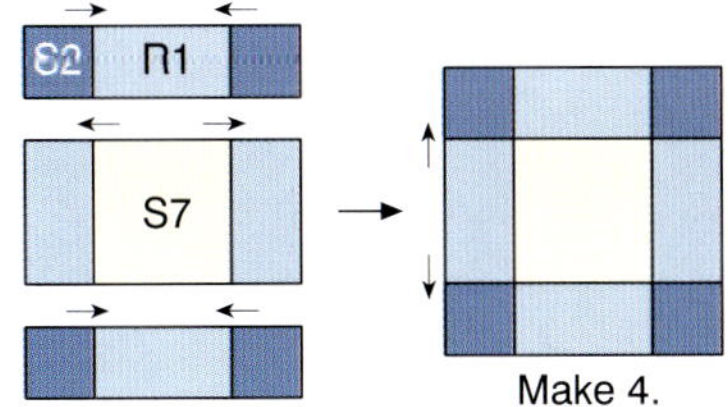

Make 4.

3. Join a side section to each side of the center panel. Join a Puss in the Corner block to each end of the 2 remaining side sections. Join to top and bottom. Quilt center should now measure 29½" x 29½", edge to edge.

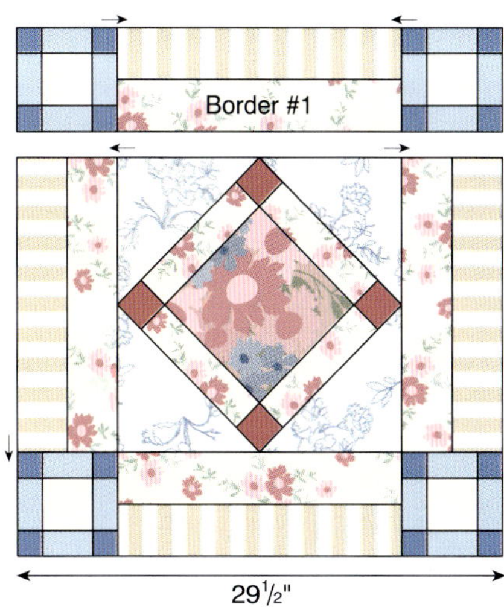

Step 3: Border #2

Cut 4 border strips, and make four 4" Pinwheel blocks.

From Fabric B, cut:
- 4 border strips, 4½" x 29½"

From Fabric C, cut:
- 8 squares, 3" x 3", for Pinwheel blocks

From Fabric D, cut
- 8 squares, 3" x 3", for Pinwheel blocks

Piecing

1. Make 4 Pinwheel blocks.
- Place Fabric C and D squares right sides together. Cut diagonally and sew resulting triangle pairs together. Press seams towards the darker fabric. Make 4 for each block, 16 total.

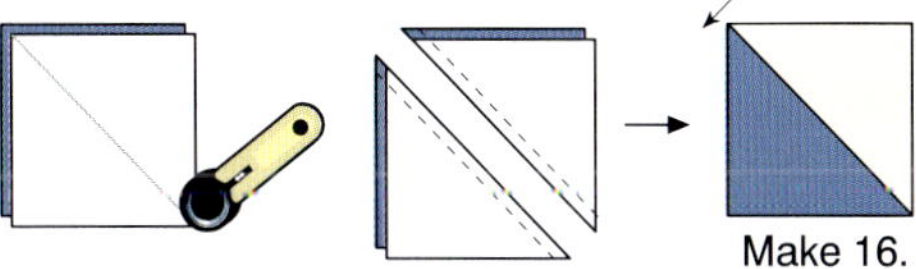
Make 16.

- Using the Precision Trimmer 6™ ruler, trim the completed square to 2½" x 2½", edge to edge.

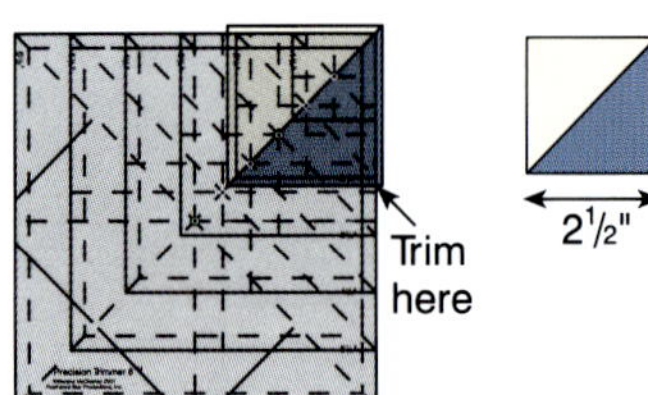

- Piece blocks as shown. Press center seam open. Blocks should measure 4½" x 4½", edge to edge. See page 73 for piecing Pinwheels.

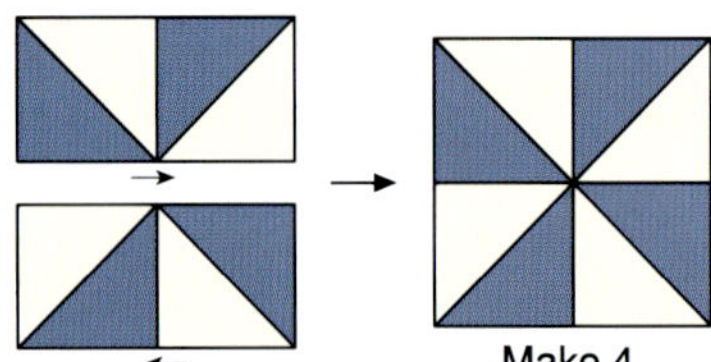

2. Join a Fabric B strip to each side of quilt center. Join a Pinwheel block to each end of the 2 remaining strips. Join to top and bottom. Quilt center should now measure 37½" x 37½", edge to edge.

Step 4: Border #3

Make twelve 6" Evening Star blocks, and cut rectangles to join them together. In Barb's quilt, the 4 corner stars are darker than the other 8.

Cutting for the 4 corner stars:

From Fabric A, cut:
- 4 squares, 3½" x 3½" (S7), for centers

From Fabric D, cut:
- 16 squares, 2" x 2" (S2), for corners

From Fabric C, cut:
- 16 rectangles, 2" x 3½", for star point units

From Fabric F, cut:
- 32 squares, 2" x 2", for star point units

Cutting the 8 remaining stars:

From Fabric C, cut:
- 8 squares, 3½" x 3½" (S7), for centers

From Fabric G, cut:
- 32 squares, 2" x 2" (S2), for corners
- 32 rectangles, 2" x 3½", for star point units

From Fabric F, cut:
- 64 squares, 2" x 2", for star point units

From Fabrics H, cut:
- 4 rectangles, 6½" x 11½"
- 8 rectangles, 6½" x 7½"

Piecing

1. Make 4 star point units for each of the 12 blocks.

- On the wrong side of two 2" squares, draw a diagonal line from corner to corner. (Be sure to use 2" squares that you've selected for star points—other 2" squares will be used for block corners.)

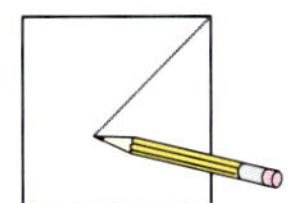

- With right sides together, place one 2" fabric square on one corner of a 2" x 3½" rectangle. Stitch on the pencil line, then trim away the excess, leaving a ¼" seam allowance. Press seam toward the triangle. Repeat for other end of rectangle to make a star point unit that measures 2" x 3½", edge to edge. Repeat to make 48 units.

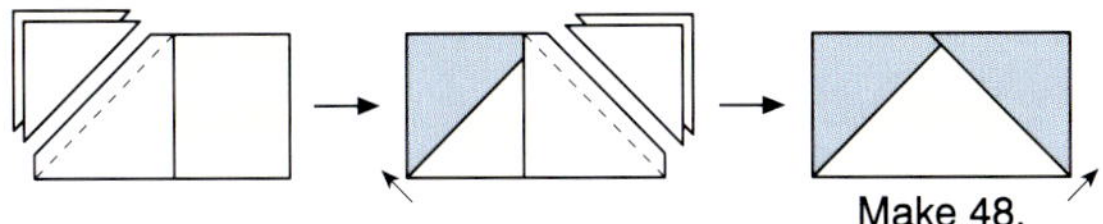

- Piece blocks as shown. Sewn blocks should measure 6½" x 6½", edge to edge.

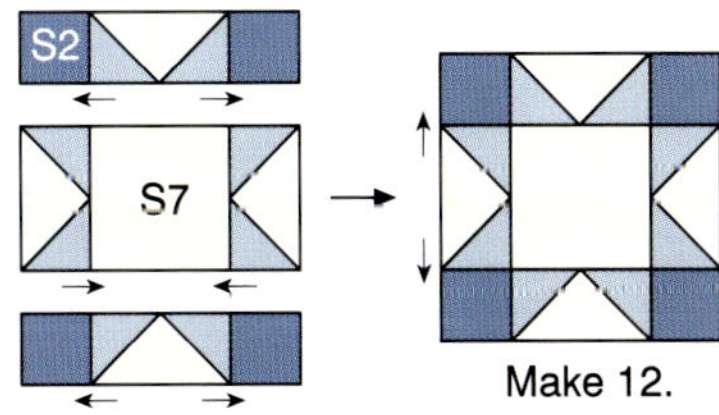

2. Join 8 completed Evening Star blocks with Fabric H rectangles as shown to make 4 border strips. Each should measure 6½" x 37½", edge to edge.

3. Add 2 border strips to sides of quilt center. Join a star block to each end of the 2 remaining strips. Join to top and bottom.

Quilt Assembly Diagram

See finishing instructions on pages 20-21.

Garden Dance

Inspiration for a Blended Quilt is often sparked by just one wonderful fabric. Sue Gross found inspiration in a scenic print featuring an elegantly-dressed couple dancing

in a garden. Selectively cut, it was the perfect scene for the center square. The next fabric chosen was a floral bouquet print with similar colors for the outer border. These two focus prints established the color palette, and Sue went to her extensive fabric collection for the rest of the prints. Though medallion-style quilts from the 1700s and 1800s were typically very large, Sue has adapted the style to make a smaller quilt that could hang on a wall, cover a table, or be used as a throw. The size could easily be increased by adding more borders.

Garden Dance

DESIGNED AND QUILTED BY: **Susan Gross**

FINISHED QUILT SIZE: **63½" x 63½"**

Materials

Fabric requirements are based on 40" fabric width.

- Fabric A, scenic print: 9½" square
- Fabric B, large-scale spaced-floral for Border #5: 1¾ yds.
- Fabric C, light green print for Borders #2 and #4: ¾ yd.
- Fabric D, assorted medium prints for Center Panel and pieced borders: 8-9 fat quarters
- Fabric E, assorted beige and tan light prints for pieced borders: 6-7 fat quarters
- Fabric F, toile for largest triangles in Center Panel: ½ yd.
- Binding: ⅔ yard
- Backing: 4¼ yds.
- Batting: 72" x 72"

Quick Cutting Guide

For more detailed information, see complete cutting instructions given in each Step.

Fabric	Shape	Piece/ Template	Total Needed	Rotary Cutting		
				# to Cut	1st Cut	2nd Cut
Fabric A	□	Center square	1	1	9½" x 9½"	
Fabric B	▭	Border #5	4	4 lengthwise strips	6½" x 51½"	
Fabric C	▭	Border #2	2	2	2" x 33½"	
	▭	Border #2	2	2	2" x 36½"	
	▭	Border #4	4	6	2" x width of fabric*	
Fabric D	◺	Triangles	4	2	7¼" x 7¼"	⧄
	▭	Rectangles	4	4	3½" x 13¼"	
	□	S7	12	12	3½" x 3½"	
	◺	T4	36	18	4" x 4"°	
	△	T6	16	16	3½" x 6½"§	
	□	S9	20	20	4¾" x 4¾"	
	◺	T4	16	8	3⅞" x 3⅞"	⧄
Fabric E	◺	T4	36	18	4" x 4"°	⧄
	◺	T4	32	32	3½" x 3½"§	
	◺	T4	16	8	3⅞" x 3⅞"	⧄
	△	T6	32	8	7¼" x 7¼"	⊠
	◺	T9	16	8	3" x 3"	⧄
Fabric F	◺	Triangles	4	2	15" x 15"	⧄

*Sew strips together, end-to-end, into one long strip. From this long strip, cut 2 strips, 48½" long; and 2 strips, 51½" long.

°These are cut large, and will be trimmed to size after piecing.

§Leave as squares or rectangles for now. These will be used in a "sew and flip" technique.

Directions

Read these instructions thoroughly before you begin. The directions given here vary somewhat from the quilt in the photo. In writing the pattern, some changes were made to make cutting and sewing easier. See *Basic Quiltmaking,* beginning on page 14, for general quiltmaking directions. All cutting measurements include ¼"-wide seam allowance. Instructions are for rotary cutting. Some pieced units are made larger than needed and then trimmed to size. For traditional piecing, refer to templates S7, S9, T4, T6, and T9 in Template section beginning on page 128.

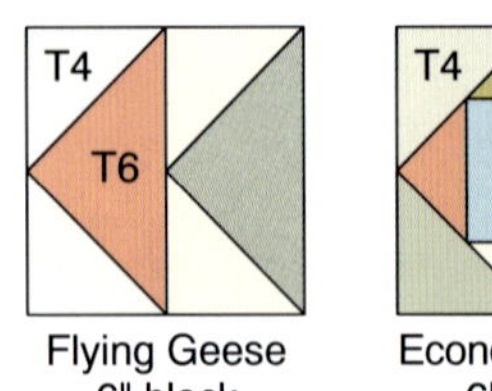

Flying Geese 6" block

Economy Patch 6" block

Step 1: Center Panel

Audition and cut all the Center Panel elements; then place them on your design wall before stitching.

From Fabric A, selectively cut:

- 1 square, 9½" x 9½"

From assorted Fabrics D, cut:

- 2 squares, 7¼" x 7¼"; cut each square once diagonally to make 4 half-square triangles. Sue cut the triangles selectively, centering the square on a round motif so each triangle has a half-circle to "frame" the center square. For a perfect fit, trim triangle points with the Precision Trimmer 6™ ruler as shown.

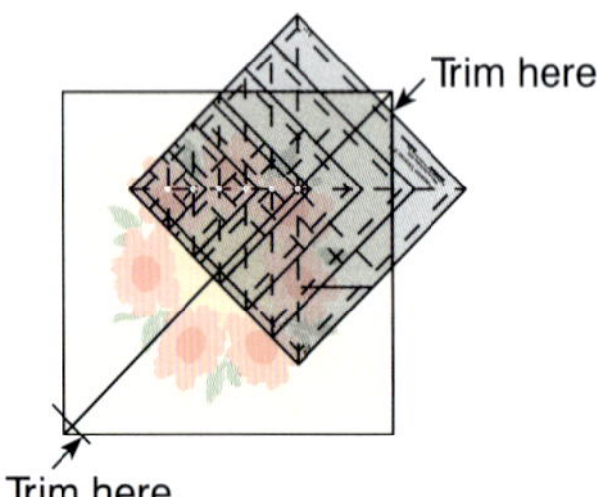

- 4 rectangles, 3½" x 13¼"
- 4 squares, 3½" x 3½" (S7)

From Fabric F, cut:

- 2 squares, 15" x 15"; cut each square once diagonally to make 4 half-square triangles.

Piecing

1. Sew Fabric D triangles to Fabric A center square as shown, opposite sides first, then the other two.

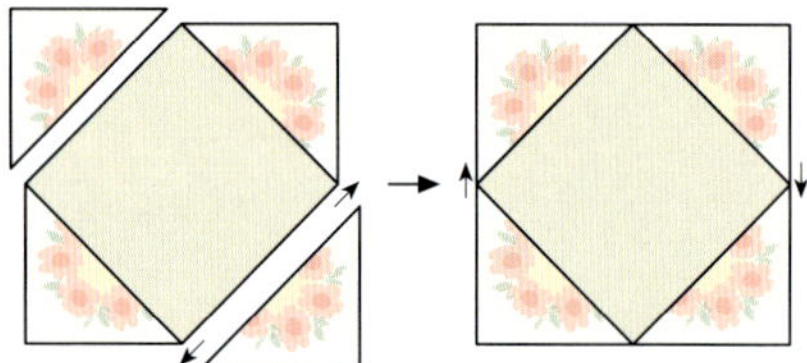

2. Add 2 Fabric D rectangles to sides of quilt center. Join a 3½" square to each end of the remaining 2 strips. Join to top and bottom.

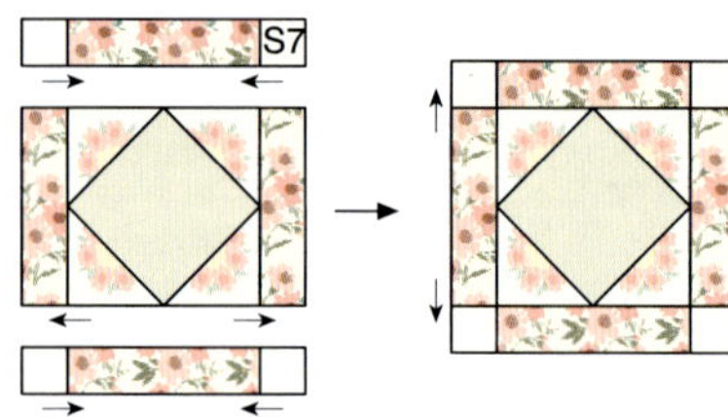

3. Sew Fabric F triangles to center square as shown, opposite sides first, then the other two. These have been intentionally cut larger than they need to be. For stitching, match the midpoints of the triangles to midpoints of the center square. After adding the large triangles, the total quilt center should measure 27½" x 27½", edge to edge. Trim to that dimension if necessary.

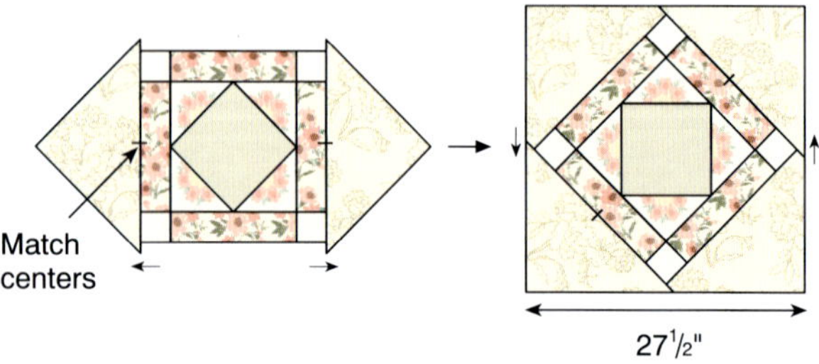

Step 2: Border #1

Cut and piece Sawtooth border; then join to quilt center.

From assorted Fabrics D, cut:

- 4 squares, 3½" x 3½" (S7), for corners
- 18 squares, 4" x 4", for making Sawtooth units

From assorted Fabrics E, cut:

- 18 squares, 4" x 4", for making Sawtooth units

Piecing

1. Sawtooth units. Cut 36 assorted 4" squares once diagonally to make 72 half-square triangles.
   - Stitch triangles together in pairs to make 36 Sawtooth units. These will be larger than needed. Trim down to exactly 3½" x 3½" using the Precision Trimmer 6™.

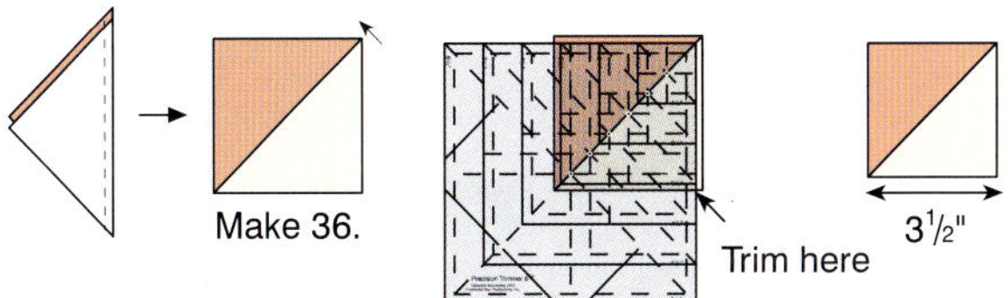

   - Arrange 3½" squares and Sawtooth units around the center square on the design wall. When you like the color balance, stitch the units together in rows as shown. Join to center; sides first, then top and bottom. The quilt should now measure 33½" square, edge to edge.

Step 3: Border #2

Cut strips and join to quilt center.

From Fabric C, cut:

- 2 strips, 2" x 33½"
- 2 strips, 2" x 36½"

Piecing

Add 2 short Fabric C strips to sides of quilt center. Then join the longer strips to top and bottom. Quilt center should now measure 36½" x 36½", edge to edge.

Step 4: Border #3

Make 4 Chain of Squares border units and 16 Flying Geese units; join in border rows and to quilt center.

From assorted Fabrics D, cut:

- 16 rectangles, 3½" x 6½", for "sew and flip" Flying Geese
- 20 squares, 4¾" x 4¾" (S9), for Chain of Squares

From assorted Fabrics E, cut:

- 32 squares, 3½" x 3½", for "sew and flip" Flying Geese
- 8 squares, 3⅞" x 3⅞"; cut each square once diagonally to make 16 half-square triangles (T4) for Chain of Squares
- 8 squares, 7¼" x 7¼"; cut each square twice diagonally to make 32 quarter-square triangles (T6) for Chain of Squares

Piecing

1. Make four Chain of Squares border units. Arrange pieces on the design wall before sewing. Join Fabric E triangles and Fabric D squares in diagonal rows, then join the rows together. Each sewn unit should measure 6½" x 30½", edge to edge.

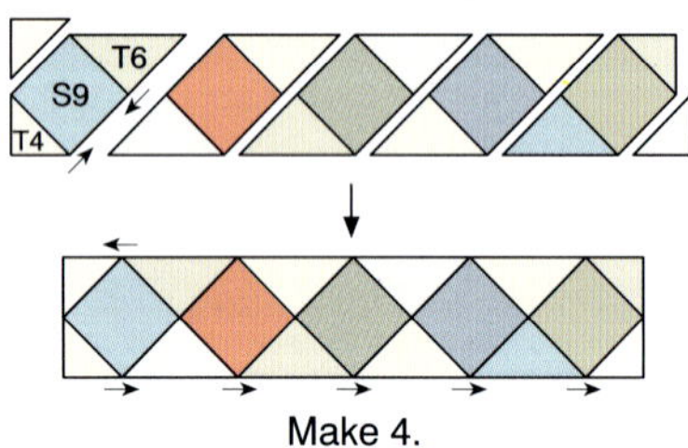

Make 4.

2. Make 16 Flying Geese units.

- On the wrong side of 32 3½" Fabric E squares, draw a diagonal line from corner to corner.

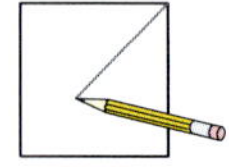

- With right sides together, place one 3½" Fabric E square on one corner of a 3½" x 6½" Fabric D rectangle. Stitch on the pencil line, then trim away the excess, leaving a ¼" seam allowance. Press seam toward the triangle. Repeat for other end of rectangle to make a Flying Geese unit that measures 3½" x 6½", edge to edge. Repeat to make 16 units. (See page 78 for another method of making this unit.)

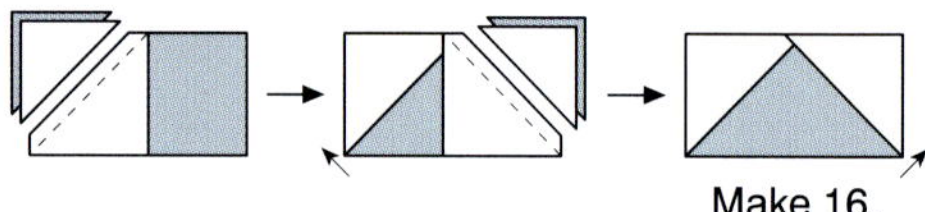
Make 16.

3. Arrange sewn units on design wall to determine the best color balance.

- Join Flying Geese together into 8 units of two each.

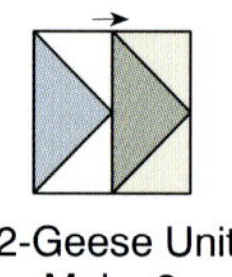
2-Geese Unit
Make 8.

- Sew a 2-Geese unit to each Chain of Squares unit.

Make 4.

- Join 2 of these border strips (each should measure 6½" x 36½", edge to edge) to sides of quilt center.
- Sew remaining 2-Geese units to ends of remaining 2 borders, and join resulting border strips (each should measure 6½" x 48½", edge to edge) to top and bottom of quilt. The quilt should now measure 48½" x 48½".

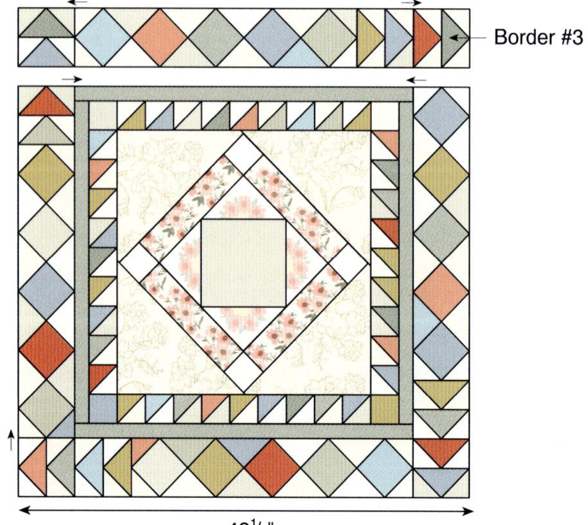

Step 5: Border #4

Cut strips and join to quilt center.

From Fabric C, cut:

- 6 strips, the width of the fabric by 2" wide. Sew the strips together, end-to-end, into one long strip. From this long strip, cut 2 strips, 48½" long; and 2 strips, 51½" long.

Piecing

Add 2 short Fabric C strips to sides of quilt center. Then join the longer strips to top and bottom. Quilt center should now measure 51½" x 51½", edge to edge.

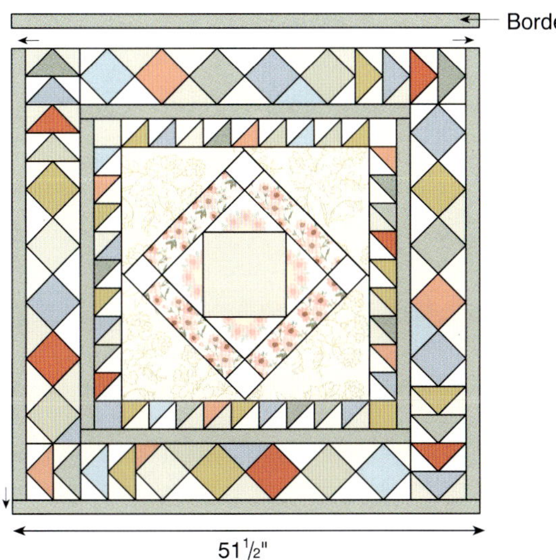

Step 6: Border #5

Cut border strips and make four 6" Economy Patch blocks.

From Fabric B, cut:

- 4 lengthwise strips, 6½" x 51½"

From assorted Fabrics D, cut:

- 4 squares, 3½" x 3½" (S7), for block centers
- 8 squares, 3⅞" x 3⅞"; cut each square once diagonally to make 16 half-square triangles (T4)

From assorted Fabrics E, cut:

- 8 squares, 3" x 3"; cut each square once diagonally to make 16 half-square triangles (T9)

Piecing

1. Make 4 Economy Patch blocks. Join T9 triangles to center square as shown, then add T4 triangles in the same manner. Edge-to-edge measurement should be 6½" x 6½".

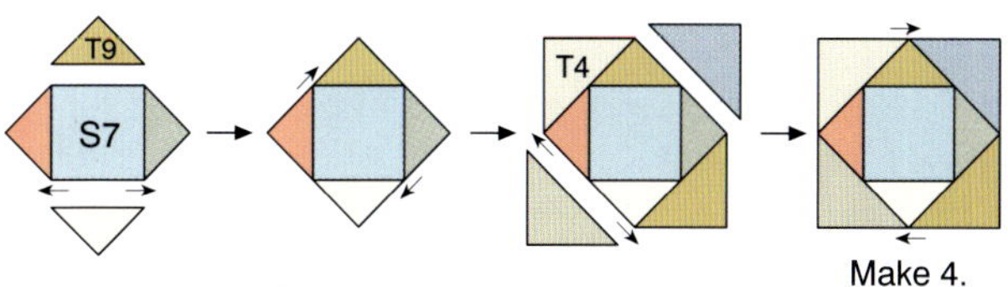

2. Join a Fabric B strip to each side of the quilt.
3. Join a pieced Economy Patch block to each end of 2 remaining Fabric B strips, and join to top and bottom of quilt as shown. Press seams toward Fabric B strips.

Quilt Assembly Diagram

See finishing instructions on pages 20-21.

Garden View

The rectangular center panel for this medallion-style quilt was cut from a fascinating toile print by Sharon Yenter for In the Beginning Fabrics. The image on the fabric comes from an antique quilt owned by Ann Stohl. In the antique quilt, the pieced blocks are set with 3"-wide sashing strips. The fabric used is a fairly complex, large-scale toile, but because it was cut in pieces, it was hard to know what the whole design was like. After several hours of photocopying the quilt, then cutting and pasting the images together, Sharon was able to assemble the entire glorious scene! The intricate design she found is amazing and a perfect center for this rectangular medallion.

This is a scrappy little quilt. The two most important fabrics are the Garden View toile and the dark-background, large-scale, spaced-floral with a stripe running through it. Both were selectively cut for some parts of the quilt and randomly cut for others.

GARDEN VIEW

DESIGNED BY: **Marsha McCloskey** • QUILTED BY: **Cindy Paulsgrove**

FINISHED QUILT SIZE: **48½" x 51½"**

Materials

Fabric requirements are based on 40" fabric width.

- Fabric A, scenic toile, for Center Panel and some piecing: 1 yd.
- Fabric B, dark-background, large-scale, spaced-floral with a stripe for Border #3 and some piecing: 1 yd.
- Fabric C, assorted green, teal, and purple medium prints for piecing: 6-8 fat quarters
- Fabric D, assorted beige light prints for piecing: 6-8 fat quarters
- Fabric E, assorted purple light prints for piecing: 2-4 fat quarters
- Fabric F, medium-scale spaced-floral for Border #2 and some piecing: ¾ yd.
- Binding: ½ yd.
- Backing: 3½ yds.
- Batting: 57" x 60"

Quick Cutting Guide

For more detailed information, see complete cutting instructions given in each Step.

Fabric	Shape	Piece/ Template	Total Needed	Rotary Cutting		
				# to Cut	1st Cut	2nd Cut
Fabric A		Center	1	1	12½" x 15½"	
		Border #3	4	4	2" x 27½"	
		S10	4	4	6½" x 6½"	
Fabric B		S9	4	4	6½" x 6½"*	
		Border #3	2	2	3½" x 27½"	
Fabric C		S7	4	4	3½" x 3½"	
		T9	28	28	2" x 3½"°	
		T4	16	8	4" x 4"§	
		T4	16	16	3½" x 3½"°	
		T6	38	38	3½" x 6½"°	
Fabric D		T1	72	72	2" x 2"°	
		T4	76	76	3½" x 3½"°	
Fabric E		S4	4	4	3½" x 3½"†	
Fabric F		Border #2	2	2	3½" x 18½"	
		Border #2	2	2	3½" x 21½"	
Fabrics B-F		S7	6	6	3½" x 3½"	
		S2	24	24	2" x 2"	
		T9	24	24	2" x 3½"°	
		T1	48	48	2" x 2"°	
		Border #3 (S7)	10	10	3½" x 3½"	
		Border #3	2	2	3½" x 9½"	
		Border #3	1	1	3½" x 15½"	
		Border #3	1	1	3½" x 21½"	

* These are cut for a "sew and flip" technique. Use the S9 template measurements for traditional techniques.
° Leave as squares or rectangles for now. These will be used in a "sew and flip" technique.
§ Leave as squares for now. These will be cut again during piecing process.
† These are cut for a "sew and flip" technique. Use the S4 template measurements for traditional techniques.

Directions

Read these instructions thoroughly before you begin. See *Basic Quiltmaking*, beginning on page 14, for general quiltmaking directions. All cutting measurements include ¼"-wide seam allowance. Instructions are for rotary cutting. Some pieced units are made larger than needed and then trimmed to size. For traditional piecing, refer to templates S2, S4, S7, S9, S10, T1, T4, T6, and T9 in Template section beginning on page 128.

Square-in-a-Square
3" block

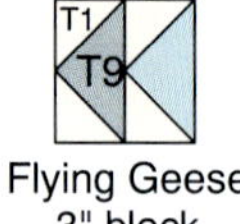

Flying Geese
3" block

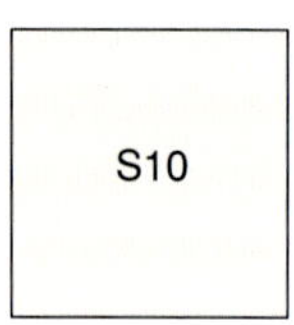

6" square

S2 T9 T1 S7

Evening Star
6" block

T4 S9

Square-in-a-Square
6" block

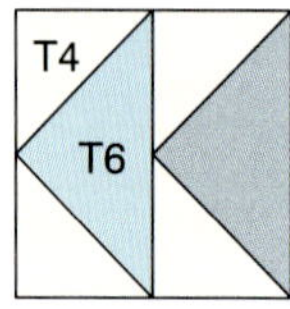

Flying Geese
6" block

Step 1: Center Panel

From Fabric A, selectively cut:
- 1 rectangle, 12½" x 15½"

Step 2: Border #1

Cut and piece border strips.

From Fabrics C, cut:
- 4 squares, 3½" x 3½" (S7), for corners
- 28 rectangles, 2" x 3½", for Flying Geese units

From Fabrics D, cut:
- 72 squares, 2" x 2", for Flying Geese and Square-in-a-Square units

From Fabrics E, cut:
- 4 squares, 3½" x 3½", for center of Square-in-a-Square units

Piecing

1. Make four 3" Square-in-a-Square units. (These are "sew and flip" instructions. For traditional methods, use templates S4 and T1.)

- On the wrong side of sixteen 2" Fabric D squares, draw a diagonal line from corner to corner.

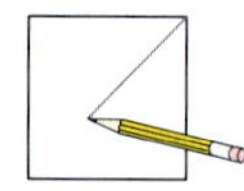

- With right sides together, place two 2" Fabric D squares on opposite corners of a 3½" fabric E square. Stitch on the pencil lines, then trim away the excess, leaving a ¼" seam allowance. Press seams away from the center. Repeat for opposite corners so there are 4 triangles sewn around the square. The unit should measure 3½" x 3½", edge to edge. Repeat to make 4 units.

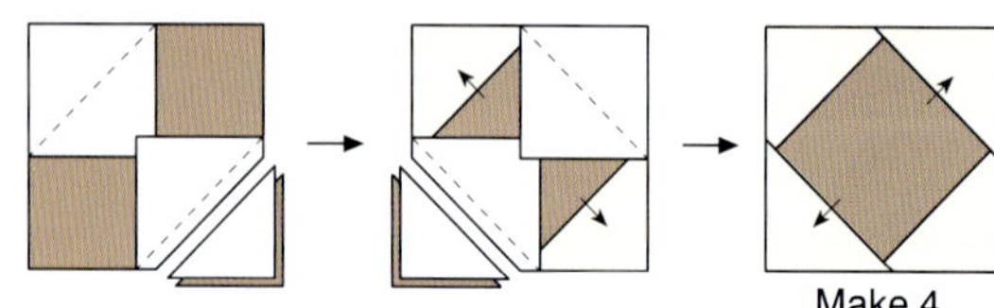

2. Make 28 1½" x 3" Flying Geese units.
   - On the wrong side of 56 2" Fabric D squares, draw a diagonal line from corner to corner.

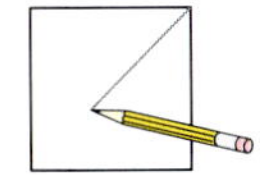

   - With right sides together, place one 2" Fabric D square on one corner of a 2" x 3½" Fabric C rectangle. Stitch on the pencil line, then trim away the excess, leaving a ¼" seam allowance. Press seam toward the triangle. Repeat for other end of rectangle to make a Flying Geese unit that measures 2" x 3½", edge to edge. Repeat to make 28 units.

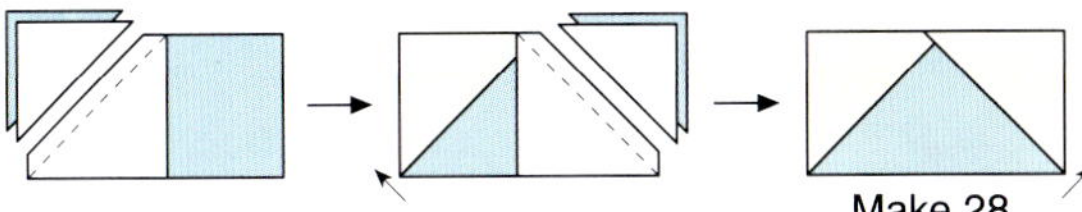

3. Using 2 Square-in-a-Square units and 16 Flying Geese units, make 2 border sections for sides as shown. Edge-to-edge measurements should be 3½" x 15½". Join to sides of center rectangle. Using 2 Square-in-a-Square units, 12 Flying Geese units, and four 3½" Fabric C squares, make top and bottom border sections as shown. Edge-to-edge measurements should be 3½" x 18½". Join to top and bottom. Edge-to-edge measurements for the total center panel should be 18½" x 21½".

Border #1 Assembly

Step 3: Border #2

Make 2-triangle units and cut strips; then join to quilt center.

From Fabrics C, cut:

- 8 squares, 4" x 4", for 2-triangle units

From Fabric F, cut:

- 2 strips, 3½" x 18½"
- 2 strips, 3½" x 21½"

Piecing

1. Cut 8 assorted 4" squares once diagonally to make 16 half-square triangles. Arrange them on your design wall for color placement. Stitch triangles together in pairs to make eight 2-triangle units. These will be larger than needed. Trim to exactly 3½" x 3½" using the Precision Trimmer 6™. Use four 2-triangle units for Border #2 and save the other 4 for Border #3.

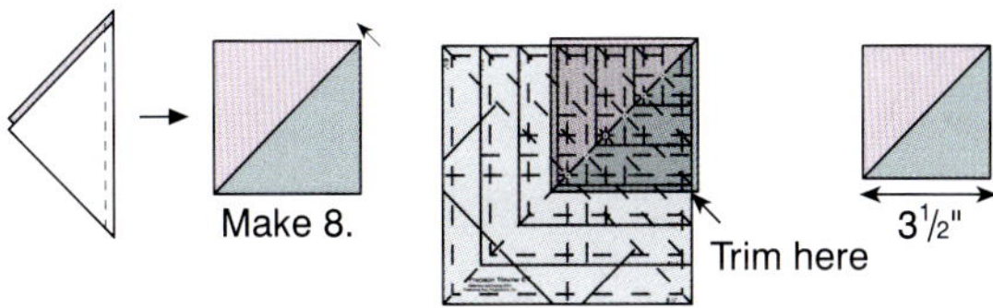

2. Join the two longer Fabric F strips to the sides of the quilt center.
3. Add a 2-triangle unit to each end of the shorter Fabric F strips, then join to top and bottom. Edge-to-edge measurements for the total center panel should now be 24½" x 27½".

Because of the offset arrangement of Evening Star blocks in opposite corners, Border #3 is made in large sections. Cut the large pieces and piece the smaller units, then arrange them on the design wall before stitching.

Evening Star Blocks

Make six 6" Evening Star Blocks. Cutting instructions are for one block. Repeat 6 times with different fabrics in each block.

From assorted Fabrics B-F, cut:

- 1 square, 3½" x 3½" (S7), for center
- 4 squares, 2" x 2" (S2), for corners
- 4 rectangles, 2" x 3½", for star point units
- 8 squares, 2" x 2", for star point units

Piecing

Following the directions for the Flying Geese units in Border #1, make 4 Star Point units for each of 6 blocks. Join these units together in rows with 2" and 3½" squares as shown. Join rows together. Edge-to-edge measurement should be 6½" x 6½".

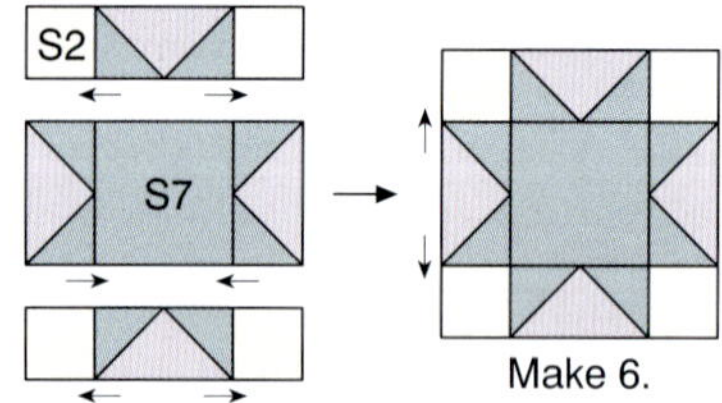

Make 6.

Square-in-a-Square blocks

Make four 6" Square-in-a-Square blocks. (These are "sew and flip" instructions. For traditional methods, use templates S9 and T4.)

From Fabric B, cut:

- 4 squares, 6½" x 6½", for centers

From a Fabric C medium green print, cut:

- 16 squares, 3½" x 3½", for corners

Piecing

1. On the wrong side of sixteen 3½" squares, draw a diagonal line from corner to corner.

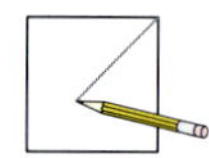

2. With right sides together, place two 3½" Fabric C squares on opposite corners of a 6½" Fabric B square. Stitch on the pencil lines, then trim away the excess, leaving a ¼" seam allowance. Press seams away from the center. Repeat for opposite corners so there are 4 triangles sewn around the square. The unit should measure 6½" x 6½", edge to edge. Repeat to make 4 units.

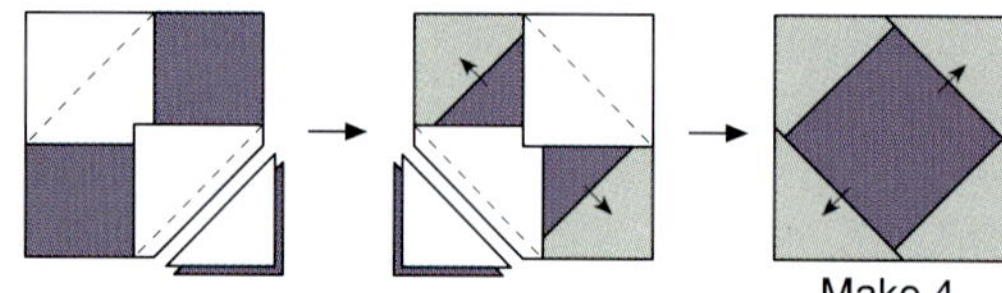
Make 4.

Flying Geese units

Make thirty-eight 3" x 6" Flying Geese units.

From Fabrics C, cut:

- 38 rectangles, 3½" x 6½"

From Fabrics D, cut:

- 76 squares, 3½" x 3½"

Piecing

1. On the wrong side of 76 3½" Fabric D squares, draw a diagonal line from corner to corner.

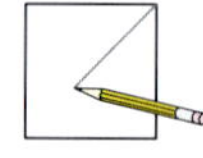

2. With right sides together, place one 3½" Fabric D square on one corner of a 3½" x 6½" Fabric C rectangle. Stitch on the pencil line, then trim away the excess, leaving a ¼" seam allowance. Press seam toward the triangle. Repeat for other end of rectangle to make a Flying Geese unit that measures 3½" x 6½", edge to edge. Repeat to make 38 units.

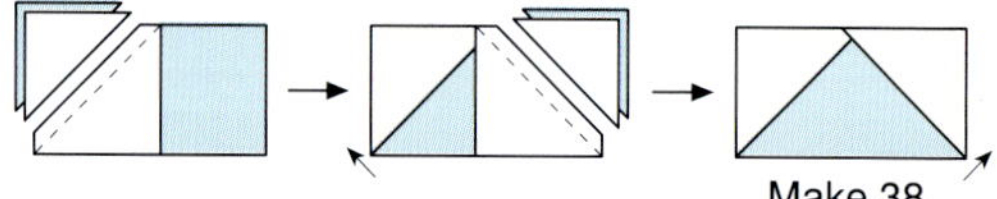
Make 38.

Vertical Stripe units

Make two 6½" x 27½" Vertical Stripe units, and cut 4 corner squares.

From Fabric A, cut:

- 4 strips, 2" x 27½"
- 4 squares, 6½" x 6½" (S10)

From Fabric B, selectively cut:

- 2 strips, 3½" x 27½"

Piecing

1. Join Fabric A strips to each side of Fabric B strips.

Make 2.

2. To fill in the remaining area of the top and bottom border units, cut assorted Fabrics B-F in 3½" squares and 3½"-wide strips. As long as the space is filled, any combination of strips and squares can be used. In the quilt pictured, there are:
   - 10 squares, 3½" x 3½" (S7)
   - 2 rectangles, 3½" x 9½"
   - 1 rectangle, 3½" x 15½"
   - 1 rectangle, 3½" x 21½"

3. Study the Quilt Assembly Diagram at right. Rearrange all the Border #3 parts on the design wall until you have a pleasing composition.

4. As shown, make 4 corner units, 2 side units, and a top and a bottom unit. Join side units to quilt center. Join corner units to each end of top and bottom units. Join these to top and bottom of quilt center.

Corner Unit
Make 4.

Side Unit
Make 2.

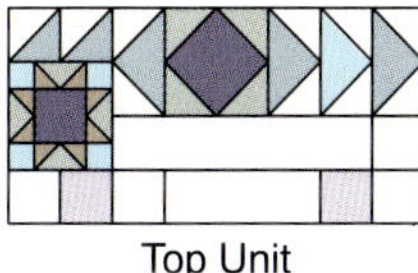

Top Unit
Make 1.

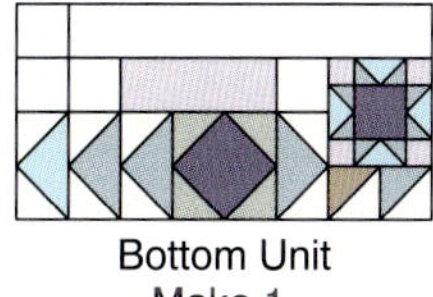

Bottom Unit
Make 1.

Quilt Assembly Diagram

See finishing instructions on pages 20-21.

Templates

2½"
S3
2"
S2
1½"
S1

3 5/16"
S6
3"
S5
2 5/8"
S4

6½"
S10
4¾"
S9
4½"
S8
3½"
S7

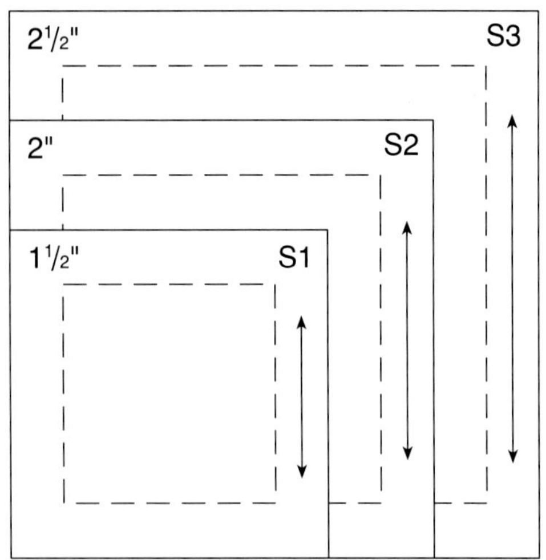

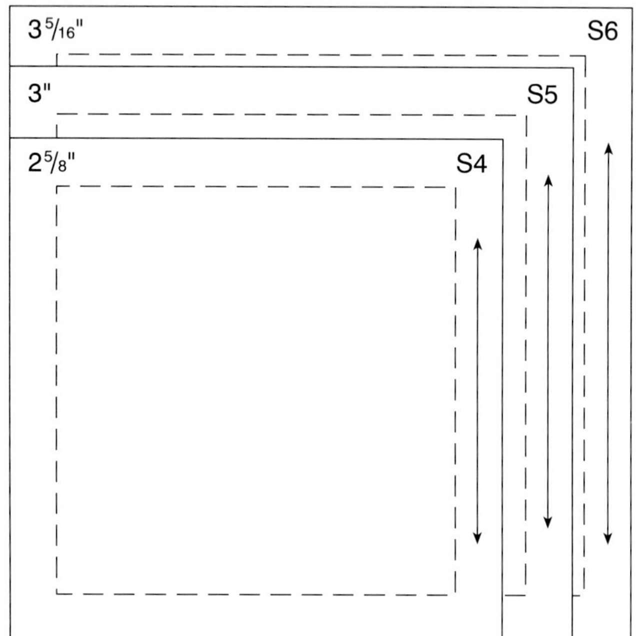

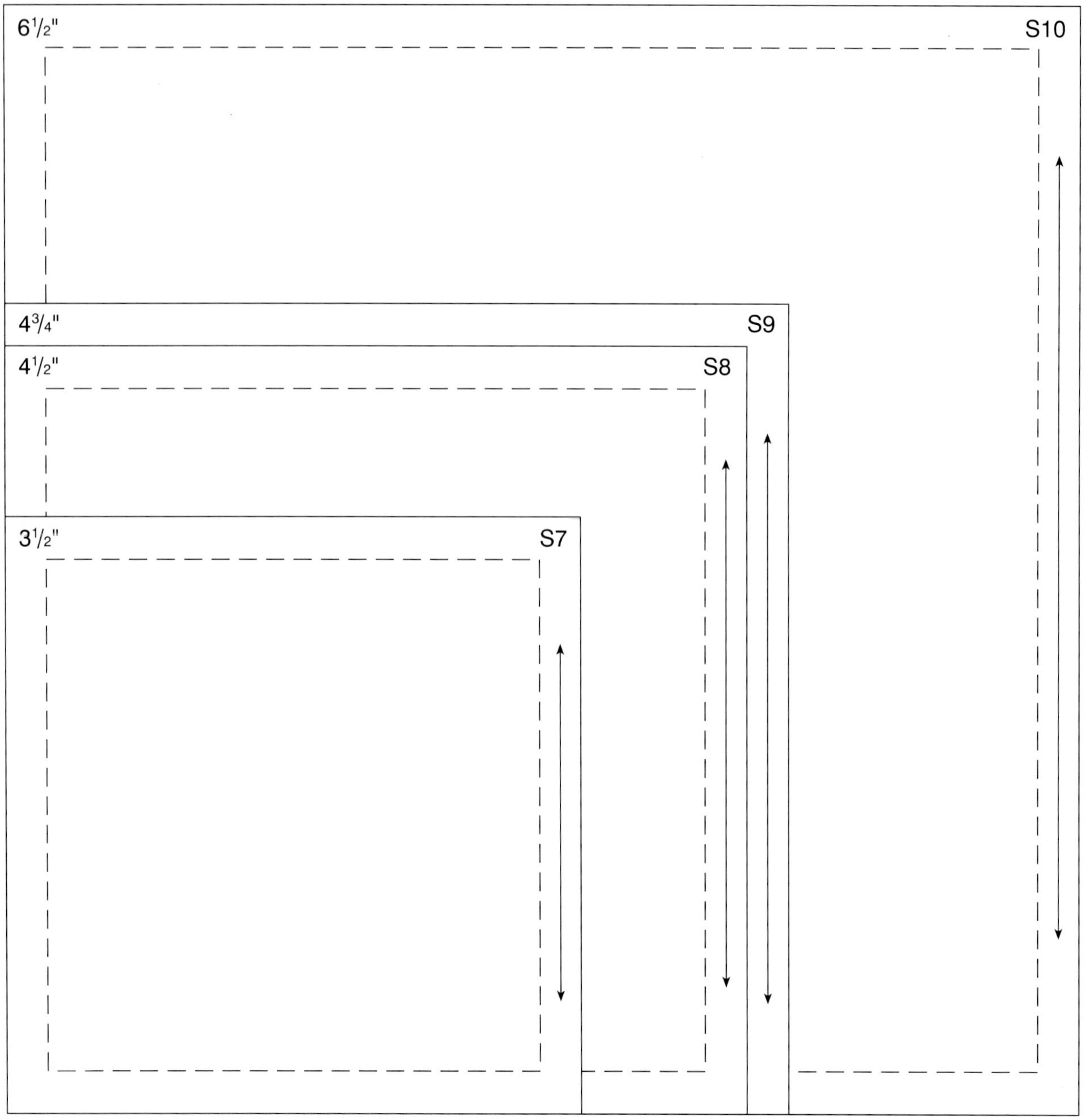

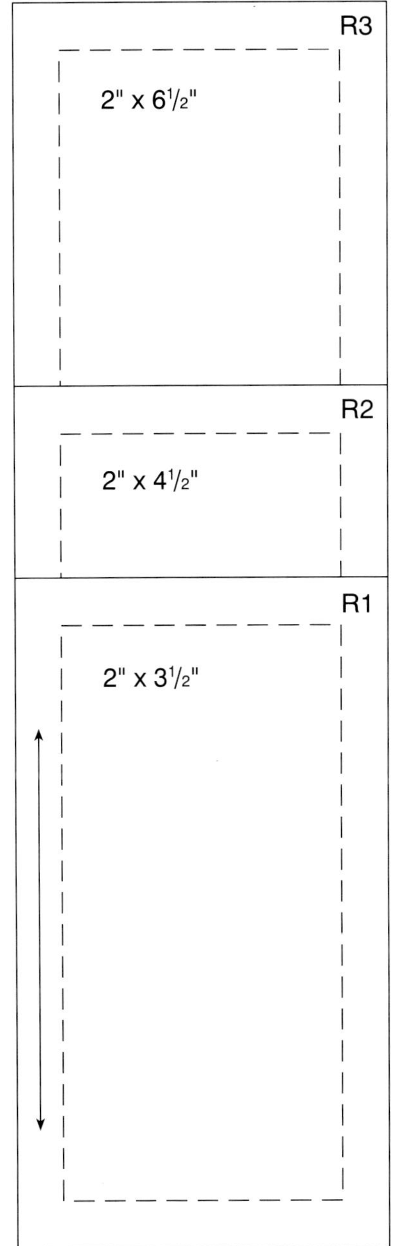
R3
2" x 6½"
R2
2" x 4½"
R1
2" x 3½"

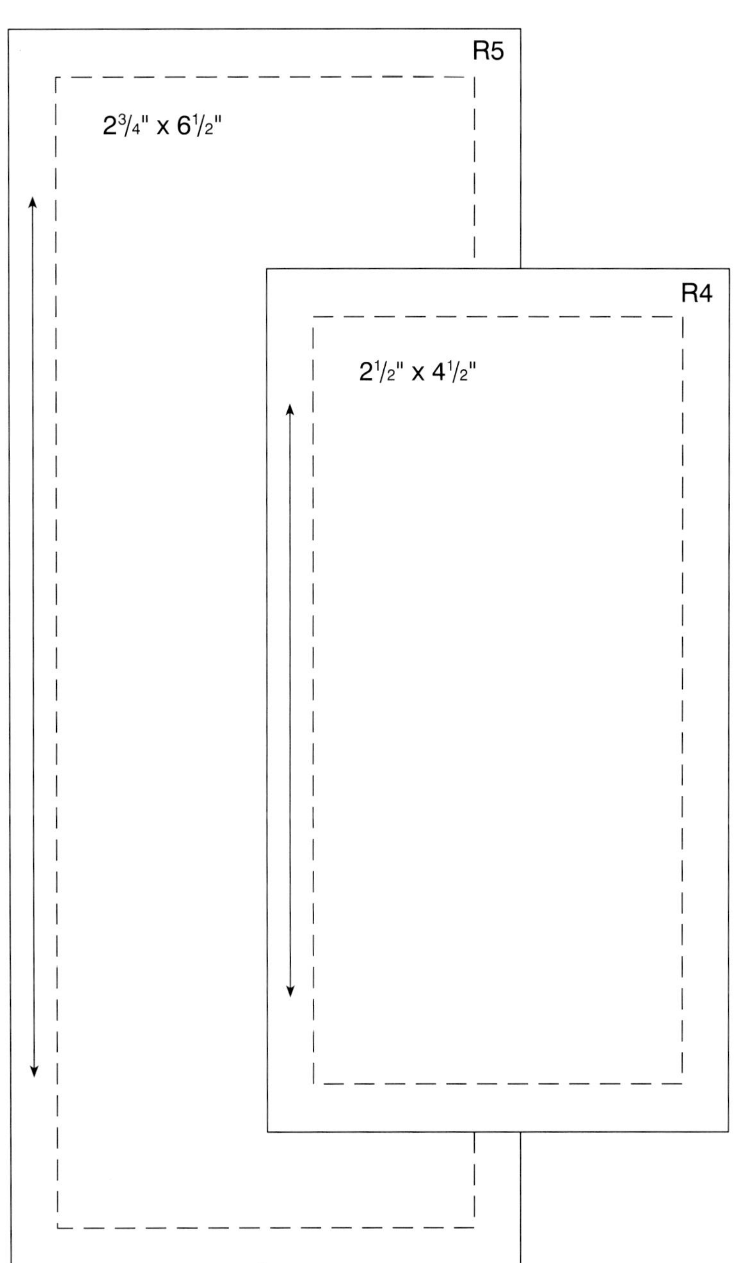
R5
2¾" x 6½"
R4
2½" x 4½"

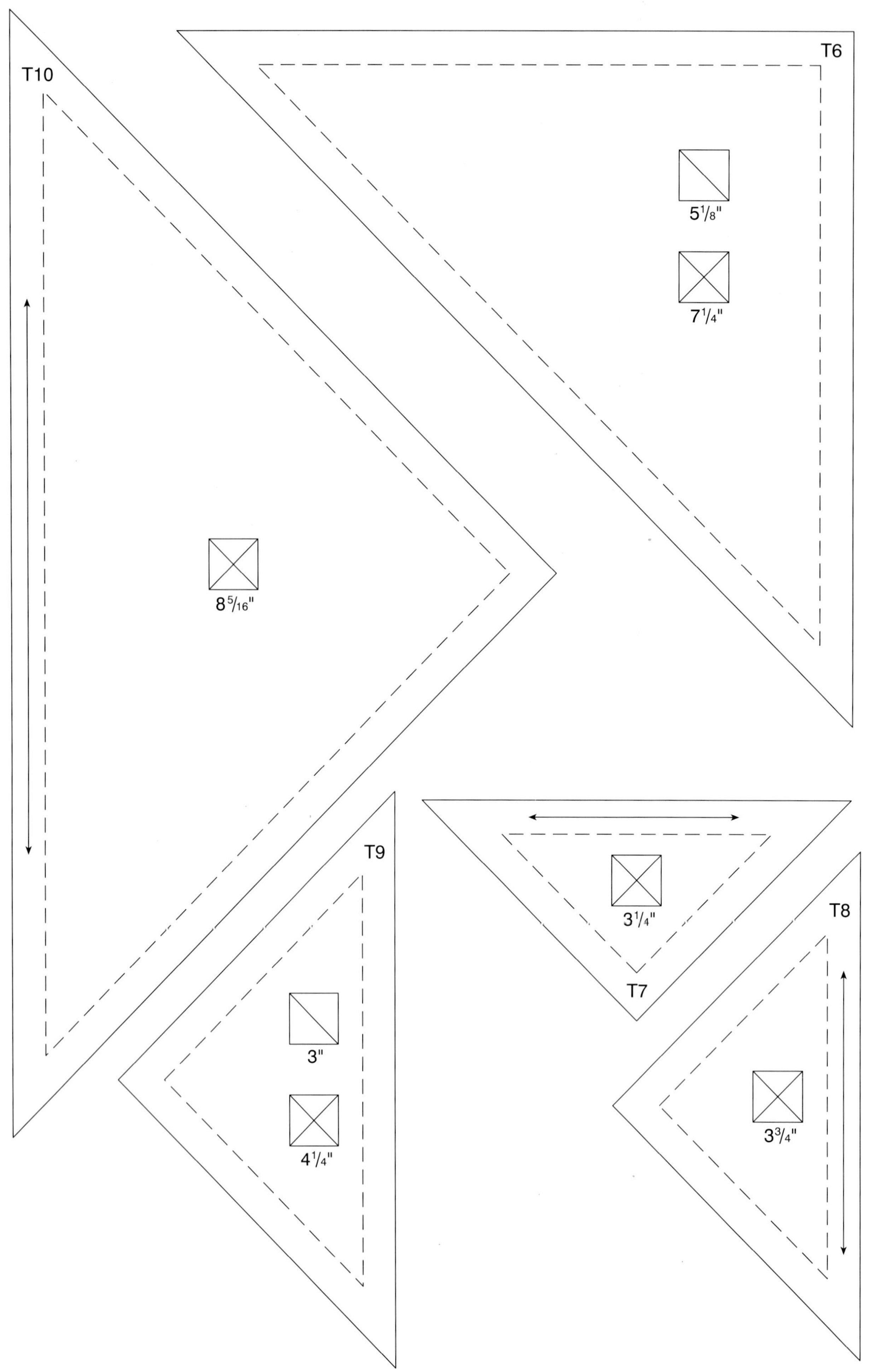
T10
T6
5 1/8"
7 1/4"
8 5/16"
T9
3"
4 1/4"
3 1/4"
T7
T8
3 3/4"

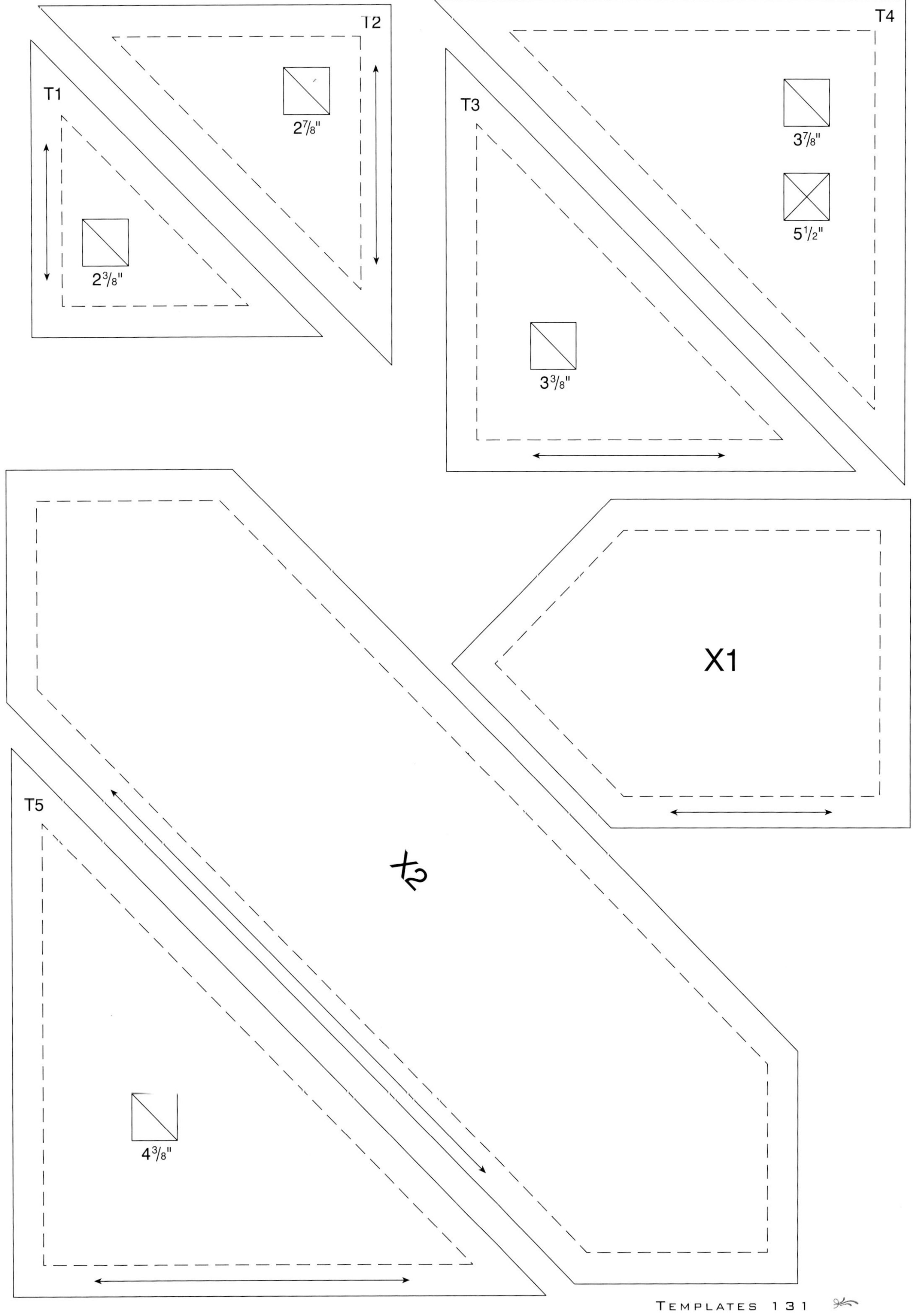
T1
2 3/8"
T2
2 7/8"
T3
3 3/8"
T4
3 7/8"
5 1/2"
X1
X2
T5
4 3/8"

Credits

Creative Director: Sharon Evans Yenter
Editor: Wendy Slotboom
Technical Editor: Laurie Shifrin
Art Director: Barbara Schmitt
Illustrators: Wendy Slotboom and Brian Metz
Photographer: Michael Craft
Photo Styling: Sharon Evans Yenter, Barbara Schmitt, and Melissa McCulloch

Acknowledgments

Every book project requires the creativity of many people. First, I'd like to thank the talented quiltmakers who accepted the "blended" challenge and made the uniquely beautiful quilts in this book. In alphabetical order: Margy Duncan, Sue Gross, Vicki Hurst, Cathy Mathes, Melissa McCulloch, Jackie Quinn, Ann Stohl and Barbara Schroeder, Rachel Vanderlaan, and Barb Vose.

A big thank you, too, to Sharon Evans Yenter, my friend and co-author on the first Blended Quilts book, for having the vision to make these books a reality, and to the ever supportive staff at In The Beginning.

Published by In The Beginning, Inc.

Resources

Fabric collections and books by Sharon Yenter; and fabrics, books, and Precision Trimmers™ by Marsha McCloskey are available at your local quilt shop, or you may inquire at:

In The Beginning Fabrics
8201 Lake City Way NE
Seattle, WA 98115
206.523.8862
www.inthebeginningfabrics.com

Quilt Wall® is available at your local quilt shop, or you may order from:

Keepsake Quilting
PO Box 1618
Center Harbor, NH 03226-1618
1.800.865.9458

Blended Quilts II From In The Beginning

In The Beginning, Seattle, Washington USA

ISBN 0-9706900-5-3
Printed in Hong Kong

Canals in Camera

Canals in Camera

JOHN GAGG

LONDON

IAN ALLAN

First published 1970

To my various crews, without whom all this canal exploring would be neither as extensive nor as pleasurable

SBN 7110 0148 0

Published by Ian Allan Ltd, Shepperton, Surrey, and printed in the United Kingdom by Crampton & Sons Ltd., Sawston, Cambridge.

Contents

Introduction

THERE ARE increasing numbers of books on the history of canals, and several accounts of specific cruises. This book doesn't attempt to be either of these. It is, rather, a personal " canal-cruising " look, in words and pictures, over almost the whole of the canal system.

The idea of gathering together these photographs and comments arose because I felt that most boaters aren't really interested in heavy historical books about canals, nor can they work up much enthusiasm for accounts of individual cruises on canals they have never seen. But from their reactions to general pictorial articles of mine in various boating magazines, I felt that the ordinary canal user might prefer an ordinary man's pictures and thoughts about the very locks and weirs and bridges and tunnels and aqueducts and embankments and cuttings which are the daily sights of any canal journey—not to mention the incidents, enjoyable or alarming, that punctuate every cruise.

So here is this countrywide meander. I've been able to see most of our canals lately, so I offer Foulridge Tunnel cheek by jowl with that telegraph pole halfway up a bridge on the Shropshire Union, and the cheery lock-keeper of the Northampton flight alongside his gesticulating colleague on the long climb up at Lapworth. Here is the distinctive worm paddle-gear of the Warwickshire Grand Union, the awkward racks of the slow-filling Atherstone flight, the torrential gate-paddles of the Trent and Mersey and the Staffs and Worcs, and the wicked broken shoulder of the bottom lock at Hurleston. I photograph or think about the tropical creepers hanging down the sides of Grub Street cutting, the surprisingly lonely main line of the Birmingham Canal Navigations, and of course the polythene bags and lock-tail anglers and even small boys dropping stones from bridges and grown-ups pushing old cars over banks.

I'm afraid I hop from canal to canal disconcertingly. But I felt that tackling particular *aspects* of canal travel would be more acceptable to the ordinary boater. In this way the reader is really with me all the time, since he too knows his bridges and locks and tunnels and other landmarks, and indeed he may bump into them at any time in these pages.

So this book is for browsing, as we browse along the canals. And I believe that I have browsed among the very items that the growing army of canal voyagers come across and think about and laugh about and sometimes swear about during their travels. I hope the reader will enjoy them with me.

JOHN GAGG

Anyone with an interest in inland waterways—whether armchair or active—should join the Inland Waterways Association (114 *Regent's Park Rd., London NW*1). *Without this lively body there is no doubt that our canal system would be less widely known and used than it now is.*

The chief canals now in use

with associated rivers

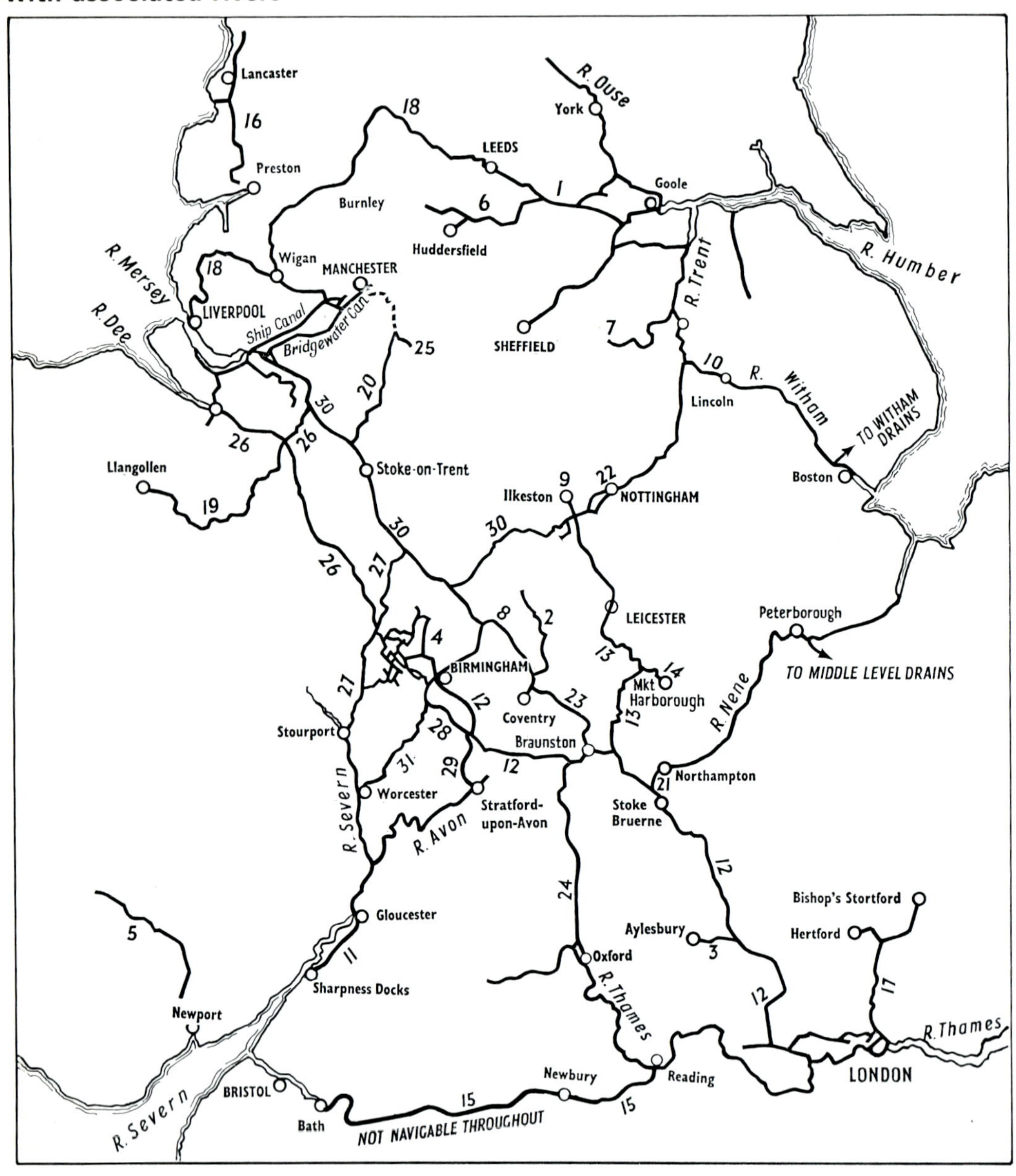

1 Aire and Calder
2 Ashby
3 Aylesbury Arm (Grand Union)
4 Birmingham Canals
5 Brecon and Abergavenny
6 Calder and Hebble
7 Chesterfield
8 Coventry
9 Erewash
10 Fossdyke (and Witham Navigation)
11 Gloucester and Sharpness
12 Grand Union (main line)
13 Grand Union (Leicester line)
14 Harborough Arm (Grand Union)
15 Kennet and Avon
16 Lancaster
17 Lee and Stort (Navigations)
18 Leeds and Liverpool
19 Llangollen
20 Macclesfield
21 Northampton Arm (Grand Union)
22 Nottingham
23 Oxford (north)
24 Oxford (south)
25 Peak Forest
26 Shropshire Union
27 Staffordshire and Worcestershire
28 Stratford (north)
29 Stratford (south)
30 Trent and Mersey
31 Worcester and Birmingham

Not shown: the Caledonian and Crinan Canals in Scotland, and the short Exeter Canal.

1 Boxes of Water

As you travel along canals there are many things to see, but undoubtedly the locks are the most intriguing. So I'll start with those—for in any case without them there would hardly be any canals at all.

Locks must in fact be among the simplest yet most effective inventions ever made. They enable the seemingly impossible to be achieved—the raising of boats from one level to another, and even up to hill-tops and down the other side again. They alone allowed canals to be dug across uneven country, to conquer mountains, to drop down river valleys and climb up the opposite slopes. They enabled the canal navigators to take their waterways where no navigable waters could normally exist. And they allowed them to fulfil one of their main aims—to link river systems by crossing higher ground in between.

There are few locks, of course, in the flatter eastern counties, but they begin to gather thickly towards the midland plateau and in canals up in the Pennines. Locks carry several different waterways up to the focus of our narrow canal system in the Birmingham area. They take the Grand Union over the Chilterns through the Tring gap. They climb down in quick succession through Worcestershire to the Severn. They take the Leeds and Liverpool Canal up among the moors till it cuts through Foulridge Tunnel to drop down the other side. They lift the Oxford Canal gently over the tip of the Cotswolds, and drop the Staffs and Worcs at graded intervals from the Trent and Mersey down to Stourport.

All over our uneven countryside waterways climb and fall with the aid of their locks. There are still well over a thousand of them in use on our canals alone, applying the same principles as when some Chinaman first thought of them nearly a thousand years ago.

These principles are almost laughably simple. A lock is like a step in the waterway—a box of water which allows a boat in at one end, and raises or lowers it so that it can leave at the other end at a different level. For this purpose there must be doors at each end of the box, and openings through which water can be let in and out. And basically that's all there is to it. The doors are called gates, the openings are called sluices, paddles or cloughs (" clows ") according to the area of the country, and they are opened or closed by means of simple cog-wheels turned by means of a handle. The boat rises or falls with the water-level until it is ready to go on its journey at the new level of the waterway.

The principle is simple, and in theory the operation is simple, but in fact locks, gates, paddles and methods of operating them vary intriguingly throughout the canal system. Tackling the job correctly is one of the problems facing the beginner on canals, and although there are various safeguards, it is unfortunately possible to make a hash of the operation. This can—especially where locks are close together—cause chaos on the waterway and the towpath, inconvenience to other people, and damage to locks and boats. And since, these days, lock-keepers are rare, the canal traveller is usually on his own.

The worst possible thing for a boater to do is to be in a hurry. But anyone in a hurry oughtn't to be there, and probably won't be. He'll be haring off to the Costa Brava, and good luck to him. The canaller, covering his leisurely fifteen to twenty miles a day, has time to stand and think at the lock, and even to sit on the balance-beam of a gate and wait for the water to settle. For " working a lock " does need a bit of thought at times.

In the next 45 pages there will be locks galore, from the Kennet and Avon to the Leeds and Liverpool, and the narrow canals in between. There will be gates and paddle gear, footbridges and balance beams, windlasses and cog-wheels. But first, to whet the appetite and flex the muscles, some varied locks from various canals.

To start with, one of the deepest narrow locks in the system—Somerton Deep Lock on the Oxford Canal. This is what it looks like from a boat going in from the lower canal level—a couple of towering cliffs like the Grand Canyon, and a tight fit like a hand going into a glove. Like all locks on narrow canals, this one is about seven feet wide and seventy feet long, just taking the traditional narrow boat. With the boat entering through the bottom-end gate the lock is said to be "empty", while the far gate here is holding back a water-level twelve feet higher. There is a single gate at the bottom end of this lock, as at many on the Oxford. But most narrow canal locks have a single gate at the top and a pair of mitred gates at the bottom, like those showing on the Tardebigge lock on page 12.

RIGHT: Now one of the widest locks. In fact a confusing mixture of locks and lochs makes up the widest canal in Britain—the Caledonian. It consists of chunks of canal joining up a string of lochs across Scotland, and the artificial locks are monsters by English standards. There are 29 of them in the 21½ miles which are artificially cut, and they measure 160 feet long by 35 feet wide. So if ever a fleet of narrow boats got up there, each lock might well hold ten of them with room to spare at the end. The locks are now worked automatically, and the canal is often used by fishing boats. The one here is entering the first of five locks at Fort Augustus, and I must confess I visited this canal by road.

BELOW: Coming down in size, but still pretty large for Britain, this broad lock is one of an interesting pair linking the Worcester-Birmingham Canal with the Severn. Although the locks of the canal are narrow, its terminus is in Diglis basin in Worcester, and the connection with the river is then through these barge locks, each 76' by 18' 6", so the basin offers an interesting mixture of narrow canal boats and much larger ones coming from the unpredictable river into the haven of the basin. There have been times when the river has risen above the top level of these locks.

ABOVE: Back from the excursion among the big ones, and 56 locks further up the Worcester-Birmingham, this narrow lock is in fact the deepest on the narrow canals. Instead of the more usual six feet or so, the top lock of the Tardebigge flight drops boats fourteen feet. Originally there was an experimental boat-lift here, but this was replaced by the lock. We shall see more of Tardebigge, with its famous flight of thirty locks, but some idea of the depth of this top one can be gathered when you realise that my boat is at the bottom of it here, but you can't even see it.

BELOW: A full lock here for a change, but there's also an empty one at the side of it. For this unusual sight is at Hillmorton, near Rugby, where the only three locks on the northern Oxford are fairly close together, but each lock is in fact a pair side by side. Here I'm coming uphill while another boat in the other lock is going downhill at the same time. It certainly saves waiting when boats can pass each other in this way. The machinery between the locks enabled one lock to be used as a side pond to the other, to save water if necessary.

ABOVE: Although most of the popular cruising canals are narrow ones with seven-foot locks, the Grand Union is one of the exceptions. It has 166 broad locks, 14 feet wide, between London and Birmingham, though some in Warwickshire were only widened in the thirties. The locks are the same length as narrow locks, but being twice as wide they can take two narrow boats side by side, and this is how narrow boats carrying goods often work. In between locks the one with a motor tows the butty without a motor. Here is a pair leaving Cow Roast lock at the highest water-level of the canal in the Chilterns.

RIGHT: Another broad lock, and a deep one again, at Stenson on the Trent and Mersey. This is a narrow canal over most of its length, but the first six locks from the Trent are broad, and would take barges as far as Burton. Stenson is a fierce lock, as the leak at the far end already suggests. You need to hold tightly on to a boat, and because of the twelve-foot depth, if you want to climb out from the boat you have to use a vertical ladder set in the lock side.

ABOVE: This is a most unusual lock, but more and more boaters may see it as the Kennet and Avon Canal is opened up. It's Sheffield Lock, on the already navigable eastern section, and it is an example of the intriguing turf-sided locks of this canal. As can be seen, the sides are sloping, and getting on and off boats is a precarious business, though they are kept from grounding by the rails. The lock is quite a shallow one, and it is actually at its lowest in the picture.

BELOW: The Leeds and Liverpool is the northern broad rival to the Grand Union for cruising, though most of its locks are only 62 feet long. You'll be seeing more of this canal later, as it strides magnificently over the Pennines. The hire cruiser in this picture has left the highest level to pass down the Barrowford locks and then through several Lancashire towns. About a mile above these locks is Foulridge Tunnel, seen on page 105.

Two more unusual locks. The first (UPPER) is a diamond-shaped one on the Oxford Canal at Aynho. There are two of these on the Oxford, and each one is just below a pound where the River Cherwell has entered the canal and left it again. Each diamond lock has quite a small rise, and the shape—which can be awkward for boats—was constructed so that despite the small drop in level, the same amount of water would pass through the lock as through a deeper normal-shaped lock.

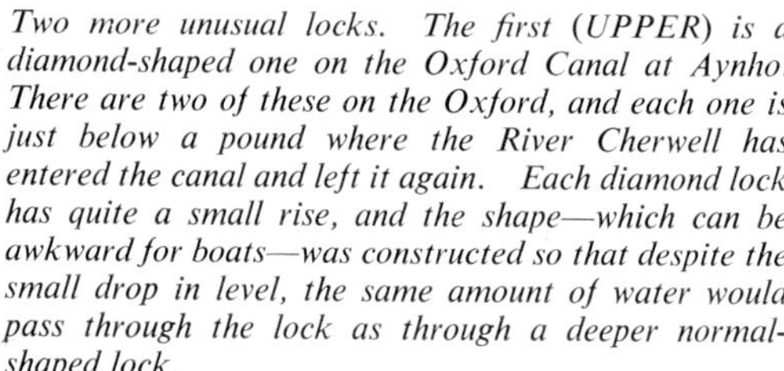

LOWER: This is one of the very few "guillotine" locks on the canal system, where the gates rise upwards. There are many on various rivers, however. This lock is in fact a complete box of steel at Thurlwood on the Trent and Mersey, built because of subsidence. Unlike most guillotine locks, it has a rising gate at each end, and to prevent both gates from being raised at the same time there is a complicated locking device in use. There is an ordinary lock alongside, and like those at Hillmorton the locks along this stretch of the Trent and Mersey are often twins.

ABOVE: Locks were not always built merely to raise the water-level. In the days of separate canal companies they were often placed at junctions to prevent water from being lost from one canal to another, or just to block the entrance and take tolls. These are known as stop locks and this one is Autherley junction where the Shropshire Union begins. The rise in water-level is in fact only six inches.

2 Flights and Staircases

When a canal reached a particularly steep slope, the canal diggers either had to make the locks deeper or build more of them. But the deeper a lock is the more water it uses, and the harder it is to work through. So in fact most of our locks raise a boat only about six feet and, as we have already seen, the deepest narrow lock is only fourteen. Thus where canals meet hills the boater tends to meet locks in quick succession.

The Worcester-Birmingham Canal especially has an impressive number of locks as it drops down to the Severn, and indeed it is one of the most heavily-locked canals in the world. Including the two large locks into the river which I showed on page 11, there are 58 in only sixteen miles, and 30 of them gather together below the village and tunnel of Tardebigge.

A group of locks like this, close together, and with only short pounds between them, is called a flight. And Tardebigge only just beats the Devizes flight of 29 broad locks on the Kennet and Avon. But the latter are at present out of use, though they form a spectacular sight, with wide side-ponds to take the water between locks.

Most flights are smaller than these giants, to some people's relief, though there are 23 at Wigan, 21 near Wolverhampton, and another 21 at Hatton near Warwick. A delightful flight of 13 takes the Northampton Arm from the Grand Union towards the Nene, under M1, and there are many pleasant small flights of five or six locks all over the system.

The really startling sight, however, is where locks are so close together that the top gate of one is the bottom gate of another, and rears up out of the water like a wooden cliff. Locks arranged like this are called a staircase, and the biggest in Britain isn't likely to be passed by most canallers, since it is on the Caledonian Canal—eight huge locks in a row. But there are two together at Bascote on the Grand Union which catch many a novice—and provide a great deal of fun to lookers-on. For when locks are stuck together in this way, where do you put the water from the top ones?

The answer is, if there isn't a side-pond to run it into, that you can only put it into the lock below. And if that's full, it must be emptied first. And so on, and so on.

The " Five-rise " at Bingley on the Leeds and Liverpool illustrates this with a vengeance. For if all the locks are full, they have to be emptied in turn, starting from the bottom. And then again, and then again, if there's to be room for the water coming down from above.

Next to Bingley, the best-known staircases are two lots of five at Foxton on the way to Leicester, with a short passing place between them. But the water here runs in and out of side-ponds alongside the steep slope. And if you nose around you may find the remains of an incline on which boats once rode in tanks instead, pulled by a snorting fixed steam engine.

To round off, there are locks at Bratch on the Staffs and Worcs which can't quite make up their mind whether to be a flight or a staircase. The pounds between are too short for boats, so they extend into side-ponds as well. Part of this flight can be seen on page 125 but, here are some views of other flights and staircases.

RIGHT: The slightly annoying thing about the Tardebigge locks is that they're not quite close enough together to make walking ahead as easy as hard-working lock-operators would like. So by the time they've finished they've walked quite a distance compared with, say, Hatton, where the pounds are shorter. But it's a lovely quiet flight, and without killing yourself you can do all 30, plus the remaining 26 into Diglis Basin at Worcester, in one day. Paddles are easy to work, and there's not much distraction if you pick the right day. There's a lot of water coming down the weirs in this picture, so that it is running over the lock-gates.

BELOW: Another truly rural flight, but going north this time. This is Audlem, on the Shropshire Union, where 15 locks through especially picturesque banks drop the Shropshire Union down to Cheshire. It's not so rural on Sundays, when great flocks of boats are rushing down on their way to the Llangollen. But at other times you can hear the birds singing above the burble of the water through the paddles. And Audlem, near the bottom of the flight, is a quiet little shopping town.

LEFT: Just above the junction with the Leigh Branch from the Leeds and Liverpool Canal, the locks of the Wigan flight climb up towards the Pennines, though there are still Blackburn, Burnley and Nelson in the 30 miles before the summit level. These locks are hard going, and not exactly crowded with eager travellers, but like a lot of canal stretches through industrial areas they are curiously deserted, possibly because industry has turned its back on the waterway. But the anglers appreciate this, and there are always a few scattered up this slope somewhere or other.

BELOW: A fascinatingly patterned builder's yard, and the electrified British Rail, signal the first lock of the 21 which take you down from the Birmingham warren past Wolverhampton to the rural canals to the north. Unlike the Wigan locks, the Wolverhampton 21 are narrow, but apart from a few spots they, too, are remarkably quiet. A retired canal character may appear to help you down, and he leaps alarmingly about, wielding a windlass more vigorously than many a younger man. You pop out of this long flight at Aldersley, and a little way along is the beginning of the Shropshire Union.

ABOVE: As a gentle introduction to staircases as opposed to flights, this pair of locks at Bascote in Warwickshire is strongly recommended. Most books forget to mention that it's a staircase, so you have to work out your own salvation, which usually means that water from the top lock is poured over the sides of the bottom lock. There are in fact side-paddles, but no-one seems to use them. They can be seen on the right of each lock in the picture. Some idea of the height of the gates between the two locks can be gathered when it is realised that they must be twice the normal height to allow for both depths. Bascote is on the quieter locking stretch between the Two Boats *at the foot of Stockton (see page 117) and the* Cape of Good Hope *just before the notorious Hatton starts.*

BELOW: After the staircase of five at Bingley, the two pairs of five narrow staircases at Foxton take the prize. Indeed, some may think that these are far more interesting, because there's always the ghost of the steam engine tugging boats up the ghostly slope in the trees at the side. There's one small passing-pound between the two groups of locks, and wide side-ponds taking the water off. You can devise your own ingenious ways of taking your ropes under the hefty footbridges as you go down.

3 Lock Gates

Locks have two vital components—their gates, and the paddles which let the water through.

Lock gates can be monstrous structures, from the huge but electrically-operated ones of the Caledonian, through the vast, slow hand-operated Crinan gates, down to the tiddly little stop-lock ones at Hawkesbury and Autherley and elsewhere. Mostly they are built of wooden planks on a massive framework of wooden beams, though some clangy ones are made of metal, especially on the southern Oxford at Napton. Sticking out from the top gates, and over the land, is a balance-beam, which serves the dual purpose of bringing some sort of a counter-balance to the gate-hang, and providing the traveller with a lever to push on.

Balance-beams are a study in themselves, tackled later in this book. Gates come in all shapes and sizes. Broad canals have a pair of gates at each end of their locks, meeting in the middle and pointing slightly up towards the weight of the water, which thus keeps them pressed against each other. Even then, some of it sometimes manages to squeeze through, and the old boatmen's trick was to pour their fire-ashes down to be carried into the gap.

On narrow canals the top end of the lock almost always has only one gate covering the whole of the end, and this is obviously a bit harder to move than the double gates at the bottom end. The Southern Oxford Canal, as mentioned already, has a single gate at the bottom as well.

Gates are fascinating things. There may even be a variety of plants growing from their beams, not to mention ancient messages from boatmen to each other occasionally carved on them. But they sit there doing a vital job—some of them rather precariously, judging by the way they wobble and creak.

The snag is, they have to be opened and closed. In theory this is easy, since they turn on a heel-post sitting in the bottom of the lock and anchored at the top, and merely need pivoting by a push on the balance-beam. But for variations on this theme, turn to page 32.

There's just one little thing to watch about the top pair of gates when going downhill. As the water drops and your boat with it, a lethal great slab of concrete often emerges, which serves to hold the top gates from bursting in under the water pressure. This is vital to them but can be fatal to you. For if your boat is sitting too far back, it can end up with its stern in the air on this concrete sill, with perhaps its propeller and rudder damaged. So don't let a chap in front of you in the lock keep you too near to the back end.

Perhaps the most stirring view of a lock-gate is to stand on top of one in one of the staircases mentioned in pages 16 to 19. Since it forms the barrier directly between one lock and another it is twice the usual height. Looking straight down it is rather like peering over Beachy Head. There's an awful lot of wood down there—especially when you come to open it.

ABOVE: This is a fine typical view of the bottom gates of a Grand Union lock, complete with lockside houses, steps up from the lower pound, mooring bollards (modern), and in this case a fascinating but unusual fall of surplus water over the gates. This is the bottom lock at Buckby, seven locks down from one of the summit levels of the Grand Union. There's a pair of great mitred gates at each end, with some rather old-fashioned paddles that take their time in letting the water through. There are some new wooden gates here and there in the Buckby flight, though, and it is interesting to see that the craft of gate-making still goes on.

BELOW: This pair of gates is in fact the next pair that the boater sees after leaving Buckby locks travelling south, but they are 15 miles and Blisworth tunnel further on. They are the top gates of Stoke Bruerne flight, just by the Waterways Museum and the Boat Inn, *and a solid gnarled pair they are, with their four gate-paddles and two ground-paddles at the side. The sill which I mentioned earlier is clearly visible here, and it is fairly obvious what would happen to a boat lying too far back as the water dropped. In fact narrow boats are sometimes deliberately allowed to settle on these sills as a quick but improper way of examining the propeller and rudder.*

ABOVE: Although rather battered and patched, this pair of gates shows clearly the way they meet in the middle to bear the weight of the water pressing on them. The ends of the gates are angled so that they fit exactly together, and the more the higher level of water presses, the more tightly they bind. When the paddles are opened you can often hear a sort of creak or groan of relief from the meeting gates as the water level drops. This pair of gates holds the water in the bottom lock of the Aylesbury arm.

LEFT: Well across country from Aylesbury is this solid piece of craftsmanship at the end of the top gate at Marston Doles lock, next to the top of the Napton flight of the Oxford Canal. There are several of these end-posts around here, mounted on the ends of the single top gates, and very helpful they are for a lock-worker to give a push to assist the chap at the balance-beam at the other side of the gate.

ABOVE: Further down the same Napton flight are the metal bottom gates which interest students of canal engineering. A far as practical boaters go, they are certainly amongst the easiest gates I know, some of them opening almost at the push of a finger. The look of this particular pair has been marred by the addition of an experimental piece of paddle-gear, which may be much easier to work, but which sticks out like a sore thumb, especially with the famous mellow ruined windmill in the background.

RIGHT: Looking for an example of a single top gate—almost always the rule on narrow locks—I came on this rather sad one, in surroundings which tell their own story. This is the last usable lock on the Chesterfield, at Worksop. The next one is impassable, and all of this interesting waterway from Worksop to Chesterfield is now closed. But from the Trent to Worksop enthusiasts keep it fairly busy.

LEFT: This is outside British Waterways' territory, but on an artificial cut nevertheless, even though it is concerned chiefly with drainage. This is Cowbridge lock, near Boston on the Witham Navigable Drains. Like the Trent and Mersey lock on page 15, it is of the guillotine type, though with the rising gate at one end only. Quite a few boats use this lock, coming from the Witham through the British Waterways' lock at Anton's Gowt, and via Cowbridge into Maud Foster's Drain, which gives them quiet moorings in the heart of Boston.

BELOW: Another guillotine, and a famous one this time, but no longer in use. This ancient monument used to seal off the Stratford Canal from the Worcester-Birmingham at Kings Norton, and now remains poised in precarious preservation there, and subject to much photography. Unhappily the house at the side has been felled since my photograph, and the smoothed-off pile of rubble in its place is hardly worth using film on.

4 Working the Paddle Gear

The vital tool, without which hardly any lock can be used. This is the blister and labour-saving version, with twin sockets to fit either size of paddle-spindle, and a revolving handle for delicate palms.

THE WHOLE EXISTENCE of locks depends on the boater being able to let water in or out of them, so that the boat can rise up or be lowered. And that's what the sluices, paddles or cloughs are all about, lurking there in the gates or in the ground at the side.

It's all a very simple idea, really—holes at each end of the lock which you can open or close—but in fact the paddles up and down the British canal system are a study in themselves. They are also, to some extent, wrapped in mystery, since normally we see only the apparatus above the gate or the ground, and we don't know what's going on under the water. But the bits we can see can vary intriguingly.

Somewhere, however, there's a spindle sticking out, on which we fit our handle, called a windlass or key. This thing is a very valuable piece of property on a boat, and it pays to carry a spare or two, for the beds of canals near lock-gates must be well lined with lost windlasses.

Even this simple tool deserves study. The spindles on most narrow canals are smaller than those on broad canals, and you really need two different windlasses on board. The old boatmen's windlass is a lovingly-kept solid piece of metal, polished by years of use in horny hands. But for softer travellers nowadays you can buy one with a revolving handle, so that you can return from a trip with the palms of your hands intact. Moreover, you can also buy a windlass with two sockets to it, so that you can use the same one for both sizes of spindle.

There's one word of warning here. The spindles on paddle-gear are usually slightly tapered, and sometimes extremely worn, so that far from being square they are almost round. So if you are rash enough to have a windlass with an absolutely square socket you may run into trouble, for there's nothing more dangerous than a windlass that flies off the spindle just as you are applying pressure. It can break an arm. The safest type should have a generous tapered socket, which is much more likely to stay snugly on the spindle of the paddle-gear. And by the way, another way of breaking an arm is to leave a windlass unattended on the spindle of a lifted paddle. For paddle-gear has been known to slip before now and fling the windlass at the innocent boater.

Having got the windlass firmly on the spindle, you wind away. In most cases, you are in fact turning a cog or a group of cogs which then pull up a toothed rack attached to the paddle way down below the water. As the rack appears above your cogs, so the paddle uncovers the waterhole wherever it may be, and the water rushes in or out of the lock.

This sounds quite straightforward, but it has its catches, quite apart from slipping windlasses. For example, not all paddle-gear works as smoothly as the description suggests. It may be bent, or rusty, or worn, and require a hearty effort before it decides to get moving. But often it is liberally coated with grease, which you have to brush past when crossing the lock. Wise boaters, indeed, have a pair of old " locking gloves ". These come in especially useful when a paddle has been wound up, for there is almost always a device to stop it from dropping down again. This may be a ratchet which, if it is turned over into the right position, automatically engages and holds the paddle-rack up. But the most endearing little gimmick is a piece of metal hanging on a chain, which you have to insert by hand into the cogs to stop them unwinding themselves again. This invariably transfers its grease gradually to the passing boaters. Another cunning gadget is a sort of sliding spanner on the Napton flight, which slides upwards to hold the spindle, but drops down of its own accord when you start to wind the paddle down.

The straightforward up-and-down paddle-rack is found both on gate-paddles and on the paddles which are in the ground at the side. When it is on a gate, the operator may have to perch precariously on a step, or even on a footbridge overhanging the lock (as on the southern Stratford). And sometimes he may find difficulty in turning his windlass without hitting himself in the stomach. But usually there is a long connecting spindle between the winding position and the gear out on the gate, so that the winder can stand safely on land. On some gates on the Trent and Mersey he winds from the extreme end of the balance-beam, the connecting spindle being cunningly hidden underneath, so that newcomers have difficulty in finding it.

When this simple type of gear is in the ground at the side, gremlins may live down there. When the winder starts up, a water-spout sometimes swishes out of a hole conveniently placed to spray him. And very often weird subterranean noises can be heard.

On the Grand Union in Warwickshire, a burst of canal improvement in the thirties produced some fascinating ground paddle-gear, worked beautifully but invisibly by a worm device—the whole lot being enclosed, and prevented from running back by an enormous hunk of chained metal looking like the spare end of a spanner, to be clipped over the spindle. On some of these white towers, which look particularly spectacular stretching up the steps of Hatton, a sort of Neptune's trident emerges from the top, so that at least the lock operator knows whether the paddle is up or down. Where there isn't one of these, you can always peer through a little peep-hole to see how things are going.

The Leeds and Liverpool doesn't believe in dragging paddles upwards all the time to open the water-holes, but goes in for great slabs of wood to be levered sideways. This is done by winding a long toothed metal arm along the balance-beam.

Anyhow, somehow or other, this variety of gear uncovers holes. If these are underground the water comes rushing into the lock like a whirlpool, and can push a boat around if released too quickly. It also, in narrow locks, has the illogical effect of sucking a boat up to the top gate, although one would expect it to push the boat towards the bottom one. When filling a lock, in any case, the boat must be well secured, and if it is a broad lock, it's a good idea to open the paddle on the same side as the boat first of all, for this often has the effect of holding the boat against the wall.

When gate paddles are opened, the water can often be seen pouring in like a waterfall, and if there are ground paddles also, they should be opened first to bring the level up, or there may be danger of the gate-paddle water swamping the boat if it's too near to the gate.

Perhaps one final word about paddles may be said before we have a look at some. Strange as it may seem, boaters have been known to have paddles at both ends of a lock open at the same time, leaving them wondering why the lock isn't filling. This doesn't do the canal any good if the locks are close together, since it can empty the pound up above. But it's a thing that happens to the best of us, often by pure accident because we didn't notice a paddle still up. It is a fact that working a lock calls for eyes all round all the time—not only to check on the paddles, but to check also on the gongoozlers who materialise from nowhere and are liable to get knocked in when nobody is looking.

ABOVE: Let's start off with the unusual sight of water visibly entering when a paddle is being opened. Usually it boils in deep down in the lock, shooting up to the surface or sweeping along underneath and coming back again to take the boat forward. But some canals, such as the Staffs and Worcs and the Trent & Mersey, specialise in gate paddles of this type, where the water is diverted sideways, presumably to avoid flooding open-fronted boats. The whole operation can be seen clearly here, at the first lock leaving the Stourport basins on the way northwards.

What can you call a collection of ground paddles? A "creaking"? A "grunting"? Some of them certainly take a bit of getting moving, but once the initial jerk is over, and if you keep the windlass going, up they come. There's a fair variety of these all over the system, but they all, somehow, connect with a shutter over a channel underground which lets water in or out of the lock low down in its sides.

A very common kind, captured on the Staffs and Worcs Canal, but having the Birmingham Canal Navigations initials embossed on it. This is fairly well geared, and the ratchet to keep the paddle up actually has a small handle on it which saves oily fingers.

Curious sloping twin ground paddles, but unhappily no longer in use. This striking old pair are on the Huddersfield Narrow Canal high in the Pennines.

When a paddle is up, the rack stands out above its top like this (LEFT). Another form of ratchet can be seen here. All these ratchets have excellent finger-trapping qualities.

A magnificent iron specimen at the broad river lock from the Stratford Canal into the Avon (RIGHT). The gate-gear can be seen beyond, and also the chain which fastens the gates against hooligans.

Few canal travellers reach this antiquated ground-paddle, which is at Ashline where Whittlesey Dyke rnus into the Middle Level. The waterway is actually below sea-level, and leads, with a struggle, through to the Great Ouse.

There seems to be no rule as to when there are to be gate paddles and when ground paddles, and often there are both. The gate paddles work less mysteriously, for you can actually see the bar running down from the gear to the shutter in the gate below. At times, as can be seen on page 27, they release a visible waterfall if the ground paddles haven't been used first to raise the water-level.

An unusual and well-geared example at the diamond-shaped lock at Aynho on the Oxford. As already mentioned, instead of a ratchet there's often a sliding spanner affair on the Oxford, which grips the spindle to prevent the paddle from dropping.

Another helpfully large bit of gearing in the staircase locks at Grindley Brook on the Llangollen. Working the paddles here requires quite a bit of logical thought to avoid flooding the towpath.

ABOVE: A hefty and protected contraption on the Calder and Hebble at Brighouse in Yorkshire. This is one of the unusual cases where the windlass is provided. This canal is a magnificent one, though liable to floods.

RIGHT: Exposed cogs and racks are obviously likely to wear and rust, as the many awkward ones around bear witness. So British Waterways have introduced various experimental types, which may be both easier to work and easier to maintain. This one is on the Oxford Canal.

LEFT: In the thirties the Grand Union locks in Warwickshire were widened to barge width (though this scheme was never fully finished). One blessing that came from it was the striking ground paddles, working on a worm gear and enclosed in these sloping containers. They need more turns than usual, but the turns are fairly easy. One of the snags is that you can't see at a glance whether the paddles are up or down, so some of them have been fitted with rods, as seen here, which emerge from the top of the casing. Even without these, however, it's possible to peer into a hole at the side and make a check. The one in the photograph is well on the way up the notorious 21 locks at Hatton, and others can be seen in the distance.

BELOW: The Grand Union locks at Buckby and Braunston were already broad in the thirties, and their paddle-gear didn't receive the benefits conferred on the ones further north. They have some particularly cantankerous examples of paddles, and some have been removed completely, making the filling or emptying rather slow in places. On the Braunston six, the upper gates have a pair of gate paddles in each gate and a ground paddle at each side. The lower gates, as seen here, have a gate paddle apiece.

LEFT: The Leeds and Liverpool provides an unusual and simple alternative to the usual sliding shutter, pulled upwards and lowered again. Instead, there is the great slab of wood, as in this lock at Gargrave. It is levered sideways by a cog engaging a long toothed horizontal rack. The slab gradually uncovers the hole in the gate as it slides. Gargrave is on a fine rural stretch above the basin at Skipton on this trans-Pennine canal.

BELOW: Carelessness, stupidity, or just plain forgetfulness can cause chaos at any lock, but where there's a staircase, as at Grindley Brook just mentioned, the possibilities are even greater. But the problem of explaining to newcomers how to work such locks is almost more difficult than the working itself. Anyhow, see if you can fathom this notice at the side of the Watford staircase on the way up to Leicester. In fact this staircase is not as difficult as some, for there are long side-ponds to take the water, so there isn't the problem of having to put it into the lock beneath.

5 Heaving on Balance Beams

MANY CANAL TRAVELLERS claim that the ultimate enjoyment of canal cruising is lying flat on one's back on a great balance-beam, listening to the gurgle of water through the sluices.

There certainly do seem to be two different approaches to the working of locks. There are those who rush madly about shouting at each other and wearing themselves out after half-a-dozen locks. And there are those who calmly walk up, open the necessary paddles, and then either sit or lie down until the water levels up. And since it's impossible to hurry the water once the paddles are open, you may as well join the second group.

But balance-beams for lying on are not as common as they were. On the narrow canals, indeed, they tend to be on the slim side at the best of times, and far too many of them have been replaced by miserable metal girders, too narrow to lie on, cutting to sit on, and not even very satisfactory to push on. So the broad canals provide the best bets for balance-beam relaxers, and the Grand Union and the Leeds and Liverpool offer some beautiful wide flat slabs. But even the Grand Union in places seems to have gone in for chunks of concrete trapped in cages instead to provide the necessary weight.

Pleasant to look at and to sit on, but not to lie on, are the occasional round beams, such as the great tree-trunks on the Nene, some enormous ones on the Exeter Ship Canal, and some ex-telegraph-poles on the Kennet and Avon. But the oddest beams are probably those that have had to be modified when widening road-bridges. They are either very stubby and fat to give the weight without the length, or else they have been bent to clear the bridge wall, like the well-known one just before the terminus of the southern Stratford. Though in some cases, as in Blackburn, there are no beams left, and the gate is opened like some on the Trent, by turning a wheel which pulls on a toothed arm.

Usually, however, there is a straightforward beam of some kind which has to be pushed. But even in the pushing, variety abounds. The ideal beam is just about the height of one's backside, so that it is possible to lean on it gently until it begins to move. But some beams were obviously built for dwarfs, and are only a foot or so above the ground, so one has almost to kneel to get at them. Others, where the lock-side drops sharply enough to the pound below, may be high in the air when the gate is open.

In many places there are brick ribs to tuck the feet against when slowly inching forward a recalcitrant beam. But sometimes these aren't just where you want them. And in any case, generations of beam-heavers have often gouged out hollows which at times are nicely filled with mud. It must be said, too, that often desperate single-handed boaters have made holes in beams with their boat-hooks, improperly poking bottom gates shut as their boats move out.

Somehow all these beams get pushed and all these gates are moved. And though some beams take a few hearty heaves before they reluctantly begin to give, once moving a steady shuffle should eventually do the trick with the toughest of them. Sometimes, when the gate is partly open, it gives a sort of defiant last hiccup, but persistence usually wins.

ABOVE: A good clear number on a good strong balance-beam reminds the boater here that he is in his 54th lock down the Stratford Canal—if he started at the Kings Norton guillotine. The restored Southern Stratford, by the way, is like the Oxford Canal below Banbury: although narrow, it has single gates at both top and bottom instead of the more usual double gates at the bottom. One more lock below this balance-beam, and the traveller enters a tunnel-like stretch beneath the panting cars pouring into Stratford, and emerges in front of the Memorial Theatre.

BELOW: A cold, hollow and cheerless metal beam greets this party of primary school children visiting the Waterways' Museum at Stoke Bruerne. But like all the surroundings at this pleasant canal spot it is usually kept painted and tidy (though paint chips off metal only too easily). This is late winter, when the museum sign is laid up. In summer the moorings are busy with boats, and the Boat Inn *opposite does a roaring trade. Quarter of a mile beyond the museum the famous Blisworth tunnel begins.*

ABOVE: Among the Leeds and Liverpool's industrial stretches, which contrast with its moorland miles, is a built-up but quiet length through Blackburn, where a lively I.W.A. rally once brought the canal into the public eye. Where the wide Bolton road passes over the foot of a flight of locks there is no room for balance-beams to swing. Instead, curved toothed racks pull open the gates when the fixed handle is turned, and just to protect carelessly-hanging clothes or calf-muscles, the teeth disappear into a metal shield. The lock-worker can nip across one of those sturdy Leeds and Liverpool footbridges to avoid going out on to the main road.

BELOW: This is a starker solution to the widened-road problem. The murderous A5 at Gailey carries traffic struggling to get from M1 to M6, and Gailey lock by an unusual tower has to bend its beams accordingly. This crude piece of meccano looks rather out of keeping with the canal scene, especially at this spot where boats often moor at nights, and where there are several reminders of canal history. A lively youth club here also makes use of the canal with canoes.

ABOVE: Few canal travellers will recognise this lock—or indeed use it. But a few ships and yachtsmen in the south-west know the Exeter Ship Canal, which was one of the earliest canals in Britain. It is really a by-pass to the River Exe, with only two locks, one of which, confusingly, is called Double Locks. These odd shaped metal beams are at one end of this lock, but the other pair of gates have enormous pole-like arms to help them to open. This is a peaceful canal, and even if you can't take your boat there it is worth a walk on the towpath.

LEFT: It can't be! But surely it is! This looks like a useful change for superannuated telegraph poles, especially if they can play their part like this one in opening up more locks on the Kennet and Avon. Slowly but surely this broad canal across southern England is coming to life again, and Sheffield Lock, seen left, is on the eastern stretch which now runs from the Thames at Reading to the tail of Tile Mill lock. One of the snags is that canal boats need to travel via the Thames, and thus must obtain a Thames licence and conform to Thames regulations. There is a reduction of 50% on British Waterways' licences for boats used only on the K and A.

LEFT: This beam at Sandon on the Trent and Mersey is unusual in that it carries the shaft of the gate-paddle to the extreme end of the arm. Many windlass-wielders at this and other T & M locks fail to notice this at first, as a spindle lurking underneath the arm is a rarity. But somehow the gate-paddle has to be raised, sending a torrent of water into unsuspecting front cockpits.

BELOW: The lynx-eyed canaller will spot a paddle up at the far end of this top lock of the Northampton flight, which he'll need to put down if he wants to fill the lock. This is a typical simple narrow canal lock, with small but sturdy beams, and hand-rails for crossing the gates. This picture, too, shows the ribbed track for the beam pusher. The lock-house is a landmark for boats struggling up the sixteen other locks below this one, though often they may be helped by a particularly cheerful lock-keeper. The locks are easy to work, however, and are strongly recommended, not only as an exercise, but as a link with the delightful River Nene.

6 Crossing the Lock

All this business of winding up paddles, opening gates, and getting boats in and out of locks is fascinating to do and to watch. No two crews ever seem to tackle it in the same way. And thus you see a tantalising variety of methods in operation.

Many crews, of course, are there to relax, and they amble along in perfect contentment, not caring whether their locking is efficient or inefficient so long as they're in the fresh air. But other crews regard canal travel as a challenge, and apply time and motion study methods to the task of working locks both efficiently and rapidly.

Certainly the job is one worth the attention of the time and motion boys, for getting through a lock can range from the laborious, lengthy, and often hilarious, to the speedy zoom carried out by the real craftsman, who is often, it must be said, on a narrow boat.

A bicycle is one of the best tools for efficient lock-working, for it enables a crew-member to cycle ahead, with the occasional header into the canal where the towpath has fallen in, and prepare the next lock if there is no-one coming in the other direction (or, sometimes, I'm sorry to say, even if there is). But another and even more efficient aid to quick and economical lock-working is a way of getting across a lock as quickly as possible. This applies particularly when two people are crewing a boat, with only one working the locks and one steering.

The point is that the chap working the lock must be at both sides at the same time, to work paddles and open and close gates. And since there's only one of him, he must be pretty nippy.

There are three solutions open to him. The longest and safest is to walk down the lock after opening one paddle or gate, across the opposite (closed) gate, and up the length of the lock to open the other paddle/gate—with of course a double journey in some circumstances. The most precarious method—used by agile boaters of all ages—is to leap across from an open gate to a still-closed one, and if still in circulation to proceed on to land and open the other gate (needless to say, this applies only to pairs of bottom gates on narrow canals). The third way, of course, is to hope for a footbridge. (There's a fourth, improper, way whereby the boat forces open the bottom pair of gates.)

Now footbridges can be a mixed blessing. Many boaters prefer to take their boats in and out by means of their ropes, and it's a hazardous job passing a rope under a fixed footbridge at the tail of a lock, lying on your belly and hoping. And I wouldn't really recommend the lassooing method I nearly learnt at Foxton once. So you hope for a split in the bridge, as on the Stratford, or a gap at one end, as on the diving-board bridges in some places. But you don't often get them.

So you meet many boaters who haven't a good word to say for footbridges. I suppose it depends whether you're a boat-roper or not, or a gate-leaper or not. Anyhow, here is a selection of footbridges from my collection, wide and narrow, precarious and solid, elegant and chunky. Mind how you cross them.

LEFT: This is the standard way of crossing the closed gates from one side of a lock to the other—on the gates. Sometimes there's a foot-plank, which occasionally is barely above water-level, or at other times you walk along the top of the gate. There's usually a handrail, but this may be in sections to make room for the gate paddle-gear, if any. Some such gates seem to have been specially designed so that it's impossible to walk across them without collecting a quantity of black oil from the the cogs of the paddle-gear, unless you lean precariously out as you pass them by. Or maybe you have to lean out anyhow because the rails have been bent by some over-eager boat. This is one of the more civilised gate-crossings, at Keynsham on the Avon end of the Kennet and Avon.

BELOW: When gates are open, the problem is very different, and this is where the footbridges come in. The occasional footbridges on the Staffs and Worcs expect canal travellers to be agile. There are numerous narrow ones with nothing to hang on to at all. On the other hand, the designers didn't ask us to contort ourselves trying to pass a rope underneath. Slits are provided for the tow-rope, though unfortunately they have sometimes been made ineffective now by more recent strengthening devices. Below, the precarious pair of metal leaves hangs out over the depths, and looks as if it is built for a tight-rope walker. The adjoining road bridge wall acts as a handrail.

ABOVE: Increasing numbers of boaters are exploring the Birmingham Canal Navigations. From Gas Street or Farmers Bridge they cruise up wide, straight, if not too clean waters, with surprisingly open views and surprisingly few buildings on the banks. This is the Main Line, but there's a warren of waterways on either side at two other levels. The Main Line itself eventually rises to one of these levels at the three Tipton Factory locks, near the bridge shown on page 81. These locks are black with oil, and leave their trade-mark on your boat. But the most intriguing thing about them is this footbridge. Solid, marked by ropes, looking as if it will last for ever, it is somehow symbolic of the Black Country. And it still remains cantilevered, with a gap at one end for ropes to slide under.

BELOW: Here is exactly the same principle in an entirely different setting—but not too far away from Birmingham. It is on the Worcester-Birmingham Canal on its way down to the Severn. Looking rather like a diving-board with handrails, it seems to be fixed in the same way, and even springs up and down a little as the lock worker dashes across. Again those who prefer to take their boats in and out with tow-ropes are grateful for the gap. This canal, on the few stretches not filled with locks, is surprisingly broad and rural, with wide views.

ABOVE: At Sandon, on the Trent and Mersey, a broader wooden footbridge gives more confidence than the Staffs and Worcs tight-ropes. But there are still no handrails, and passing a rope under a wide bridge is harder than getting it under a narrow one—for there is no rope-gap either. Here is a chance for the boating cowboy to try his lariat practice, swinging the rope round until it whips under and comes up on the other side.

BELOW: The Macclesfield Canal concentrates all its locks at Bosley, climbing through twelve there towards its spectacular views westwards. These locks are sturdy ones, and this pleasing metal footbridge offers a simple handrail too. The canal crosses the Dane below the locks, on a high embankment, and at the top of the mile-long flight a feeder from the Bosley reservior comes into the 16-mile pound which takes the canal to Marple.

ABOVE: At opposite ends of the 21-mile summit level of the Leicester Grand Union, two well-known sets of locks climb up. The Foxton flight at the northern end—seen on page 19—has footbridges and handrails all the way down its two staircases. The picture above is of the Watford Flight at the southern end. Four of its seven locks are joined in a staircase, and they are crossed by these strong bridges with heavy guard-rails, possibly because the drop between staircase locks is a formidable one.

BELOW: Although only a footbridge, this lock-crossing is reminiscent of the curious split road-bridges on the Stratford Canal, one of which is seen on page 78. It is on the Trent and Mersey at Stone, not far from the Sandon bridge. Stone, incidentally, gets its name from a monument once placed there to commemorate two murdered princes. It is now a busy spot for boat-building and hiring.

ABOVE: Among the canals whose builders obviously thought lock-workers needed protection when crossing, the Leeds and Liverpool must rank high. This lock-bridge in Leeds is typical of many more—a solid baulk of wood clamped down at both ends, and with outward-sloping railings and no concession to horses. In Leeds, as in other cities, the canaller can be perfectly peaceful as he starts along a canal as solid as the Pennines themselves.

BELOW: Is this the most elaborate lock footbridge of all? It is on the Shropshire Union where it passes almost unnoticed through the heart of Chester. This is a little-travelled length of the canal, across the Wirral Peninsula to Ellesmere Port. There is a link with a stretch of the Dee in Chester, and a staircase of three locks alongside the city walls. The locks are cut from solid rock.

7 Water over the Weir

One of the most noticeable differences between locks on rivers and locks on canals is that the river locks often have a terrifying weir at the side of them, where the main flow of water roars down to the lower level while the boats make their way through the lock. These rushing and often very wide little waterfalls were used long before locks were invented, in order to build up the river for fishermen or millers. When boats wanted to pass them, they would have to shoot downwards through a gap opened in the weir barrier, or be dragged forcibly upstream through the same gap. And all this had to happen very quickly, so that the water-level up above didn't drop too low and make the miller or the fisherman angry.

In those days there was many an argument or fight between boatmen and millers in particular, and the millers used to hold up the boats for hours or days before condescending to let them through.

Many canal locks, of course, have no weirs, since there is not a flow of water along a canal as there is along a river. But in fact there may be some small flow there. Indeed, the Llangollen Canal has quite a current in it, since it acts as a water feeder. And all canals have to be kept filled at their upper levels from reservoirs or pumps of some kind, in order to keep water in them all the time. This upper level water is always making its way slowly downwards as locks are used.

Canal levels are normally taken care of by overflows which you can spot in the banks in many places. But as well as these there may also be overflows at the sides of locks, especially where there are several together in flights. These not only look after any surplus water that may be coming down, but also balance up the levels in the short pounds between the locks. It's surprising how quickly pounds can drop through careless boaters leaving gates open or paddles up, or merely through leaking gates.

Thus in some way or other water may be able to flow out of one pound, past the side of the lock, and down into the next pound. This only happens, of course, if the water in any pound is above the correct level, which is fixed by the lip of the overflow weir. When enough has escaped, the level is below this lip, and no more flows.

These weirs, where they exist, vary like all other things in the canal system. Sometimes the water flows past quite openly in a wide channel, as on the Grand Union in Warwickshire or the northern Stratford Canal, pouring straight down over a lip at the end like a little Niagara. On some of the Leeds and Liverpool flights it rushes past the lock like a mountain torrent. On the Northampton flight it runs downwards in a curving narrower channel, sloping all the way and quietly running out into the lower pound. At Napton and elsewhere on the Oxford the water runs—if it is running over the weir at all—over a broad lip, then disappears under the ground. The weirs at Tardebigge are a bit of a mystery and a bit of a nuisance. It isn't very obvious where they start in the upper pounds, but they come boiling up just below the lock gates in the lower level, and bang boats about a little as they leave the lock.

The most striking weirs are on the Staffordshire and Worcestershire Canal. At several locks there are large round or semi-diamond-shaped contractions at the side of the top lock gate, with water pouring over their lips all round, and a large domed grating to stop branches and bottles and cans from going in. The water then disappears underground and reappears somewhere in the pound beneath.

Although the Tardebigge weirs may be the

worst, almost all weirs—if they happen to be running fairly strongly—affect the steering of boats, since they naturally run out into lower pounds somewhere near the lower lock gate. Thus boats that are about to enter the lock, and are nicely lined up to go in without hitting anything, get pushed a little cock-eyed by the force of the weir water. And many a steerer has been disappointed in what he thought was going to be a perfect journey into the lock. Similarly, boats leaving the lock may be gliding beautifully out, only to find their bows pushed over and their stern scraping the shoulders of the lock. But that's one of the reasons why canal boats are —or ought to be—so well protected by rubbing strakes, metal cappings, and fenders (though no boat builder yet seems to have solved the problem of completely protecting the two rear corners).

Here, then, are a few of the weirs to be seen on the canal system.

The Lapworth flight is a curious collection of locks, where the boater is asked to leave the bottom gates open whichever way he happens to be going. Nobody seems quite sure why this is, and certainly the flight is well protected by weirs, which run alongside the locks and drop furiously down into the lower pound. The northern Stratford is very different from its southern part, and was never closed. In fact it forms an alternative route into Birmingham, though the Lapworth locks come rather too soon after the Hatton ones on the Grand Union. The Stratford and Grand Union Canals come close together at Lapworth, and there is a short link with a lock, at the junction shown on page 97.

TOP: As you work quietly but busily down the close-together locks of the Northampton flight, with their occasional raised lift-bridges, there always seems to be a drop of spare water coming down with you, and often that seems to be the only moving thing besides you and your boat. It seems a far cry from the Grand Union at Gayton just above, but you find that you need the same-sized windlass despite the narrow locks. The weirs by the locks on this flight are narrow and gentle streams, meandering into the field and sloping their way gradually downwards. They rarely cause much trouble as they discharge into the lower pound.

ABOVE: Goodness knows by what devious subterranean means the weirs down Tardebigge make their way past the locks, but they come bubbling up much too close to the lower gates, like some miniature Loch Ness monster. Sometimes there seems to be a lot of water on its way down the famous 30 locks, even running over the bottom gates, as can be seen on page 17. Indeed, I once saw it invading the towpath. These weirs have a greater effect on boats entering or leaving a lock than most do.

ABOVE: The Chesterfield almost matches the Lancaster and the Brecon/Abergavenny as a completely isolated canal. But it is in fact possible to visit it from other canals by tackling the tidal Trent. There's a vigorous collection of enthusiasts boating on it, and four miles from its start at Stockwith it skirts the highest point in north Notts at Gringley-on-the-Hill. This weir at one of the locks beneath the hill is a broad, quiet one, rather like the lower part of the canal itself.

BELOW: By contrast, the weir here comes down like a mountain torrent, which is perhaps appropriate to the Leeds and Liverpool. It is near Apperley Bridge and the British Waterways' yard at Dobsons Locks. It has two locks to bypass, which maybe accounts for its speed. Like many locks on the L and L, they are joined in a staircase. This is a popular fishing spot, and there are good meals at an inn along the road.

ABOVE: One of the strikingly unusual weirs on the Staffs and Worcs, which seems to specialise in unusual things, such as bridge name-plates, split footbridges, sandstone cliffs, and amusing place-names. There are several of these circular or semi-diamond-shaped weirs at the sides of locks, with water swirling mysteriously through the metal grid and into the ground, to reappear in the pound below. One that is easy to see from the road is by the Stewponey Hotel.

BELOW: There seems to be no pattern in the weirs on the southern Stratford Canal, and the lively restorers appear to have sorted them out as they went along. This remarkably rural canal near busy roads drops gently down, and here at Lock 28 near Rowington simple concrete retaining walls guide the water out below the lock. This is a curiously isolated area, with few places to call at, though there is a pleasant village at Lowsonford three locks further down.

8 On and off the Boat

SINCE SOMEBODY usually has to prepare locks for the boat to get into them, it's necessary to land crew members in advance. Conversely, after lowering the final paddles and closing the gates when leaving the lock, whoever has done the job has to get back on to the boat. This isn't always as easy as it sounds.

At Nell Bridge, for example, where the A41 from Bicester to Banbury now hides a smaller and fascinating little predecessor of a bridge beneath itself, there is a popular lock with a small farm shop and a petrol station up the road. But there is no way of getting on or off a boat at the lower end of the lock, since the towpath doesn't go under the bridge. So in order to deal with the lock—or after closing it if going downhill—somebody has to take his life in his hands and cross the busy highway, which is no fun after a peaceful stretch of the Oxford Canal.

The Trent and Mersey and the Stratford often play this trick of no towpath under a bridge, too, though not usually with a wide main road bridge. So the lock-worker has to leave the boat before the bridge in order to get to the lock, and vice-versa. At Buckby top lock on the Grand Union, crew members might well have had to brave A5, but luckily somebody thought of this and squeezed some steps in between the bottom lock-gate and the main road. Similar narrow, steep steps are sometimes found in such confined places.

Bridge or no bridge at the foot of the lock, lock-workers always have to climb up or down between boat and lock above. And often impressive steps are provided for this purpose. You're never quite sure what you're going to get, however. The most convenient ones run straight up parallel with the canal side, so that someone can leap off the boat and run up with a rope if necessary, or at least with a windlass. Conversely they can trot down and on to the boat as it leaves. On parts of the Grand Union, for instance, you can do this for a few locks, but may then find that the next one has its steps well away from the lock-side and curving down from the end of the balance-beam instead.

Like all canal things, then, steps vary. Some are old and crumbling and covered with vegetation. Some canal-builders didn't bother with steps at all, and left the lock-worker to scramble about as best he could. In summer, where there is only a grassy slope, many a boater has tobogganed down on the slippery grass, and landed at the lower level earlier than he expected.

The top end of a lock, of course, doesn't have the problem of steps, but it has the same need to land and take on lock-workers. To make this rather more hazardous—at least for the boat—kindly maintenance-men have sometimes put old railway lines to protect the concrete curved shoulders of the lock entrance. These are excellent weapons for carving up a boat's hull below the water-line, if it pulls up a bit tardily to land someone. These deadly protectors are also used in a number of places on the edges of canals, and many a boat-owner has wished they were back where they came from.

RIGHT: There are some smart and well-kept steps to help the busy crew member working the Watford flight on the Leicester Grand Union. Part of this flight is a staircase, with one lock leading directly into the other, and a fairly steep rise therefore between them. After this flight there is a long and lonely pound to the Foxton locks down the other end, and the wise boater stops at Watford to refuel. He can get a meal over the fence at the M1 service station, and some petrol from an A5 garage on the other side of the canal. More of the flight can be seen on page 41.

BELOW: Grand Union steps are on the whole still in good condition, though they vary in shape. British Waterways have recently placed bollards at some little distance from lock entrances so that boats can be moored while the lock is worked. But many seem to be ignored, and along the Hatton flight, for example, they have already been lost in the undergrowth in places. The photograph shows one of the Hatton locks with the typical paddle-gear, and one of the older bollards still surviving at the foot of the steps. The 21 Golden Steps to Heaven at Hatton can be astonishingly peaceful, and not too exhausting if taken at the leisurely pace suggested in the picture.

ABOVE: Old and weather-beaten and worn and crumbling, a little mountain of steps climbs up under the bridge to the lock-edge of Somerton Deep Lock on the Oxford. Although, at twelve feet, this is often quoted as the deepest narrow lock in the system, as we saw on page 12 it is in fact beaten by Tardebigge top lock at 14 feet. Nevertheless, it's a fair climb up or down, and a considerable rise or fall for the boat. Its depths were seen on page 10.

LEFT: Neat, steep and tidy, and even white-washed edges to the steps for the hasty—Sandon lock on the Trent and Mersey, whose balance-beam was seen on page 36, and whose lock footbridge was seen more clearly on page 40. This lock is nearly ten feet deep, as the steps suggest. Nearby for the leisurely is Sandon Park, with five hills and extensive views. There is either a building or a monument on top of each of the hills.

9 Cottage by the Lock

IN THE GOOD OLD DAYS of towpaths filled with horses, boats filled with goods, hastening boatmen and warring canal companies, each canal was dotted with lock-houses. There were also other canal buildings for various purposes such as taking tolls, but by far the most common were the cottages by the locks, occupied by lock-keepers or lengthmen.

Nowadays they are sadly depleted. Not so many lock-keepers are needed with so much less traffic. People are not easy to come by to live in the remoter cottages. And in any case there's certainly not enough money to keep all the buildings and people going. So gradually the numbers thin.

The speed with which lock-cottages disappear is sometimes alarming. You can travel on a canal one year and there is a little house by the side of a lock, and the following year it has vanished. That's what happens with an official demolition, but the unofficial things that happen to lock cottages once they are empty are unbelievable. Hooligans seem to be able to sniff out an empty house for miles. And in no time at all—as at Calcutt in Warwickshire, for example—they make it look like something left over from a war.

This is sad, and is made worse by the fact that these cottages are usually away from others, and nobody sees any of this happening. But canal enthusiasts get annoyed about it, because some would be only too glad to take over such places if only the wheels of authority worked quickly enough. Occasionally this has happened, and along a canal you can find interesting people sometimes living in former official houses, and keeping them alive and pleasant. This is a change from the soulless mounds of rubble elsewhere.

But the trend is downwards. One year there is a lock-keeper locking the gates at the bottom of Atherstone; the next his cottage is battered and empty, and the practice of padlocking locks at dusk has ceased anyhow. One year the cottage by the unique guillotine stop-lock at Kings Norton helps to make a delightful photograph; the next year the lock remains but the cottage is flat. Perhaps the most embarrassing occurrence is when you find a lock-keeper in a cottage one year, and a private individual who you think is a lock-keeper the next.

Certain well-known lock-cottages—and even lock-keepers—still continue, however. The extremely well-kept one at the foot of Napton, for example, will surely be there for many years yet, with its cheery though firm lock-keeper. Some of those on the Leeds and Liverpool look as solid as the Rock of Gibraltar. The striking one at the top of the Northampton flight, which looks as if it is wearing a wide-brimmed hat, will surely go on, looking very much like its counterpart at the top of Foxton.

Just as separate canals had their own styles of bridges and locks and gear, so they had their own kind of lock-cottage. The most remarkable, probably, are the barrel-roofed ones of the southern Stratford, with their curiously foreign look. Almost all are now in private occupation, but well kept. Here and there there are even fairly new cottages, such as on the Grand Union in Warwickshire, and one I recall on the Lee and Stort near Harlow. But most are old, possibly not easy to modernise, and not always easy to get at from the road. They are intriguing to see, however, and here are a few of them.

ABOVE: Is this yet another dying lock-house? When the photograph was taken, this house by the second lock up the Atherstone flight was boarded up. Yet only a little while before it had held a lock-keeper. Like so many such cottages it is not easy to get to, and it may already have vanished. The flight it lives on sticks in the memory for a number of reasons. Some of the locks must be the slowest-filling in existence, especially for their last few inches. There are also side-ponds still working, which will take half the water from a lock and store it for further use. This was a water-economy measure, but no-one seems to worry about it now, and some of the side-pond paddles are broken.

BELOW: The Napton cottage, looking up at the distant arms of the windmill, may well win a "best-kept-lock-cottage" competition. It always seems to be extremely clean and attractive, and the surroundings of the lock are the same, despite the toilet-emptying building, the rubbish-incinerator and the disposal bags for tins and bottles. Indeed, these facilities are a model which might be followed elsewhere. The only trouble with this spot is that some boaters seem to come and stay for some days, causing occasional chaos as others queue up for the lock-flight at weekends.

ABOVE: Boaters can sometimes buy garden produce at canal-side cottages. There may be honey or lettuce at Napton, and here at this Stratford barrel-roofed cottage lettuce may also be available. It is by Lowsonford lock, famous in Temple Thurston's Flower of Gloster. *There's a pub called the* Fleur de Lys *across the canal, but it is often too busy with cars to spare a glance for the boats. But the canal is unbelievably quiet, despite the nearness of so many roads and towns.*

BELOW: The northern part of the Stratford is very different from the revived National Trust southern stretch. It stayed open when the southern section was derelict, because it provides an alternative narrow-boat route to Birmingham. From Kingswood junction there is an active flight of locks very close together at first, but beginning to open out a bit by the time No. 7 lock is reached here. There is one of the unusual split bridges beyond the cottage, and many boaters remember the retired lock-keeper here, with his reminiscences of the Kennet and Avon Canal.

ABOVE: Steaming up the Llangollen with the summer crowds—or wisely going there rather earlier in the season—you pass through two fine lift-bridges at Wrenbury, followed by another one which seemingly stays up all the time. And then there's Marbury lock, with its reconstructed bridge. The cottage is so close to the lock that a fence has been put at the lock-edge, presumably to safeguard children at some time. But it makes working the lock rather awkward for boaters, reminiscent of Great Haywood lock. This is a gentle spot, ideal for the quiet waiting for a lock to fill.

BELOW: Shardlow, Braunston and Stoke Bruerne are rivals in the "typical canal village" field, though all of them now have been rather swamped by later developments. Shardlow, near the beginning of the Trent and Mersey, is still a landmark on the canals, and its pubs and houses could tell many fascinating tales. There is a good and friendly boatyard there, one of whose boats figures several times in this book. And the Malt Shovel *provides simple meals for passing boaters. The lock—the second one from the Trent—is a broad one like the rest up to Burton.*

ABOVE: The Calder and Hebble is not one of the most publicised waterways, because it isn't easy to get to, and doesn't offer a round trip route. But for those who can reach it, it has some magnificent moorland stretches above the industrial areas, though there are a fair number of locks. It once connected with the west through the Huddersfield Narrow Canal, but now the boater will go to the lively scenery of Sowerby Bridge and turn back again. This lock-house, dwarfed by a gasometer, is at Brighouse in one of the less salubrious stretches.

LEFT: This is the lock cottage with the broad-brimmed hat, and it stands out on the horizon to boaters working their way up the Northampton flight from the River Nene. As I recalled on page 36, often the lock-keeper will come cycling down to meet a boat and help it through the close-packed stack of locks. This final lock calls for a breather, not only because of the exertions of the flight, but also because the Grand Union lies ahead beyond the extensive moorings at Gayton.

10 Narrow Boats and Barges

I SEEM to have started this book rather the wrong way round by looking at locks at considerable length before saying very much about the boats that go through them. Maybe this is because boats are familiar and expected things on waterways, whereas locks are unnatural and perhaps unexpected, and certainly intriguing. But boats too—especially on canals—are intriguing, and in any case the canals were built for them. And although anglers and farmers and even swimmers use our canals too, they still exist chiefly for the boats that travel on them.

Brindley and Telford and company would be startled at the boats on canals now, and they might even think that some of them are really far too flimsy for the hard use they get if they go anywhere very far. There are in fact two broadly different types of boats around. There are great and growing numbers of pleasure cruisers, either specially built for canal cruising or suitable boats from other waters. Then there are the true canal boats. Some of these are still at work, especially on broad canals, but large numbers have been converted into holiday boats or even homes. These are mainly former working boats from narrow canals, properly called narrow boats and not " barges ".

There's quite a bit of friendly snobbery about this. The narrow boaters, thumping along in their seventy-foot hulls, do tend to look a little haughtily at the sixteen and twenty and twenty-five-foot cockle-shells scuttling out of their way as they plough down the middle of the cut.

But this is dangerous ground to write on, for their owners rise rapidly to defend narrow boats when necessary, and they have a vigorous club into the bargain.

On the broad canals commercial boats continue to run and are officially supported and catered for. But the narrow canals are a sadder story, which doesn't really belong in this book. But briefly, the continued use of narrow canals by traditional narrow boats has for many years been a growing problem. Some say forthrightly that the authorities don't want narrow boats, and will do nothing to encourage them to be there. Others point out that even if the British Waterways Board really wanted narrow boats to continue, they simply haven't the money to keep the canals deep enough for them.

Whatever the truth of the matter, traditional commercial boats, fully laden, are finding it increasingly difficult to move in more and more stretches of canal. And in places the canals are shockingly shallow. As fast as one notorious length is dredged, others become as bad. Yet enthusiastic groups of people, despite frequent setbacks, continue to find and carry cargoes. And nobody can deny that their boats provide some of the most exciting sights on the canals, as well as by their very presence helping to keep the channels deeper than they might otherwise be. Any hold-ups at locks while a butty is worked through, or any forcing of smaller boats into the shallows at the side, are a small price to pay for the continuing sight of these often beautifully-painted and interesting pairs, which after all belong to the canals far more than any small plywood cruiser ever did.

The commercial narrow boats converted into pleasure boats are in their own way even more interesting. Many are most lovingly built and cared for, and whether alone or at rallies are as picturesque an experience as can be seen anywhere. Seventy feet is an awful lot of boat, however, and needs a whole lock to itself, an exceptional slice of the channel, and a considerable share of a mooring. And while full-length conversions may be excellent for schools, youth clubs, hotel boats and similar large groups, it may be that shorter versions are more suitable for families and more appropriate for conditions on the narrow canals today.

Certainly many narrow boats have been cut down and converted, and indeed a number of firms are building traditional narrow hulls of shorter lengths. At Market Harborough on the Leicester, and Norbury on the Shropshire Union, for example, some interesting construction of this kind can be seen.

The future for the full-size, fully-laden narrow boat must be worrying many of their owners now, however. I've seen them anxiously questioning other travellers as to the state of the pounds on the Trent and Mersey around Armitage, around Penkridge on the Staffs and Worcs, on the southern Oxford, on the Coventry near Nuneaton, and other black spots. Often they will be found moored two or three feet away from the towpath, for the simple reason that they can get no nearer. But they go on scraping their bottoms the length and breadth of the canal system, and it would be a sad day indeed if they were to disappear.

The barges on the broader Lee and Stort, the lower Grand Union, part of the Leeds and Liverpool and the canals of Yorkshire have no such difficulty, and will no doubt go on carrying their cargoes for many years to come, even though they are still considerably smaller than the great vessels on the much wider and prosperous canals abroad. A European looking at our narrow canals must be tickled pink by the seven-foot width of our locks, and he must wonder how any boats so small could ever have been paying propositions. And that, of course, is basically the reason for the decline in commercial narrow boat carrying—though many people would vociferously claim that there are other and avoidable reasons too.

You can often catch these odd-shaped boats ploughing down the Aire and Calder to Goole, and they must be some of the strangest craft to be seen on the canals. They seem to derive from the tub-boats often used for coal in the early days, and they are just like square boxes which lock together behind a special bows section. The whole lot is pulled by a tug and looks like a short train. When they reach Goole, each one can be yanked out of the water and its contents tipped out at one go.

ABOVE: Looking further south, this barge was caught on the River Lee at Ware. It's a frightening size compared with narrow boats, though it would be dwarfed by many barges on the continent. The Lee Navigation runs from Hertford down to the Thames, and is broad and enjoyable in its upper rcaches. A few miles below Ware the Stort joins it from Bishop's Stortford.

BELOW: Back north again, but this time in the north-west, this barge was a pleasant surprise at Wigan, on a canal which so often looks empty yet is so often recommended for commercial traffic—the Leeds and Liverpool. The only moving boats I saw one day were being unloaded at Wigan power station, then moving off down the Leigh Branch from the junction shown on page 98. As far as I could see, the chap heading for the locks was the only one aboard, but this takes a bit of believing with a boat this size. The Leeds and Liverpool wide boats are limited in length by 62-foot locks above Wigan, but 72-foot boats can travel on the Leigh Branch.

ABOVE: From the broad canals to the narrow, and a more difficult search for commercial traffic, as the picture changes almost from month to month as old contracts fade out and new ones are vigorously sought. Despite the disappearance of some well-known carrying firms, however, Blue Line seems to go on all the time. Three pairs of its narrow boats ply the cut, and often as you pass Braunston you see one or other pair moored, loaded or empty, in between carrying coal down south. The boats are attractively maintained and their steerers are well-known to regular Grand Union boaters.

BELOW: Another indefatigable name in narrow boat carrying has been the Birmingham and Midland Canal Carrying Co. Their boats have been seen in several different roles, and this boat heading down the Audlem flight on the Shropshire Union had been converted to carry oil from the north-west to the midlands. Its butty—the one without the engine—has to be pulled by hand down the locks after it, and this is one of the laborious aspects of narrow boats working in pairs.

ABOVE: The most likely sight for boaters on narrow canals is a British Waterways' narrow boat on some job or other. Some are quite short versions, but there are full-size ones also. This one has been putting new lock-gates in the Watford flight on the Leicester section of the Grand Union, and is now coming down, with M1 alongside, towards Norton junction.

LEFT: Other British Waterways' craft likely to be seen where welcome dredging operations are in progress are hoppers such as these, loaded up with mud and unmentionable debris and towed off somewhere to get rid of it. These two, unable to get nearer to the bank, are tied up at Goldstone Wharf on the Shroppie, opposite a well-known canal pub. The waterway beyond gives some idea of the broadness of this canal and the open views from it.

ABOVE: Looking now at narrow boats converted for homes or pleasure, this is a typical example of what is usually done. Often the addition of the superstructure is done by enthusiasts, and this narrow boat moored in Aylesbury shows the extensive accommodation that can be provided. There is a limit to the head-room because of the canal bridges, and it's wise to slope the sides inwards for the same reason. But with nearly seven feet of width and seventy feet of length, there's a lot of space to play with.

BELOW: One of the earliest books an canal holiday cruising was about a narrow boat called the Flower of Gloster, *and here the name lives again on a modern conversion owned by a Liverpool man. The traditional roses and castles, which once decorated all narrow boats, have been reproduced on this boat, so that although it is serving a very different purpose from that which it was built for, it is still carrying on the colourful image. Both the boat and steerer in the picture are often seen on the canals and at rallies. Here they are in a lock on the Staffs and Worcs above Penkridge.*

ABOVE: Here are two rather unusual conversions, both doing rather unusual things. The Lady Hatherton, *which I seem to have met in a number of places (including unexpectedly on a sharp bend once), was originally said to be a director's boat on one canal. It has a beautifully built and maintained cabin, as well as a much more graceful shape than traditional blunt narrow boats. Here I found it helping to blaze a trail up the Kennet and Avon when two locks were re-opened to extend the navigable stretch to Tyle Mill.*

BELOW: This conversion, which looks as if it was from a tug, was purchased by a primary school in Hertfordshire after serving as a hire boat on the Grand Union. It was brought round by a voluntary crew up the Lee and Stort Navigation, and its use with children under eleven shows considerable imagination. Here the parents welcomed it when it first arrived at Sheering Mill Lock.

11 Canoes and Cruisers

WHETHER Brindley and Telford turn in their graves or not, the canal system is used from end to end by "non-traditional" boats nowadays. And they come in a most remarkable variety of shapes and sizes. Several times I've seen rafts made of oil-drums—unlicensed, of course—and canoes are frequent travellers for quite long distances, usually laden with camping-gear.

Rowing-dinghies, sailing-dinghies, inflatables with outboards and faster runabouts are popped in and out of canals for a few hours at a time all over the country—many of them without contributing a penny in licence-fees, and almost impossible to track down. But most of today's canal-users are cruisers ranging from about fifteen feet upwards, on which people can live in varying degrees of comfort.

These boats when not in use live in little flocks at Iver and Bletchley and Braunston and Market Drayton and Nantwich and Burnley, and at growing numbers of similar harbours and boatyards all over the country. Or else they are tied up in ones and twos by gardens and pubs and fields everywhere.

They range from home-made houses on army pontoons to beautiful craftsman-built architect-designed luxury cruisers in gleaming chrome and boat-builders' mahogany. They come in wood and steel and increasingly in fibre-glass, and they are driven by outboards and jets and inboard engines with outdrives, and even a variety of home-made paddle-wheels. The outboards drink fuel like a drunkard drinks beer, and their owners may enjoy many a long walk across fields with a five-gallon tank. The inboard petrol engines are more economical, even if they take up more room and require more safety precautions. Diesels are safer, and chug along noisily for hours on the cheapest fuel of all.

And inside all these boats of many shapes there is an equal variety of accommodation. In some a remarkable number of inhabitants seem to bed down like a happy shoal of sardines. In others there are showers and even baths, hot and cold, fridge, oven, electric light and flushing lavatory, with room to hold a small dance if required. Beds range from spartan hammocks with sleeping bags to thick foam-rubber sprung mattresses with blankets, sheets and the lot. And feeding habits vary between the army mess-tin and a full kit of table-linen, cutlery and crockery.

A fair proportion of these pleasure boats—and the ones which do the hardest work—are those hired out by over 100 hirers. Some own just one or two boats, but at Brinklow and Braunston and Christleton and Drayton and Leighton Buzzard and Kinver and Tardebigge and Stourport and Norbury and Burnley and elsewhere there are larger fleets, as well as at the British Waterways bases at Oxford and Nantwich.

Some of these boats are extremely comfortable and surprisingly inexpensive, especially away from August. Most hirers are canal enthusiasts themselves—they had to be in the early days!—and are very helpful to beginners.

Even the driving and steering of this great variety of private and hire boats varies fascinatingly. There are small cruisers with a wheel at the front like a motor-car. There are others with tillers like traditional narrow boats—even when the boats themselves bear no resemblance. There are little outboards steered from afar by lengths of metal piping. There are great wheels looking as if they have come from the Queen Mary, and little imitations hardly big enough to get a grip on. And there are rudders of all shapes, from the full-scale one to the home-made addition to an outboard that merely serves to wrap up the polythene bags more firmly.

Every boater to his taste and the length of his purse. About the only things most canal boats have in common are their seven-foot width and their six-foot headroom—in case they ever reach Harecastle or the bridge below the first lock on the southern Stratford. The total result of all these varied and personal boats is quite delightful. And whatever Brindley might say—or even the narrow boat enthusiasts—they somehow, with all their quirks and oddities, fit surprisingly well into the canal scene.

Perhaps the most startling sight when cruising on a canal is the appearance of a canoe. Yet this isn't at all rare, and it seems to be a growing popular pastime for youngsters to explore the canals in this way. The lad here, seen near Leamington, is obviously just out for the day, but often larger canoes carry camping equipment and travel for long distances. They are probably most common in the Warwickshire area where sizable lock-free stretches can be found around Hawkesbury, and on the southern Shropshire Union. But canoeists are quite prepared to lift their craft out and round locks when necessary.

ABOVE: A very common form of small pleasure craft—and an inexpensive one, too—is the home-built cruiser based on a surplus army pontoon. How these stand up to some of the tougher canal journeys I don't know, but undoubtedly there are many about, with every imaginable kind of superstructure on them. This one was seen moored at the side of Tixall Broad, also shown on page 125.

BELOW: 16 and 20-foot plywood cabin cruisers are probably the most common of all on the canals. They can squeeze in a couple of children as well as their parents by using the cockpit with the hood up for sleeping, but they are most useful for two people. Many small cruisers of this kind are seen in this line of moored boats on the Brecon and Avergavenny Canal at Govilon, probably because this canal is rather shallow for bigger boats. Some idea of the countryside visible from the canal can be seen in the background.

ABOVE: If I might be purely personal on this page here are two of my own boats, which also figure—though I hope not too often—elsewhere throughout the book. This one, in Itchington Bottom lock, is a 24-foot Dolphin with centre cockpit, giving quite comfortable accommodation for four, yet easily driven by an outboard motor. I had metal rubbing-strips added on the sides and a few extra internal cupboards. There's a Honda charger roped to the back deck here, which is useful on longer journeys for keeping the battery charged for starting and lighting.

BELOW: This is the Dolphin's successor, at the Bridge Inn on the Trent and Mersey near Burton. It was built to our exact layout by Dobsons of Shardlow, and exhibited at the Boat Show. It has an amazingly resilient fibre-glass hull, and some rich mahogony elsewhere. There's a large if noisy cockpit at the back where the Perkins Diesel throbs away, seeming to consume hardly any fuel at around 12p a gallon. There's hot and cold running water, a fridge, a shower, electric light, and a peaceful front cockpit where all you can hear is the ripple of the water.

ABOVE: So far the pleasure-boats shown have been rather different from traditional canal narrow boats—though my own Nike Three *always seems to me a happy compromise. But there are quite a few pleasure cruising boats built on narrow boat lines, though usually much shorter. Here is one in a delightful setting on the Trent and Mersey before it reaches the Stoke-on-Trent industrial stretches. It has a narrow boat tiller and a rope stern fender, and makes a pleasing traditional shape.*

BELOW: Further north still, and in an entirely different setting, is a hire cruiser from Burnley passing through the Blackburn locks on the Leeds and Liverpool. There is a large rear cockpit, but passengers must dodge the swing of the tiller if they travel there. They may prefer the front cockpit, which can be seen on page 14 as the same boat locks down through Barrowford.

ABOVE: The hardest working pleasure boats on the canals are of course the hire cruisers, and wherever you go you meet them. They are out week after week from March to September, and I must say I admire those firms which work to keep them looking smart nevertheless. Among them are the popular Blue Line Cruisers, and one of their boats is seen here moored at the foot of the Napton flight of locks on the Oxford Canal. Maidboats from Brinklow, narrow boats from Tardebigge, cruisers from Bletchley, Sawley, Stourport, Chester, Market Drayton, Norbury and dozens of other bases explore the canals all summer, some of them reaching great distances from their base.

BELOW: An unusually shaped type of hire boat has recently appeared on the Oxford Canal—the Mariner class, offered both by British Waterways and by Morgan Giles. It is an example of a builder of sea-boats turning to inland waterways, and has caused much discussion among regular canallers, about both its accommodation and its propulsion. As the picture suggests, hire cruisers are popular with families. Children enjoy boating, though the non-swimmers and smaller ones should wear life-jackets as these children are doing.

ABOVE: We shall look at boatyards and basins in a moment, but there are plenty of other places where you can see boats moored in large numbers. In contrast to the boats collected at Govilon on page 65, a very different set will be found gathered at different places on the Leeds and Liverpool, which seems to be specially favoured by tough boats of the converted lifeboat type. Being a broad canal, such boats can, of course, navigate the locks. A popular place for seeing a variety of them is above the famous five-rise staircase at Bingley, and some of them can be seen in the picture. There is a 17-mile pound without locks available for them to use on the way towards Lancashire.

BELOW: Round the corner from the Blue Line boat on page 68, the foot of Napton is always a busy place for boats, though in this case they are mostly there for short stays only, or even just queueing up for the locks on busy Sundays. Many people stop here to visit the village or the windmill or the Crown, *or to shop or take on water. A few, of course, stop to turn round at the sight of the locks.*

12 Boatyards and Basins

WHEREVER YOU GO on canals there are wharves and basins. In Birmingham especially there must be hundreds of them. But most of them now exist in name only, if that. Where names still exist you may have to dig in the summer under vegetation. But here and there, where they happen to coincide with a pub or more likely a new boatyard, they are still going strong.

People tend to think of " boatyards " as being small harbours, as they need to be when by the sea. But on the canals there was never the necessity for sheltered areas surrounded by walls, and usually boats were dealt with or loaded merely at solid edges at the side of the channel.

This has been a bit of a handicap to many of the pioneers setting up boatyards for pleasure cruising, for they really needed more than just a length of bank to work from. They wanted to get boats away from the canal itself, and in particular to be able to provide safe moorings for their customers. And newcomers are often surprised when they go to a " boatyard " to discover that it has no harbour or separate moorings of any kind away from the channel.

In one case, indeed, in order to provide moorings, a firm at Market Drayton dug out vast quantities of earth and made itself a large lay-by, but this must have been a costly process. At Norbury Junction on the Shropshire Union and Finsley Gate on the Leeds and Liverpool, for example, firms were rather more fortunate in finding wider areas of canal which gave them a little elbow-room. And at Brinklow and Rugby other firms make use of arms of the canal for moorings.

Perhaps the most remarkable spot—and exceptionally well-placed for exploring the canal system—is at Braunston, where the Oxford and the Grand Union virtually cross each other. With the Leicester and Northampton Arms not so far away, boaters have six different directions to go in. Here, in former reservoirs, are extensive piers, and all the services a boater needs.

It's surprising, perhaps, not to see large boatyards using all the few remaining canal basins, which seem sometimes given over to a few sporadic moorings, including boats that never seem to move anywhere at all. The fascinating extent of water at Stourport, for instance, or the basin at Worcester could surely take more boats if staging were erected. The beautiful basin at Nantwich is apparently going to be developed, and though it may be sad to fill up with boats what were peaceful open areas of water, the pressure for both moorings and services is growing all the time. And stretching more and more boats along the canal side is unsatisfactory from servicing, security and navigational points of view.

The canal basin at Aylesbury has been developed as moorings, despite the long climb up to the Grand Union, but perhaps it's a pity the canals don't have along their banks the extensive gravel pits which some rivers enjoy. For here, as on the Great Ouse and Nene, for example, would be ready-made harbours which can be turned into the most delightful moorings imaginable.

Although it is a pleasure to tie up at Nantwich or Stourport or Worcester or Ellesmere, many popular canal spots are ill-served by moorings and boatyards. Probably the worst example is Oxford, where the basin has been filled in, and the canal now fizzles out ignominiously. Even Stratford, with its wonderful terminus opposite the Memorial Theatre, has only unsatisfactory moorings among tree roots in the river, though luckily the boatyard on the outskirts of the town will welcome you. Banbury, too, on the Oxford has a bus station where its canal basin used to be, but there are convenient moorings alongside a car park.

In Birmingham, incredibly, you can moor in Gas Street Basin and step out almost into the bustle of Broad Street, with a large Chinese restaurant if you fancy one. But just as you are looking forward to a quiet night so near to a roaring city, you may be awakened by the noise from one or two nearby night haunts.

People who trail smaller cruisers find it less easy to locate slipways on canals than they do on rivers. There are convenient ones at Bletchley and Braunston and Market Drayton and at some other yards, but even where there are slipways there's sometimes no room for the car and trailer, but of course most river and seaside slips suffer from this same trouble nowadays.

Among the pioneer boatyards, and certainly one offering the most extensive and sophisticated moorings, is the Blue Line harbour at Braunston. The Braunston area figures in several of my photographs in this book, for it has always been a famous canal centre. There is a complex of reservoirs here, in which staging has been erected to provide individual moorings for a large number of boats of all kinds. Unlike many moorings, these are away from the canal channel, and a short if rather awkward arm makes the connection under one of the beautiful towpath bridges of this district.

ABOVE: Way up in the Pennines, the Leeds and Liverpool comes to Skipton, where the waterway takes a sharp turn. This is not exactly a basin, but there is an arm called the Springs Branch running off to the foot of Skipton castle, where boats used to load rocks from the quarries. And the whole area is quite a useful mooring for a number of boats, and for passers-by, since it's only a step to the shops of this quite busy town.

BELOW: The Lancaster Canal supports a large population of boats, despite the impossibility of getting to other canals except by sea. One snag for many enthusiasts is that there are now no locks except in the branch down to Glasson Dock, but that seems to suit some boaters, and the gathering of boats here at Galgate shows how popular the waterway is. At this wharf and basin, Norwest Holiday Cruisers now provide services and hire out boats.

ABOVE: This is the large Diglis basin whose exit locks to the River Severn were shown on page 11. Worcester Cathedral can be seen in the background, and also the Royal Porcelain Works. This is a curious place for the canal boater to arrive at because, as the boats in the picture suggest, he meets some massive sea-going vessels moored there, which couldn't possibly join him in the canal system.

BELOW: A much smaller harbour now, though in a large city. This is the end of the Coventry Canal, with quite a different population. It's a difficult five miles from the busier section at Hawkesbury, but the struggle past smelly factory backs and through weeds and debris is worth it, for you sit high above the city here in comparative peace.

ABOVE: There aren't really enough basins to go round, so many boatyards have set up efficient establishments along the canal bank, or on small branches. The large Maidboats concern, which has many boats on both rivers and canals, has its canal headquarters at Brinklow on the northern Oxford. Its fuel pumps are in the foreground here, but beyond are sheds and moorings, and round to the right is the old Stretton Arm, which is also full of boats. Maidboat cruisers will be met in many parts of the canal network.

BELOW: A smaller boatyard, that of Swallow Cruisers, uses the little basin behind the Wharf Inn *at Hockley Heath on the northern Stratford. This firm has also erected these neat moorings along the canal bank. This is a useful stopping place for refreshment and shops after climbing the Lapworth flight, and across the bridge you can even buy parsnip wine by the pint.*

ABOVE: The narrow boat conversion shown on page 61 (top) was spotted in a line of boats leading up to the basin at the end of the Aylesbury arm of the Grand Union. The final stretch of this waterway can be seen here, and at the far end is the well-known boatyard and moorings alongside the Wendover road. Boats moored here have a slog up the locks to get to the main line, but it's a convenient place for many people to keep their boats. The tall building in the picture is the new Buckinghamshire county hall.

BELOW: Prominent in this photograph of the Market Harborough basin are some of the boats which are built there on traditional narrow boat lines. The boatyard and basin occupy an interesting site alongside A6, looking down on the town, and this in fact was the terminus of the navigation from Leicester originally. When it was joined from Foxton to the Grand Union, the last five miles to Market Harborough became an arm from the through route. This is a pleasant town to visit, if you can swing the bridge seen on page 87.

13 Bridging the Cut

As you plod down the Northampton Flight you come to a short, wide, domed tunnel, with very broad towpaths on each side. Pressing on round the curve to the next lock, you suddenly realise that you have burrowed under the M1. Idling up towards Rugby on the northern Oxford the same thing happens to you as you echo your way through a square cavernous tunnel under the M45, where an ingenious farmer has made use of the wide concrete banks and the waterproof concrete roof as a shelter for animals, with a gate at each end.

You meet similar tunnels—but each with an individual character—under the M6 near Penkridge on the Staffs and Worcs, under the M1 above the Watford Flight on the way to Leicester, and under an approach road to the M5 after slogging down many locks on the way from Birmingham to Worcester.

These vast and almost overwhelming structures are, I suppose, not tunnels but bridges. But the contrast with the traditional canal bridge is almost laughable. Yet when you come to think about it, they also show the difference between civilisation today and the peaceful cruise along a canal. For up there is a constant suicidal roar of mightier and mightier lorries and more and more cars; whereas down here you can hardly hear or see a sign of them.

Apart from these new monstrosities and an odd bridge or two in towns, bridges over canals hardly seem to have changed since they were first built. Agreed, some of them have been submerged by main road widenings, such as the funny little one at Nell Bridge near Aynho. But for mile after mile all you ever see are the hump-backed bridges that the canal-builders built. Some of them are no longer used, but few seem to have been removed. In fact, almost the only signs of bridge-removal are the recent uprootings of no-longer-needed railway bridges—often leaving large hunks of masonry for the local hooligans to toss in the cut.

Some hump-backed bridges are humpier than other hump-backed bridges. Along the Aylesbury arm of the Grand Union, for example, it hardly seems possible to get a car over the top without it see-sawing on its middle. And one of the few things that disturbs a canal traveller is the hooting of cars about to cross canal bridges, because they can't see what's coming on the other side. Civilisation has now caught up with these bridges in only one way. Their approaches are nowadays plastered with signs banning track-laying vehicles, and giving the weight-limit of others. But since nobody ever takes any notice of such signs, no doubt one day an enormous lorry will fall through a bridge.

Not all canal bridges are of the artist's favourite hump-backed shape. The Shropshire Union's are more spacious and less humped. Many on the Trent and Mersey are fascinating inverted U-shapes, too meanly built to allow space for a towpath, which must have meant untying the horse every time. This economy appears on the Stratford Canal, and also on the way up to Stourbridge from the Staffs and Worcs. There the builders produced two small metal cantilevers, one from each side, with a gap in the middle for the towrope to pass through. Many of these two halves now sag together or have been fastened together, but there are still some which are perfectly capable of passing a rope through the gap.

The great majority of canal bridges are of course rural ones, built for and used by farmers. No doubt they are useless for modern machinery, and that's why so many of them are now overgrown. But they form the main landmarks of the boater, and there are very few places where a bridge is out of sight for long.

Indeed, bridges perform one vital function for the water traveller. They are almost the only means he has of knowing where he is. Each bridge has its number, and most of those numbers have been well maintained. And apart from the rare milestone or sign-post, they are the only form of identification on the route. The canal booklets show each bridge and its number, and only by reading these numbers does the voyager know how far he has travelled.

On the Staffs and Worcester Canal the bridges are graced by large oval plates which give a name as well as a number. And on the Birmingham and Fazeley between the north bit of the Coventry and Fazeley Junction, the bridges have only names. But both these unusual items have been much neglected, and Giggety, Coven Heath, Bumblehole and many more nameplates may crumble into rust, which would be sad.

There is one not-so-enjoyable feature about all these fixed bridges for the canal boater. He can't always get under them. This is his fault rather than theirs, for there should always be room—just—if he keeps well to the middle. But keeping well to the middle is easier said than done in a wind, and especially with the surprising number of bridges built on bends. So only too often the boat scrapes the sloping side of a bridge, or crunches along the towpath edge; and almost every bridge on the canals has its paint-streaks to tell the tale, and some have bits of boat in the water into the bargain.

There's another snag, too, about these bridges on bends. You may not have seen another boat for miles, but the odds are that when you do he will just be coming through the same bridge as you. And since these bridges are normally only one boat wide, one of you will have to stop. So any canal bridge can tell the tale of motors roaring in reverse at the last minute—and as like as not backing into the shallows and breaking an outboard motor sheer-pin in the process. But canal boaters are usually friendly people, and there's much waving and " after-you " goes on in these situations.

One sad thing about bridges. That nauseating tribe of wall-scribblers can't keep away from them. I suppose they feel safer there, scrawling their nonsense and their filth without much interruption. But all over the system you'll find them, from the supporters of West Bromwich and the Wolves as you pass through the bridges of the B.C.N., to the morons who seem to penetrate even to the remotest country bridge. Unfortunately the modern use of concrete gives them a suitable surface for their felt pens, and it's nobody's job to remove their objectionable rubbish. Thank goodness the traditional brick bridges resist their attentions. But British Waterways tend to resurface them with helpful smooth concrete.

Anyhow, let us look first at some of these fixed bridges, and go on then to look at the exasperating ways of the other, movable, kinds.

ABOVE: I can't think why, but this is probably my favourite bridge, maybe because I can't recall ever seeing anybody crossing it. There's nothing particularly special about it, but I suppose it represents the vast number of simple farm bridges all over the canals, yet manages to be a bit different. It crosses from one field to another on the northern Oxford as it sets out on its way up towards Rugby.

BELOW: A fine (and gouged) example of a rural bridge on the Grand Union, complete with towpath, metal protection of its corners against towropes, and tapering arch which the boater must beware of in a cross wind. The cows in the distance are grazing the lush grass on the very quiet pound south of Buckby. And if you can be along there in May the hawthorn flower will make you drunk with its scent.

ABOVE: This greatly different distinctive shape fulfills the same purpose on the Trent and Mersey at many points along the eastern stretches. The lack of a towpath underneath must have been a nuisance in the old days, but now the vertical sides do offer the boater less opportunity of scraping his cabin top than the wider but dropping curves of bridges on other canals give him. This bridge is on the way from Burton towards Alrewas and Fradley junction.

BELOW: This is one of the well-known Stratford Canal split bridges where the towrope could pass through the middle. This, like some others, has been strapped together by a piece of metal. There are several examples of this type, perhaps the most-visited one being by the entrance lock of the National Trust southern section of this canal, seen on page 97. But there is also a superior version which vast numbers of tourists see at the lock into the Avon at Stratford itself. No. 33, seen in the picture, is by the Boot Inn *on the vigorous Lapworth flight on the northern part of the canal.*

ABOVE: Busier roads need bigger bridges. Cosgrove is a well-known village on the Grand Union, and quite apart from the popular narrow boat trips and the odd little aqueduct seen on page 92, it sports one of the most striking road bridges on the canal. Although simplicity is probably best for canal bridges, an occasional bit of decoration makes a change, like Shakespeare in his niche on Brandwood Tunnel, or the decorative entrance to the disused Sapperton Tunnel on the Thames and Severn. Cosgrove bridge's fancy work, met by boaters, tends to be remembered.

BELOW: The bridge usually mentioned by everybody travelling from Birmingham to Wolverhampton is Galton Bridge, but last time I passed under it it foiled my camera by being hung with scaffolding. Anyhow, I preferred the look of this unsung one in the same great cutting. The cutting, by the way, was part of Telford's very useful work which turned the B.C.N. main line from a winding, narrow and shallow ditch to the broad straight highway that it often is now. He lowered the level around here and cut out locks so that almost all this Black Country system is now on only three levels.

ABOVE: This is the "tunnel" bridge under M1 that I mentioned near the beginning of this section. It's very much out of place on the truly rural Northampton flight, and makes an amusing contrast with the dear little lift-bridges (mostly propped up) which are almost the only other signs of life down these locks. There is little sign of life from the motorway, come to that, though you can't help knowing that there must be something up there.

BELOW: Following a barge down the Fossdyke, you come to one of the numerous unattractive railway bridges which straddle canals. There must be some reason why road bridges are pleasant and blend with the scene, yet railway bridges are always crude and ugly. Presumably it's because roads can cross by rising and falling, whereas railways can't. Certainly, with their preponderance of metal, railway bridges strike a harsh note, and maybe it's as well that a lot of them are being removed.

ABOVE: Back to the B.C.N., and with all respect to the inhabitants of Tipton, even the name somehow seems to suggest the heart of blackest industrial England. And as I mentioned with the picture of the lock footbridge on page 39, the water here is pretty oily. Factory Bridge, shown here, is just below the three Tipton Factory locks, which raise the main line from the Birmingham Level to the Wolverhampton Level.

BELOW: Here is yet another of the lock footbridges of the Leeds and Liverpool, but this time one of the familiar handrails is replaced by a sturdy moorland road bridge. Lock No. 37, at Bank Newton not far from the Priest Holme aqueduct visited later in this book, obviously doesn't expect its boaters to use the road bridge, but still provides them with a crossing of their own. These road bridges match the Leeds and Liverpool's tough locks, and will no doubt stand the weather. This one is also called Carpenter's Yard Bridge. The interesting names of many of these Leeds and Liverpool bridges are given in the British Waterways' Cruising Booklet.

LEFT: A lot of the bridge-building of the canal diggers had to go to making crossings for their own towpaths, so here are four. Either they had to cross junctions with the canal, or basin entrances, or from one side of the waterway to the other. This interesting gentle curve, below Kings Lock near Leicester, takes the towpath over the fairly young River Soar, where it comes in for the first time. Later, of course, it forms the major part of the navigation.

ABOVE LFFT: This is one of the most delightful towpath bridges, though steerers get little chance to examine it as they struggle round the acute hairpin at Hawkesbury Junction. With narrow boats, the Greyhound, and old (but disappearing) canal buildings and structures, this is a fascinating place.

ABOVE RIGHT: The northern Oxford would certainly win the prize for towpath bridges, and from Hawkesbury southwards there are several examples of this type, some rusting away, but others well preserved. Like this one, they usually bridge an old loop of the canal which was cut off by straight cuts, like the one straight ahead in the picture, at a later date. There are three more of these bridges at Braunston, one of them bridging the entrance to the Blue Line harbour now.

LEFT: At intervals, both to give the horse a change and perhaps to satisfy some long-dead landowner, the towpath changes sides. Usually there is a changeover or roving bridge, which allows the horse to walk across and under without unfastening the rope. This need lends itself to delightful curves, as in this example on the Macclesfield Canal.

14 Bridges that Move

They may be extremely photogenic, but bridges which lift or swing can give you quite a problem. If you happen to be sharing the Gloucester and Sharpness Canal with its more usual large tankers the bridge-keepers will come from their little houses to open every bridge. But you'll have to work bridges elsewhere for yourself, and this can have its hazards.

This is one of the rare canal activities which lone boaters find difficult. Once a bridge is open—especially a lifting-bridge—it's almost impossible for the opener to help with the boat. Either he can't get on it for the bridge, or else he has to sit on the bridge-beam to keep it up anyhow.

There are few things on the canals as individual as these movable bridges. Even lock-gates are limited in their individual quirks, but no two moving bridges ever seem to be the same. They may look approximately alike, but when you come to operate them their foibles begin to show. They may be easy to open but difficult to close. They may open easily most of the way but refuse to go the rest. They may even need more than one person to keep them up at all. They may leave plenty of clearance for the boat or give it a grudging two or three inches as its windscreen crawls precariously past. And all this isn't helped at bridges on surfaced roads by glaring motorists, fuming as you struggle.

Most of the lift-bridges—or drawbridges—are on the Oxford and the Llangollen Canals. Those on the Llangollen have probably been photographed more often than anything else in the system, except possibly the Pontcysyllte Aqueduct. For they are of that fascinating Dutch type with high top beams visible across the fields. You either pull on a chain to get the structure moving, or there is a handle to wind the chain on to a drum. Then you have the vital task of keeping the bridge up while the boat goes under it.

There are three versions of this type, though not so beautiful, on the northern Stratford, and in theory there is a ratchet to stop the chain unwinding and the bridge from crashing down. At Wrenbury on the Llangollen there is sort of drum-brake, but most boat-steerers proceed under such bridges with heart in mouth.

The Oxford lift-bridges are of a cruder kind, merely see-sawing up into the air as heavy balance-beams are pulled down and sat on. The notorious ones are in Banbury, where there is either a line of impatient cars or a sabotaging mob of children. The children turn up at the bridge near the bus station (ex-canal basin), and this bridge is particularly awkward because it occurs just below a lock. You can't really get at it when you're busy with the lock, yet you have to have it up before you can get into the lock.

Many of these Oxford Canal lift-bridges are fixed up when they merely serve fields, and you just hope they are fixed firmly. But keeping the others up is an operation which is risky to leave to passers-by, however willing they may be. A reliable and preferably heavy member of crew, not given to day-dreaming, is almost literally worth his weight in gold.

There is one interesting and usually uncharted private bridge in Oxford itself, operated electrically by the factory which it presumably serves. At a touch of your hooter somebody normally presses the button that does the trick. And there are other odd lift-bridges here and there, such as a brute in Northampton which practically refuses to go up the last six inches, and which is thus a tight squeeze for most boats.

The swing-bridges, apart from the aforementioned Gloucester and Sharpness ones, are not so common, except on the Leeds and Liverpool and a few on the Macclesfield. There are odd ones on the Coventry, the Grand Union, the north Stratford, the Harborough arm, and one or two more places, but they are naturally less hazardous than the drawbridges.

In theory they pivot smoothly round on their bearings when pushed, but the tracks are susceptible to the gathering of dirt and stones, and I have more than once had to use a mooring-pin as a crowbar in order to start a bridge at all. Uusally a little bouncing up and down, or judicious redistribution of crew-weight, will persuade the bridge to start swinging.

The daddy of all these is of course the famous Barton swing-bridge, taking the Bridgwater over the Manchester Ship Canal. This, as the whole world probably knows, is a bridge full of water, where a piece of canal is sealed off and turned sideways to let the ships go by.

Let's look, anyhow, at a few of these canal cruising hazards.

The Northampton Arm of the Grand Union, which figures in a number of pictures in this book, is a delightful if well-locked narrow link between the G.U. and the River Nene. The locks begin to open out in the final stretch, which concludes with a weedy passage under railway bridges by former sidings, with the river drawing closer all the time. There's a quiet mooring just above the final lock, with a rather precarious overhanging canopy of a former warehouse along the hard quay. But this lift-bridge is the really unpredictable item. On one occasion I found no means of reaching the arms to pull them down, so I had to lasso them with a rope. But even when the chain is present you may need help to keep the arms down on their stop long enough to hook on. For they have a habit of retreating a little so that your boat can scrape itself on the raised bridge.

ABOVE: This is a bird's-eye-view, from an Oxford bypass, of one of the well-known lift-bridges on the southern Oxford. It's No. 233 as the canal gets nearer to its rather sad ending in Oxford itself. The simple principle of these bridges can be clearly seen, and a normal-sized person sitting on the balance-beam will keep the bridge up long enough for the boat to pass under it. Just above this bridge there is a link with the Thames which some people prefer to use to make a slightly pleasanter journey into Oxford.

RIGHT: A much better known—and better painted—example of these Oxford bridges is this one at Thrupp, just off the Oxford-Banbury road north of Kidlington. The chain enables even the shortest crew member to start the beam moving down, and the stop which it should reach can be seen on the ground. There are popular moorings both sides of this bridge, and a useful water-tap and rubbish-disposal point. The right-angled turn, however, makes the operation an awkward business for narrow boats, and even much smaller ones have been known to misjudge it.

ABOVE: A rather misleading building on the northern Stratford at Shirley, for The Boatmans Rest *isn't what it looks like, and is merely an off-licence and shop. The hefty-looking lift-bridge is fairly well used by road traffic, and is opened by using the lock windlass on the winch seen in the picture. You wind down the chain so that the top arm descends, while its opposite end takes the bridge up into the air. At fine weekends there is a good-sized audience of gongoozlers.*

RIGHT: The more famous and often-photographed example of the same type of bridge, this one at Wrenbury also carries a lot of road traffic, which must fume at times when the Llangollen boats are going through in procession. This also is opened by means of a handle, and there is a brake to prevent the bridge from dropping too quickly. There is a popular canal pub just down the road for the Llangollen-hunters who have time to pause.

ABOVE: From lift-bridges to swing-bridges. Many canal boaters miss this one, for though it carries traffic in and out of the village of Foxton, it isn't on the main line straddled by the famous locks. It's on the arm to Market Harborough which goes off at the bottom of that flight. This of course is where the broad canal went originally, before the link with the Grand Union was constructed from a point near Foxton. Like other swing bridges, this one requires a bit of brute force and bouncing up and down sometimes, before it will get itself moving. And it's also the usual game for the lone boater to be able to get on and off his boat to carry out the operation.

BELOW: This kind of swing bridge can be seen all along the Leeds and Liverpool, and comes almost too thick and fast at times. There are no records of how many cars, if any, have plunged into the canal at these bridges, but there are no barriers to put up to stop them, and the notice comes a bit late if it happens to be facing the car driver from the opposite side of the canal. This bridge is at Kildwick, well on the way into the moors, where there's an interesting church and Hall.

ABOVE: The swing bridge is swung, but what's this coming through? Obviously this isn't quite the Shropshire Union, or even the Grand Union, but in fact the Gloucester and Sharpness, which by-passes the Severn to Gloucester. There are 16 large swing bridges, each looked after by a bridge-keeper from an unusual little house. There's clearly a different type of traffic from that on most canals in this book, and since this one goes out to the tidal Severn at one end, normal canal cruisers aren't usually to be seen. But quite a few small boats capable of going to sea make use of the G & S.

LEFT: Still fewer canal boats—or boats of other kinds, in fact—make use of this canal, one of whose locks is shown on page 35. It is the Exeter Ship Canal, historically interesting as being one of the earliest canals in Britain. It also, incidentally, belongs to the City of Exeter, and if you ferret around you can find its terminus there. All its four bridges are swing bridges, and their span, wide enough for ships, must take a bit of moving.

15 Bridges of Water

IT NEVER SEEMS to strike anybody as odd that a road should now and again have to cross a river or a stream, but when a canal does this it gets people quite excited. You can see the look of astonishment, for example, on the faces of motorists dashing down to Stratford when they see a boat sailing over their heads at Wootten Wawen. And of course people come for miles just to look at the Pontcysyllte aqueduct.

I suppose it's because we usually expect water to be running along on the ground all the time, which is what streams and rivers must always do. But you can do anything with canals. If the diggers could push them through the middle of the Pennines, or through the quicksands of Braunston, they could equally lift them up above the land when necessary. And often, to keep the level, it indeed was necessary. Usually this meant embankments, and Telford especially was a bit of a lad for these, as he threw them across Shropshire, for example, during the building of the Birmingham and Liverpool Junction Canal.

But canals, like roads, were bound to keep meeting rivers and streams, and this was another occasion when they needed to be above the level of the land. Unlike roads, they couldn't just be diverted to the nearest existing crossing. They had to plough remorselessly on, keeping themselves level. And this almost always meant bridging a valley over the river down below.

Sometimes it might have been possible to run up the valley a little and cross on the same level as the water, but this might have led to all sorts of complications. It does happen at times, though. Perhaps the most interesting example is where the Trent and Mersey cuts across the Trent at Alrewas—but a fine old situation develops when the river is in flood. And even the quiet Cherwell, crossing the Oxford at both Aynho and Shipton (with those odd diamond-shaped locks alongside) can cause bother. On one occasion quite recently the Cherwell raised the level below Nell Bridge lock so much that hire boats couldn't get back under the bridge to their bases.

Usually, then, the builders took their canals over streams and rivers (and sometimes roads) on a bridge. There are many hundreds of these aqueducts, most of them not noticed either from the canal or from the land, since they may be across mere streams. But no canal book dare forget to mention the Pontcysyllte, and I mention it more than once. This is the aqueduct of all aqueducts, 1,007 feet long, and in one place 121 feet above the River Dee as the Llangollen Canal heads into north Wales. The water is in an iron trough, and there is a towpath on one side and apparently nothing at all on the other. If you haven't a head for heights, it's best to get off and walk down to the Dee and up again.

My own favourite is the Edstone, or Bearley, on the southern Stratford. This trough in fact is the second in length to the Pontcysyllte, though nothing like as high. Its towpath is below the trough, so you can walk along with the boat level by your nose. I am told—but have never seen it—that when the railway was put under at a later date, a convenient pipe was taken from the canal to fill the engines' water-tanks.

There are massive stone aqueducts over the Lune for the Lancaster, over the Etherow for the disputed Peak Forest at Marple, over the Bristol Avon in two places (one at present dry) for the Kennet and Avon, 23 arches over the Dove for the Trent and Mersey, a beauty over the Tame for the Coventry, and so on, and so on.

Somehow, however much you argue that

canal water-bridges are just as normal and natural as road-bridges, it's always quite an exciting occurrence to cross one. I can never resist, when reaching the Tame one at Tamworth, climbing on the old wartime pillbox and photographing some member of the crew driving across, with the piers of the aqueduct showing in the river below, and probably quite a bit of debris piled up against them.

Many aqueducts, such as the ones over the Sow and the Trent near Great Haywood, the little Yarningale one on the Stratford, the Shropshire Union crossing A5, and quite a number of the others already mentioned, are only just wide enough for a boat. So if there's a crosswind or a nervous steerer, the boat is bound to clonk its way from one end to the other. But if a boat hasn't been built to allow for a good deal of rubbing and clonking, it ought not to be on the canals anyhow.

I realise, suddenly, that I've put the most curious aqueduct of all in a different section. I've classified the Barton Swing aqueduct as a "movable bridge" elsewhere—which seems to prove that aqueducts are merely bridges after all, even though very intriguing ones.

The Lancaster is a curious canal, with its top end and its lonely locks now flattened by a motorway, its startling views across the sea, and its almost river-like appearance. This is the famous aqueduct on which it crosses the River Lune after turning sharply upstream. Having crossed, it then turns back again and runs through Lancaster on its way south to its terminus at Preston. The only way to get into the Lancaster except by land is from the sea at Glasson Dock. The aqueduct was built by Rennie, and looks rather like his former Waterloo Bridge in London.

ABOVE: This boat is crossing the low 23-arch aqueduct which Brindley built over the Dove near Burton-on-Trent. This is such a broad waterbridge that many boaters don't notice anything different about the channel, for the banks are quite wide and in summer all grown up. But over to the right is the old road-bridge over the same river, and beyond is the new fast present A38. This is the stretch of the Trent and Mersey which has passed through several broad locks, but which soon becomes narrow at Dallow Lane lock and onwards.

BELOW: Here, in contrast, you can see the characteristic narrowing of the waterway, as the Brecon and Abergavenny Canal crosses over a swift-flowing tributary of the Usk at Talybont. This is near the present limit of navigation, but county councils are now interested in this canal, and maybe it will be open the rest of the way north to Brecon in time. Footbridges at Talybont need freeing first, among other things. There are fine views over the Usk from this waterway, a small group of locks at Llangynidr, and a 375-yard tunnel, seen on page 106, not far north of them.

ABOVE: You can see how the towpath is level with the bed of the canal on the Edstone aqueduct, instead of being up by the water's edge as is more usual. This iron trough is a less spectacular crossing than the Pontcysyllte, for somehow you don't seem to be far out of touch with the ground beneath, and any minute you expect a train to scrape your keel. There are large notices asking boaters to reduce speed when crossing, and indeed it would be absurd to charge across this seemingly flimsy and narrow channel.

BELOW: A mini-aqueduct, perhaps? In this case it is neither over a river nor a road, but over a mere path at Cosgrove on the Grand Union, from one part of the village to another. Hardly any boater will realise that he's passing over a walking cyclist, but it saves people in the village from having to go round by the ornamental bridge shown on page 79. Cosgrove is quite a well-known playground, where people can have trips along the canal as well as many other holiday activities nearby.

ABOVE: The Leeds and Liverpool not only provides some of the fiercest built-up passages, but also some of the wildest scenery. Here it is well up in the moors, where it seeks out the small River Aire above Gargrave and crosses it on this solid aqueduct at Priest Holme. The river and canal then run fairly well together eastwards, and the canal crosses the Aire again below Bingley. In the end it runs into it in Leeds to follow the Aire and Calder Navigation.

BELOW: Here is one of my many photographs of the aqueduct near Tamworth. The Tame is underneath, and up stream the traveller sees some huge blocks of flats which now ruin the original view of Tamworth church. All of them can be seen for miles on the run down from Fradley to Fazeley. A little way beyond the aqueduct are the two locks at Glascote, and there are some very pleasant gardens running down from several houses on the way to Amington.

16 Junctions and Crossroads

Now and again, but not very often, you actually come to a junction as you travel along the canals. In a few cases you come to what could, at a pinch, be termed a cross-roads. There may or may not be any indication of where the waterways lead to, and without a good chart you may be at a loss.

For example, in the heart of Nottingham you may cheerfully go straight on to nowhere, when in fact you should have turned sharp right under a tangle of railways to find your way back to the Trent. And in the middle of Warwickshire, at Napton Junction, you may carry on blissfully straight ahead for Birmingham, and end up in Oxford, having omitted to turn ninety degrees to the right when you should have done.

Junctions vie with lock-flights as landmarks on a journey. Most of them, of course originated when one canal company met up with another, and in those days they would have a whole paraphernalia of toll offices and stop-locks. Stop-locks were either merely boat-traps, or water-gates, or both, and they eventually ended up by being more of a nuisance than anything. They stopped water running from the higher level canal to the lower one, on the grounds that one company wasn't going to give anything away to the other. And though sometimes the difference in level was only a few inches, stop-locks had to be built.

At the famous Worcester Bar in the middle of Birmingham there was at one time no connection between canals, forcing boats to unload into another company's boats. But since the canals were on the same level, it is now possible to sail straight through a gap. This has happened also at Marston Junction, where the Ashby Canal begins, and the stop-lock no longer functions.

Another famous junction, Hawkesbury, where the Oxford after various tribulations joined the Coventry, has a stop-lock with a rise of only six inches, and so has Autherley at the start of the Shropshire Union. But these locks have to be worked, of course, in the proper manner. And at Hawkesbury you will usually have an audience of professional narrow-boaters, for this was and still is a great meeting-place.

Junctions with rivers are often a different kettle of fish. With the Severn, for example, both the Worcester-Birmingham and the Staffs and Worcs link up via large basins and barge locks, at Worcester and Stourport respectively. There are smaller locks also at Stourport, but at Worcester even a tiny canal cruiser must proceed through the great pair of locks down to the river below. But at times the river can rise to cover the locks.

At Torksey the Fossdyke leaves the Trent via a lock which has extra protecting gates for extra high river-levels, and warning notices about boats dragging anchors. And at Salters Lode you can only get out of the Great Ouse into the Old Bedford when the tide makes a level. On the upper Trent, however, the junctions are milder, though the cross-roads with the Erewash on one side and the Soar on the other is a hive of boats on summer week-ends. A little further upriver the Trent and Mersey quietly takes off at another cross-roads, formed by the Derwent and a bend of the Trent.

Not all junctions have locks, of course, though most of them seem to have anglers. At Gayton the Northampton Arm leaves on the same level, heading for the Nene, and so does the Leicester Grand Union at Norton, apart from an awkward swing-bridge, heading off on a high embankment for the Watford staircase. At Barbridge, too, the useful link between Shropshire Union and Trent and Mersey goes off decently opposite the *Jolly*

Tar. But a little further south the Llangollen provides a rather striking contrast, for you face four locks in a row at Hurleston, with a connoisseur's collection of broken stonework and jagged bolts if you don't happen to steer in smoothly.

I suppose there are more waterway junctions altogether than there seem to be on first thought. But at three miles an hour they certainly don't crop up very often.

ABOVE: Some junctions are almost unobtrusive, like the Ashby Canal one at Marston. But others are strikingly marked, and as the boater threads through the open guillotine lock shown on page 24, he is faced by Kings Norton church and this isolated house beside the signpost. If he then turned right he would pass Cadbury's and Birmingham University and get into the warren of the B.C.N., and if he turns left he enters misty and 2726-yard long Wast Hill tunnel, on his way down the long slope of the Worcester-Birmingham Canal to the Severn.

BELOW: Between Buckby locks and Braunston tunnel these interesting canalside houses stand at Norton Junction, where the canal to Leicester goes off at the left of the picture. There is a swing-bridge immediately, and a high embankment before the Watford flight leads up to this canal's summit level. A few hundred yards along the towpath to the right there is usually quite a bustle of boats at the top lock, where A5 crosses the Grand Union.

There are two vastly different river junctions on this page. RIGHT: Here is one distant from the main canal system, but leading from the whole artificial network of the Middle Level drains over in the Fen country. This is the famous Salters Lode lock, where Well Creek connects with the tidal part of the Great Ouse, for a quick dash through Denver Sluice lock into the non-tidal part. There's trouble in the Creek, however, and boats can't reach the lock from the Middle Level side. Even when they can, it's necessary for the tide to make a level outside before the gates can be opened. A few yards to the right of this lock is another tidal lock into the Old Bedford River, at present the only way into the Level from the Ouse. The Middle Level is fascinating touring ground, but access tends to be precarious.

BELOW: This is a busier and more certain junction—the barge lock from the Stourport basins into the Severn. Stourport is still one of the exciting canal towns, and it was in fact created by the Staffs and Worcs Canal. Its basins and buildings are worth anybody's time to visit. Narrow boats leave for the Severn via narrower locks close alongside this barge lock, and they can go down the Severn and into the Worcester-Birmingham Canal, or further and into the Avon at Tewkesbury.

ABOVE: The split bridge here travels over the first lock of the southern Stratford canal. This area is an unusual kind of junction, because the Stratford comes close to the Grand Union for a short distance, and the lock on the far left is in fact on a short link between the two canals. So there is a kind of cross-roads here near Lapworth. The northern Stratford goes up to the Worcester-Birmingham, the southern to Stratford, and of course the G.U. is on its way from London to Birmingham. The National Trust canal office is just beyond the bridge here, and the intriguing restored canal winds from there down to Stratford.

BELOW: This is a junction no longer—Huddlesford, where the now-closed Wyrley and Essington canal used to leave the Coventry to the right of the picture. Its tail-end is now used as moorings. The front boat is about to pass through a narrow part where presumably tolls used to be taken. There's an interesting thing about this length of canal between Fradley and Fazeley junctions. The northern half of the eleven miles is officially Coventry Canal, but the gap between that and the Coventry proper is officially Birmingham and Fazeley, which is all to do with the Coventry people running out of money at one stage. But it all comes to the same thing now, and is a winding eleven lock-free miles from the industry of Tamworth to the rural stretches of the Trent and Mersey.

ABOVE: This must be the most non-rural junction outside London, and perhaps the most famous on the canal system. It is at the top of Farmers Bridge locks in the centre of Birmingham, where the boats from Gas Street and Worcester Bar come up to the Birmingham Main Line. It was tidied up considerably for a vast rally in 1969, and is a weird No-man's-land under which trains run. It is surprisingly lonely at times, yet it can almost be said to be the hub of the canal system. You can certainly head in a variety of directions within a few miles.

BELOW: Another non-rural junction, but also surprisingly quiet. This is at Wigan, after you have come down 21 heavy locks from the east on the Leeds and Liverpool, and been delighted to see a bit of commercial carrying going on to Wigan power station. An impressive signpost points the ways to Leeds, Liverpool and Manchester, and the branch which goes off here is in fact the Leigh branch, joining up with the Bridgewater canal and opening up the way to the south. After two locks, you have one of the longest level stretches of canal to be found anywhere.

ABOVE: Not easy to get at by land, but a well-known junction to boaters and anglers. Its bridge is scarred by boats which left the turn a little too late, for Napton junction is a confusing place. Boaters up the Grand Union from London suddenly find that they must turn smartly right instead of going straight on, if they want to get to Birmingham. And some of them don't quite make it. The quarter-mile from the junction to Calcutt locks passes extremely pleasant reservoirs inhabited by coots, moorhens, sailing yachts, anglers and swimmers.

BELOW: Looking a little forlorn in winter, this junction probably has cause to be. As a junction it is in suspense, because beyond the narrow boat in the picture are the delightful Marple locks, which unhappily can't be used. So the aqueduct beyond them, and the round journey via the Ashton to Manchester isn't possible until restoration of these stretches takes place. Under the bridge is the pleasant and rather exclusive Macclesfield canal, with its distant views from the hillsides, and behind my camera are the many moored boats at Marple, and the six mile stretch of the higher Peak Forest canal along another hillside to Whaley Bridge.

Here are two junctions with the Trent. ABOVE: First the formidable entrance to the old Roman Fossdyke leading to Lincoln, Boston and the Wash. The taller protective outer gates can be seen open, for this is in the tidal part of the Trent, though little normally reaches as far as Torksey. Through the lock the canal is a haven for small boats, which can be more troubled by the Trent barges than by the tide.

BELOW: The Trent is still broad at West Bridgford near Nottingham, and you can cruise under the bridge by the new hotel and alongside the boulevarde. But you can't continue up the Trent, and you must return and turn, as I'm doing in the picture, and go into the Nottingham Canal at Meadow Lane lock. This will then take you through the city and into the Beeston Canal before going back to the river. But this is one of the less salubrious canal stretches, and you'll be thankful to get into the Trent again. Almost opposite Meadow Lane the disused Grantham Canal leaves the river.

17 Cruising Underground

If you've ever tried to dig a large hole in the garden with a spade, and realised just how long it takes before you really feel you're getting anywhere, this frustrating exercise gives a good idea of the task facing the early canal diggers when they set out to make a tunnel. The vast machines digging a new London tube take long enough, but we can hardly imagine what a business it must have been with shovels, picks and wheelbarrows.

Again, how did the tunnel-diggers know where they were going to come out? Or if they started from opposite ends, how could they be sure they were going to meet in the middle? Problems such as this, as well as the sheer physical labour involved, faced men such as Brindley, but they overcame them.

There were plenty of people who didn't believe they would succeed with some of the first tunnels. Brindley's plans for Harecastle were laughed at by many, and though they did succeed, undoubtedly the tunnels were some of the most formidable tasks in the whole of canal-digging.

Most of our canals come to a tunnel sooner or later, and some tackle some daunting hills. To cross them by locks would have meant not only many more locks, with the delay this would cause boats, but also the job of finding water to put into the top level of the canal. Thus for various reasons a builder would make the decision to tunnel instead of continuing with locks.

The longer tunnels took years to build, and often the canal operated for some time beforehand, with loads having to be taken over the hill by horse or tramway to boats on the other side. Standedge Tunnel, on the closed Huddersfield Canal, is over three miles long, but the longest tunnel now in normal use is Blisworth, on the Grand Union. This wasn't finished until five years after the canal itself.

Before motors were invented, the only way of getting boats through most tunnels was to pull them through by chains, or push them along by " legging ", since there were often no towpaths. Legging was a fascinating contortion in which men lay down on special boards put out at the side of boats, and walked their way along the sides of the tunnel. This must have been a pretty strenuous activity in the many tunnels which were a mile or more long.

Nowadays, even with motors, going through a tunnel is an experience not easily forgotten. When you enter the longer ones, the far end is hardly visible, unless it is a very bright day. And in West Hill, at Kings Norton, it is even possible to reach the middle and not see either end if there is a mist inside. You need a headlamp, of course, and to help things along some of the tunnels produce torrents of water in places, especially where there are ventilating shafts. Then there are odd little stalactites, and slimy growths on some of the side walls, so that it's not surprising that most big tunnels are supposed to be haunted. The roar of the engine, and the eerie reflections of the headlamp from the water and the varied roof and walls cause many a canaller to look forward to the other end which is slowly—very, very slowly—creeping towards him.

Passing another boat can be quite a game, for there's usually only a few inches to spare. You see a light coming towards you, and of course nothing else. And it's almost certainly shining in your eyes, just as yours is shining in the other chap's eyes. Then suddenly a boat is there. And if the steerers have any sense both boats are pretty well stopped by then. The rather alarming part is if the oncoming boat turns out to be a pair of narrow boats one after the other, for passing them seems endless.

But the longest tunnel has an ending—unless your engine breaks down—and the tiny pinpoint eventually begins to frame a distant scene. So you come out like a cork from a bottle and into the world again.

Like everything else on the canals, tunnels vary greatly, from little short ones with a towpath each side like Newbold to knobbly sandstone ones that catch your boat where they shouldn't, from begirdered and bat-infested ones like Armitage, and sinking ones like Harecastle where you have to pass a height-gauge at the entrance, to ones with kinks in them like Braunston.

Here are a few of them.

Here is the tunnel-collector's mecca—Standedge, starting at the village of Diggle and running under the Pennines where the A62 climbs from Oldham over to Huddersfield. This canal is full of clear water in many places—some of its unusual sloping paddle-gear can be seen on page 28—but the locks are all closed and fixed, and only canoes and anglers can use it. It passes through even wilder scenery than the Leeds and Liverpool, and it is regrettable that it didn't survive the ownership of the railways. The 3 miles 125 yards of Standedge, as can be seen, is locked up, but it is rumoured that tunnel connoisseurs can sometimes obtain permission to explore it.

ABOVE: This is the view after slogging south through 2042 yards of tunnel at Braunston on the Grand Union. The headlamp used for the past 25 minutes or so is just visible at the bottom of the picture, and the distant pin-point has slowly grown until it becomes a curved picture-frame for the outside view. Another boat, prudently, is waiting after seeing the light in the tunnel. Braunston is on a summit level of the canal, between the six locks by Braunston village and the seven Buckby locks (one of which can be seen from the A5 road). It is a fairly dry tunnel with an odd kink in it.

BELOW: When is a tunnel hardly a tunnel? This one at pleasantly-named Drakeholes on the Chesterfield is only 154 yards long, and burrows under a crossroads by the Swan Hotel. Not far along the canal is Whitsunday Pie lock, named after a pie baked when the lock was first built. In the other direction is Gringley-on-the-Hill, the high point of North Nottinghamshire mentioned on page 46. By the tunnel is a useful slipway for boats to visit this canal, which is cut off from the rest of the system except via the tidal Trent.

ABOVE: The longest tunnel in normal use is Blisworth on the Grand Union, not far from Braunston. It is 3056 yards long, and starts about quarter of a mile from the Waterways' Museum at Stoke Bruerne top lock. Visitors to the Museum, like the one in the picture, can walk along the towpath and peer down the tunnel. But they are unlikely to see the end without a long neck, since the canal turns a slight bend into the tunnel. In any case, even a boat often finds the end invisible except on a bright day. Often there is a fair mist inside. Canoes are barred from all long tunnels for obvious reasons, and the injunction to keep right is a necessary one.

BELOW: Blisworth has a number of air vents which often produce torrents of water from springs in the ground above. The course of the tunnel can be followed by road because of the "chimneys" built for these vents, which stretch away into the distance. One is shown here, with another visible beyond it.

This tunnel was a long and weary job, and was one of those where the canal was finished on both sides first, with goods being taken over the hill.

ABOVE: This is a very civilised tunnel, which actually has a towpath both sides. It is at Newbold near Rugby, on the northern part of the Oxford Canal, which was very much straightened at one time from the originally winding waterway. In fact, if you moor the boat at Newbold to have a meal or a snack at one of the two pubs there, you can wander round to the churchyard and see the remains of a former tunnel. Like several tunnels, and large numbers of bridges, there's a bend in the canal not far from the far end, so that you can't see approaching boats. Continuing round Rugby, the canal passes on several aqueducts over rivers and roads.

BELOW: That mighty waterway which is the last remaining route over the Pennines—the Leeds and Liverpool—had to have its tunnel. And though it can't measure up to Standedge, and it didn't quite make the mile but stopped short at 1640 yards, Foulridge is quite a spectacular place to see. It is three miles from Nelson, and half a mile from the top lock of the Barrowford Flight. Its fame lies not as usual with a ghost, but with a cow which once swam through, and lived to tell the tale after a dose of brandy. Here, as so often on the Leeds and Liverpool, the great stones used for construction look as if they will last for ever.

LEFT: The Brecon and Abergavenny Canal, as we have seen, is an isolated canal with no link with the rest of the system. The 375-yard tunnel at Ashford looks almost unnecessary, and certainly a little apologetic, but the canal itself has some spectacular views of mountains, and a 25-mile level stretch without locks. A lot of work has been done to open up this canal, especially by local authorities, and people from as far away as London keep their boats here, at least for a season or two.

BELOW: Blisworth may be the wettest and the longest in normal use, but Harecastle is undoubtedly the most memorable tunnel. The original tunnel—now very much sunken and to be seen at the side of the present one—was one of the first long tunnels in the world. It was of course built by Brindley, and the present one built by Telford is almost two miles long but already sagging in the middle. It has a towpath which has disappeared in places, and now one-way traffic is worked, so that you have to watch the notice-boards at the entrance. To add to the weirdness of it all, the water here is almost blood-red, and all around are the space-age buildings of the Potteries, which after all played a very big part in starting off the whole canal system of the country.

The gauge at the southern entrance, seen in the photograph, shows how low the roof in the middle now is.

18 Notices, Numbers, Mileposts and Bollards

AMONG THE minor furniture along the waterways, intriguing items crop up. Many old names and notices must have vanished, though a few have been salvaged for the Museum at Stoke Bruerne. But every mile or two there may still be something to see, whether bright and newly painted or hidden in the nettles.

Mileposts and stones are now perhaps the rarest, which is a pity, for some of them are very pleasant shapes. The Leeds and Liverpool ones are too much like road milestones, but the Shropshire Union few are colourfully unusual—aesthetically better, perhaps, than the equally unusual but knobbly Trent & Mersey's. The old Grand Junction plates along the route to Leicester, when anyone remembers to paint them, are simple and informative, but the Brecon and Abergavenny doesn't seem to have been able to afford more than mere numbers.

There's many a mile along the system, however, with no milepost left, and the most you can usually hope for is an indication at junctions. Some of the upright boards used for this purpose are odd, though, especially when one arrow points straight down to the bed of the canal. The most sensible indicators are straightforward finger-posts such as the one at Kings Norton. And the signs that cause canal travellers to make cynical remarks are the beautiful and expensive-looking ones put up by British Waterways to announce to passing railway travellers the name of the canal.

Number-plates, of course, are used for various purposes, the chief being to identify bridges. And mighty useful these are, as has already been mentioned. The road traveller, with his wealth of signposts and town and village names, and other ways of knowing exactly where he is, cannot imagine what it is like to travel along a canal. For miles there may be no village or even building, and only a skilled map-reader could decide where he was without the bridge numbers. These are shown in the various canal books, and are really the only way of reading the route being followed.

Most bridge numbers are pleasant little oval ones, painted in British Waterways blue and yellow, but there are more elaborate ones such as you find on the Llangollen, and many of the blue-and-white ones on the Leeds and Liverpool have letters of the alphabet tacked on the numbers, as if a lot of bridges were built as afterthoughts. In some places you will find bridge numbers missing where bridges have vanished, and on the north Oxford whole batches have gone. But in this case they belonged to bridges on the many big curves long since straightened.

On the odd bit of the Birmingham-Fazeley which they built for the ailing Coventry Canal Company, bridges have names, now sadly rusting. But the highlight of named bridges comes on the Staffordshire and Worcestershire, where large oval plaques announce Giggety Bridge and Bumblehole Bridge and many more.

Lock numbers were no doubt at one time another way of reading the route, but they are unfortunately disappearing and not being replaced. There are still quite a few left, though, either numbering the locks in sequence along a canal, or numbering them in flights or staircases as at Grindley Brook. Lock names, too, still occur quite often, if frequently fading and tottering. And it is a pity that Greenberford and Red Bull and Wheaton Aston and Gothersley and Falling Sands and Double Rail and The Odd Lock and The Big Lock and the rest of the fascinating names can't be perpetuated more solidly before they vanish from memory.

Canal notices are usually more mundane and less intriguing, and there are no longer any threatening transportation or other dire penalties—though there are modern reminders that the public are not supposed to use the towpath or toss their old cars in the cut. There are vital ones for canal travellers about closing paddles (and it is high time that there were more about closing gates, too!). A sensible one at Grindley Brook points out that the term " drop ", when applied to paddles, shouldn't be taken literally, or something will soon break. A few more such notices about winding the paddles down as well as up might save many repairs.

There are pleasant notices at water-taps telling you where the next ones are, occasional notices of special interest such as the commemorative ones on the southern Stratford, the Kennet and Avon, and at Limekiln Lock in Leicester, and of course the more widely-known notices stuck on canal bridges all over the country. The solid, everlasting letters, with their warning about " the ordinary traffic of the district ", look a bit quaint now against the monstrous juggernauts thundering around the roads—especially as nobody takes any notice of what it says on the bridges.

What else? Well, especially if you poke about in the undergrowth, you may unearth long-standing items. There are initials, boundary-marks, and so on, like the little " S.W.C." lurking at Tixall Lock, and the many G.J.C.'s around the Grand Union system. What does " DIS " mean on the Oxford (or is it " D/S "?)? What is the " S & W " next to the " H.C.C." at the end of the Huddersfield Canal in Ashton?

Finally in this jumble-sale, bollards. Wherever you go you'll find bollards for mooring, and there's even something to read on some of these, at least on the southern Stratford. But most of them are speechless, and there aren't enough of them. Many a canaller has longed at times for something like the metal Ten-ton Tessies found at the corners of the Nene locks. Some simple concrete ones have been put up recently in many places, and some of them as promptly pulled out of the ground by careless boaters. But the real beauties are the remaining wooden ones (and even some metal ones seen on the Leeds and Liverpool) which have been given incredible shapes by the chafing of generations of ropes. Some of them still hang on grimly, and might well fetch a fortune in a sale of modern sculpture.

Here's a mixed bag of canal notices gathered up and down the country.

ABOVE: There aren't quite enough of these for some people, and many similar notices use the word "drop", which doesn't mean in canal language what it means in ordinary language. But at Grindley Brook (and also, I recall, at Napton on the Oxford) somebody has been wise enough to make the paddle-lowering operation clear. The other notice, on a metal lock-beam at Stoke Bruerne, is quite a common one, but it might well add the closing of gates to the closing of paddles these days.

ABOVE: Not quite the same as the meticulous water-tap notices on the Grand Union, these—also at Grindley Brook—nevertheless make their point. Some taps tend to lurk unmarked in obscure places (or, as at Glascote, to dribble slowly), but there are always plenty of them along the route.

RIGHT: Two notices on the Kennet and Avon, better preserved than the canal itself. The forbidden horses are at Newbury, by the well-used lock, and the tablet to John Blackwell is on the busy main road bridge outside Devizes. Unlike the Newbury section, however, the canal below John Blackwell is unusable, being the magnificent flight of 29 locks which will be a major item of restoration.

This modern notice speaks for itself, and describes an operation which was the forerunner of others still going on, including the vast Kennet and Avon project.

RIGHT: The Shropshire Union—one of the last canals to be completed—saw the railway threat and tried to combat it by building straight, and then by making itself a railway company as well. It also produced many notices which still exist, such as this one near the Hurleston locks at the beginning of the Llangollen.

RIGHT: A later railway notice—this time after railway take-overs. This unexpected canal warning suggests the presence of boats from tidal or river navigations, and this is in fact the case. It appears on the side wall of the entrance to Torksey lock from the Trent to the Fossdyke, shown on page 100.

BELOW: Lock names still remain in some places, though more often just at the top and bottom of flights. Usually they are in yellow and blue, but on the Worcester-Birmingham a pleasant green background is found. Tolladine is well on the way to the Severn.

Notices on bridges, of course, are usually for the benefit of the road users, and may not be visible from the canal.

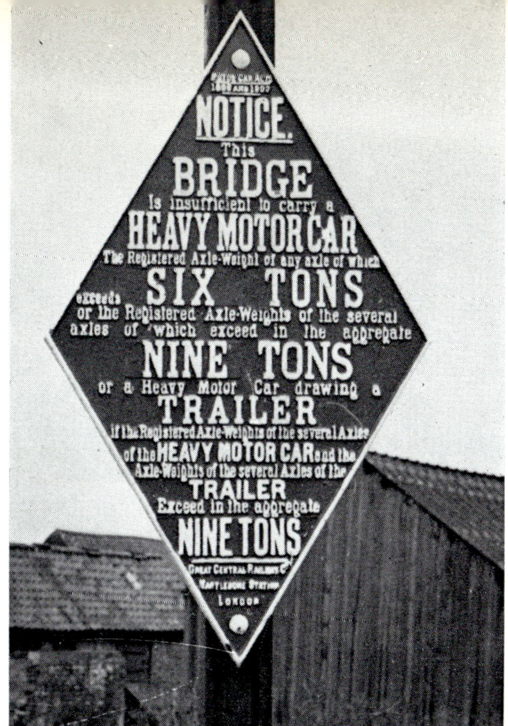

LEFT: The most common, of course, is this diamond-shaped notice, which travellers are presumably supposed to read as they flash over the hump-back, sounding their horns furiously.

The Shroppie doesn't commit itself to tonnages, but rather rashly talks about the "ordinary traffic of the district", whatever that may mean these days.

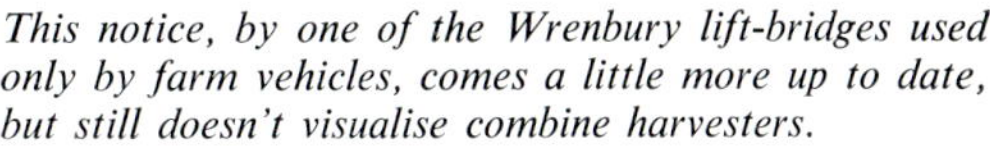

This notice, by one of the Wrenbury lift-bridges used only by farm vehicles, comes a little more up to date, but still doesn't visualise combine harvesters.

At Sheering Mill lock on the Lee Navigation, the public must often take risks, for many a car weighs more than the limit put on this road bridge by Mr Hobday.

RIGHT: The recent shattering increase in lorry sizes and weights has forced authorities to take action, and these new notices have appeared everywhere. But will they work?

From one end of the canals to the other there are numbers, and as already mentioned, the bridge numbers in particular are extremely useful. Most of them are simple blue and yellow plates, like this one on the Aylesbury arm of the Grand Union, which drops through 16 locks to the basin which is now a busy boatyard.

The Leeds and Liverpool numbers, in blue and white, seem more striking than the others. They often have letters of the alphabet appended, like this one near the Oddy locks in Leeds.

Older and rather more solid, which perhaps befits the stones it is mounted on, this number on a road bridge at Trevor gazes out at the Pontcysyllte aqueduct, and must have many a tale to tell.

The Staffs and Worcs believed in going to town a little over its bridges, and gave them names as well as numbers. Many of the name-plates remaining could do with painting, however.

Here and there locks also are numbered on balance-beams, though often the numbers merely refer to a few locks in a flight rather than to a succession along the canal. This is the top lock of the Grindley Brook staircase.

ABOVE LEFT: There are quite a few of these attractive blue and white mileposts scattered up the Shropshire Union, starting with the one at Autherley junction which faces travellers as they turn in under the attractive bridge. This one is in the Audlem flight of locks.

ABOVE: There's one at Shardlow itself, 92 miles from Preston Brook, and others here and there up the Trent and Mersey. This one is near to Great Haywood junction where the Staffs and Worcs canal leaves.

LEFT: In among the towns along the western Leeds and Liverpool, this milepost is near Nelson. It looks more appropriate to a road, but nevertheless is welcome to boaters coming from the summit level down the seven Barrowford locks.

BELOW LEFT: "Grand Union" and "Grand Junction" are names that have swapped around a bit in their time, but all are now in the present Grand Union system. This old metal Grand Junction post is at the Watford flight on the Leicester main line. There's a similar one near the Museum at Stoke Bruerne, showing 20 miles from Braunston.

BELOW: More recently British Waterways have put up pleasant signposts such as this, where the Stourbridge canal leads off from the Staffs and Worcs near oddly-named Stewponey lock. There's a similar one at Kings Norton junction, and one at Farmers Bridge junction shown on page 98.

LEFT: Bollards at lock-sides have almost vanished, and boaters must rely on their own strength, though British Waterways have put some up outside the lock entrances. This gnarled lock veteran in the Atherstone flight looks set for another few years if the hooligans let it alone, for pleasure-boat ropes can hardly have the same effect as those of heavily laden narrow boats.

ABOVE LEFT: Way down among the sandstone in the southern part of the Staffs and Worcs is another wooden veteran, not looking quite as fit, perhaps, as its Atherstone colleague. But you never know.

ABOVE: This must be the healthiest-looking of the lot, though some of the Warwickshire Grand Union ones might rival it. It is at Lock 86 at Wigan on the Leeds and Liverpool, just before the end of the long flight down. The rope-grooves are remarkable on a metal bollard.

LEFT: Not a bollard, but a common sight and reminder of the power of generations of ropes. This bridge-protector is near the Globe *not far from Bletchley, but there are many similar corner-posts, some much more deeply grooved by tow-ropes of the past.*

19 Pubs by the Water

EVERY NOW AND AGAIN you pick up a magazine containing a sentimental article about canal travel. I sometimes wonder who writes these articles, and whether they have ever left their own firesides. For the canals they describe don't seem to have any connection with mine. Their boats are always " barges ", and you half expect them still to be pulled by horses. And of course they're always stopping at " typical canalside inns " and swapping tales with gnarled boatmen.

Well, sad as it is, most of this just doesn't happen any more, though they certainly have the right idea when they say how pleasant canal travel is. But whether there is any longer such a thing as a " typical canal pub " is very doubtful (though there are still a few gnarled boatmen about). A pub now, despite the growth of pleasure-boating, would be hard pressed to make its living entirely from the waterways. Like many of the lock houses, the pubs which were remote from roads have faded away, and those near to a road have had to turn their attention to the customers on wheels.

Many, however, have not thrown aside entirely their canal backgrounds, and with sympathetic landlords they are beginning to become canal pubs again, if of a new kind. Such pubs take the trouble to build moorings for boats, and to provide a lively waterway atmosphere. But others, even where they have old canal quays alongside, almost ignore boaters, and deserve to be ignored by them.

Where once the commercial boatmen moored for refreshments or for the night, or picked up his leggers for some tunnel, the pleasure boats now moor thickly in summer (though with pubs such as the *Anchor* near Shebdon on the Shroppie, one wonder what happens in winter). Up and down the country the watery names abound. *Navigation, Boat, Anchor, Bridge, Barge, Fisherman*—there are many of each. Regular travellers know them. There's a little *Bridge* not far from Burton on the Trent & Mersey, where I once borrowed a bicycle to visit the nearby shops. The *Napton Bridge* on the Oxford provides useful meals. There are *Boats* at Stockton, Loughborough, Stoke Bruerne, Thrupp, the middle of the B.C.N. main line, and plenty of others (and *Two Boats* at Long Itchington). I can think of *Navigations* at Bedworth and Gnosall and Wootten Wawen, *Anchors* at Salterforth and the aforementioned one on the Shroppie, a *Fishermans Rest* on the Erewash and the *Boatmens Rest* on the northern Stratford which isn't a pub any more but will sell you refreshment for consumption off the premises, as the saying goes.

And now my mind is really steaming along, there's a *Sloop* and a *Steam Packet* in the heart of Lincoln, a watery name which I've forgotten alongside that narrow bit of the Middle Level just before Ashline, another *Packet* at Misterton on the Chesterfield, a *Waterside* at Mountsorrel on the Soar. I'm not so sure whether the *Jolly Tar* at Barbridge junction can be called a genuine canal name, and the *Rock of Gibraltar* on the Oxford and the *Cape of Good Hope* near Warwick look a bit out of place. And surely the *Britannia* at Thrupp has got the wrong kind of water to be alongside?

But attractive as it may be, they don't have to have watery names, and the *Red Lion* at Cropredy, the *Plum Pudding* at Armitage, the *Great Western Arms* at Aynho, and dozens of others also offer hospitality to waterborne customers. And the *Red Lion* at Crick, though it's half a mile from the cut, just oozes canal atmosphere. And hang it, I nearly forgot the friendly *Malt Shovel* at Shardlow.

One interesting development is the growing provision of simple meals. Canal cruising is really no fun for the first mate if she merely takes her cooking and washing up with her. And if you can tie up at the end of the day near to a pub which realises this, you'll be a canal family for life. This sometimes takes a bit of organising, for there are large empty spaces along the canal (which of course some boaters prefer). But maybe one day somebody will start a *Good Food Guide* to the canals, and tell us the places which provide cordon bleu cookery (or at least scampi and chips—even if, as usual these days, they're frozen in the first place).

Well, look for your gnarled boatmen by all means. But you're far more likely to find an I.W.A. flag, Stratford Canal maps for sale, teacloths with Gailey tower on them, and photographs of the Dolphin 24 which the landlord keeps moored outside. And you may well have to share all this with a large coach party of all the people you thought you'd left behind.

Never mind, you can always cast off and they've vanished.

Almost certainly No. 1 canal pub, despite the main road trade too, the Rose and Castle *at Braunston is aptly named, and it has its own long moorings (which many pubs don't trouble to have), crowded with boats in summer. The extensive Blue Line harbour is near by. Boats from all directions—six, in fact, within a few miles—converge on Braunston, which has been the canal hub of England for very many years.*

LEFT: Probably this is the best known of all the Boat *inns in different parts of the country, for it faces the popular Waterways' Museum at Stoke Bruerne. Thus it is seen by large numbers of people not on boats, as well as by the large number of boaters who plough the Grand Union. It doesn't seem to get spoilt, all the same, and with its thatch looks as natural as it must have looked long ago. It stands just above the top lock of the Stoke flight, and the boat in the foreground is one of the museum exhibits in a natural setting. Although the pub has kept unspoilt bars, it caters for boaters also with a small shop and a cafe.*

BELOW: Thirty miles and 26 locks nearer to Birmingham, the Two Boats *welcomes boaters pausing for breath at the bottom of the Stockton flight, after another* Boat *at the top, and the* Blue Lias *part way down. I recall two or three years ago mooring outside the* Two Boats *and having a pleasant meal served in the cockpit by the landlady, and it included home-made blackberry pie. There's a longer pound ahead, but locking isn't over by any means, and a formidable collection of locks is still to come before Birmingham.*

ABOVE: An unusual pub with an unusual name on an unusual waterway. This is said to be an old word for a peewit or plover, and the pub stands in splendid isolation on the Fossedyke as it nears Lincoln on its way from the Trent. It's an eerie waterway to travel on, with little to be seen over the banks in places, and only Saxilby, with its awkward slanting railway bridge, to break the journey. All the same, this old Roman canal is certainly worth a visit, and there's little danger of overcrowding on its broad straight stretches. The Pyewipe *is in fact accessible by road on a quiet lane.*

BELOW: There's nothing isolated about the Fisherman's Rest, *and it is probably almost overwhelmed in summer at weekends. It stands at a very busy boating spot where the Erewash Canal leaves the Trent, and almost opposite the Soar coming in. There are sailing clubs, canoeists, swimmers, and every imaginable river and canal boat buzzing round at times. So of course there are gongoozlers, and when you go through the lock you are likely to have an audience, at least at weekends. The Erewash is an interesting canal which nearly connected over the hills to the north-west once. It is in danger of closure, and anyone passing this spot should try to travel up it.*

LEFT: It's surprising that there aren't more pubs by this name, and in fact it's the only one I've found so far. It's by Wolverley lock on the Staffs and Worcs, a couple of miles after the traveller northwards has passed through the small canyon in Kidderminster. There's some delightful country around this pub, with steep wooded hills and sandstone cliffs—some of them right alongside your boat. This southern stretch has an entirely different character from the more open country beyond Autherley.

BELOW: Still seeking out watery names, this particular Anchor *is in a bleaker spot than the lush surroundings of the* Lock. *It looks as solid as the bridges and locks on the Leeds and Liverpool on which it stands. It is on the summit level, and only a few bridges away from 1640-yard Foulridge tunnel, whose other end is seen on page 105. The* Anchor *is a handy stop for Salterforth and its shops.*

LEFT: Beyond this unusual sign on the Birmingham to Stratford road at Wootten Wawen is the cast-iron aqueduct mentioned on page 89, a small canal basin, and the Stratford Canal, and of course the pub itself. There's a friendly welcome for canallers, and a pleasant mooring for the shops up the road, or for fuel the other way. There are usually anglers sharing the basin, and the busy traffic on the road will be almost the last sign of civilisation before the lonely drop down to Stratford.

BELOW: This one might rival the Rose and Castle *for the "best-known canal pub" title, for people from many directions pass it where the tail-end of the Coventry joins the Trent and Mersey at Fradley junction. The towpath has been widened to enable cars to reach it, and there's a caravan camp behind, but the place still remains very much of a canal pub. There are always plenty of boats about, as canallers from the south often take this route to avoid Birmingham.*

20 Looking for Landmarks

ALTHOUGH I seem to have looked at everything imaginable on canals, from locks to pubs, from boats to tunnels, and from lift-bridges to weirs, there's still a whole collection of other waterway sights well known to regular boaters. Some of them are integral parts of the canals, such as the interesting buildings at Stourport or the embankment at Weedon. Others may have no connection with the canals at all.

They all belong to the changing panorama as you look around you. Some are some distance away, but all of them are associated very clearly with some part of the canal system.

The first one that springs to my mind is a curiously shaped mast—said to be a radar mast—which dominates one section of the Oxford Canal on its summit level. Not only is it an unusual shape, but it moves about in a remarkable fashion. One minute it's exactly in front of you, and a little later it is behind you. Then it's off to the left or the right. Needless to say, it is firmly embedded in the ground, and this odd illusion is entirely Mr. Brindley's fault for taking eleven miles to travel about four, as he wandered around the contours in the Wormleighton area.

There are two other landmarks near the Oxford. One is the well known and much photographed old windmill on top of Napton Hill, standing guard over the flight of locks which are so many people's first taste of narrow canal locking. The other is the collection of masts at Hillmorton on the Northern Oxford, where you may pause and count them while working through the three pleasant twin locks which are the only ones between Braunston and Hawkesbury.

Masts of one kind or another overlook many canals, and the new odd-shaped Post Office towers do their share of this now. There's one often in view from the southern Oxford, and another on Cannock Chase looks down on the Staffs and Worcs, and can also be seen coming down the Shroppie.

Then of course there are buildings. That striking black-and-white one, for example, that actually sits across the entrance to the Witham where the Fossdyke ends in Lincoln; the tall house all on its own (pictured on page 95) where the Stratford Canal creeps through the upraised guillotine into the Worcester-Birmingham; the weird space-fiction buildings of the salt works at Stoke Prior; and the Shakespeare Memorial Theatre at Stratford, which suddenly springs into being as you emerge from the tunnel-like passage under the main road.

And churches, of course, everywhere. Nothing, perhaps, to match the River Nene, with churches always in sight both sides along the foothills, or that lonely-looking church at Marnham seen from the Trent. But there's Braunston spire popping up as you come under Bridge No. 100 travelling south. There's Brewood pointing up on your right as you plod up the Shropshire Union. Weedon's tower astonishes boaters by appearing with its top almost at water-level. And both Worcester and Coventry cathedrals are landmarks to boats entering the basins in those cities.

Some canals have hills rising over them as landmarks. And because of the canal pace the traveller has plenty of time to contemplate them. I have yet to see a hill meander about like Bredon does from the Warwickshire Avon, but the Leeds and Liverpool gives you plenty of time to examine the Pennines. From the Shroppie embankments you can see across towards Wales, with the Wrekin standing out clearly. And of course the Llangollen clings to one hillside above the Dee and enables you to look across at the opposite hills. Oddly, my favourite hill is an artificial one—that gaunt red mini-mountain as you approach Polesworth from the north. It's a relic of mining, and it's deserted and moon-like enough to send a shiver up the spine.

I suppose all canal-users have their own particular landmarks. Maybe it's the sandstone cliffs of the southern Staffs and Worcs, or the grim stone chimneys of Blackburn, or the long narrow bridge over the Soar where it comes into the canal at Kings Lock, or maybe the oddly similar one at Great Haywood over the Trent. There are Ernie Thomas's roses at Calf Heath, the cement works at Shipton-on-Cherwell, the brickwork chimneys at Whittlesey on the Middle Level, the sea of duckweed at the entrance to the Erewash, the blood-red water of the Coventry near Nuneaton, and some of those fascinating bridges in the Black Country, such as the one at Tipton, and the motto-ed one at the top of the Wolverhampton flight of twenty-one.

I could go on for ever, and anyone else could do the same with an entirely different list. For these things don't flash by like the landmarks along the roads. They creep up slowly, turn themselves around, stand still a while, then gradually retreat. And some of them—a surprising number—stay in the memory.

Leeds and Liverpool travellers near Keighley look up at Silsden Moor towering above them. In this picture Silsden Moor returns the compliment underneath sharply descending electricity cables. With the aid of binoculars the walker on the moor can make out one of the famous Leeds and Liverpool swing bridges, and it's a fascinating sight to watch boats creeping along this ribbon so far below.

ABOVE: Apart from lock cottages, few other houses stand facing the canal in the way that the Thames, for example, is lined with plush properties. But here and there, as if by accident, the occasional house appears with its garden running down to the canal bank. Sometimes, even, new ones have been built. In Rugeley and Amington, whole rows of gardens enhance the canal side. And at Acton Trussell and Colwich I remember gardens with their own moorings. The striking house in the picture is at the end of the Weedon embankment on the Grand Union, and must have some fine views of the traffic. Just beyond it the church tower manages to peep above the water level.

RIGHT: Another house, but an ancient one this time, on the bridge over the Witham in Lincoln—often called the "Glory Hole". The Fossdyke in fact ends on the other side of the bridge in the picture, in Brayford Pool, where the Witham flows in from the left. There is an unexpected and awkward swing bridge there, which at times seems to carry most of the traffic in Lincoln, and which will stop you in your tracks if you hope to get through it after seven in the evening. The Fossdyke and Witham Navigation is a little off the beaten track, and to get there the canal traveller has to tackle a little of the tidal Trent.

ABOVE: Braunston spire beckons the boater coming from three different directions. He faces it as he emerges from Braunston tunnel and works down the six locks there; it appears from Bridge 100 when coming from Birmingham or Oxford; and it stands out perhaps most clearly of all when cruising down the northern Oxford Canal from Hillmorton. There is also the remains of a windmill which will soon come into view, but there are no longer any sails.

BELOW: The Birmingham Canal Navigations, which the cynic might believe run entirely past the backs of revolting factories, in fact provide some extensive open views at times. But soon after Coseley tunnel and Deepfields junction, there is a rather terrifying sight looming up—this cross between Cape Kennedy and the father of all Meccano sets. I bracket it in my landmark mind with that tar distillery on the Staffs and Worcs, and cruise past with my collar turned up. But it may be perfectly harmless—who knows?

ABOVE: The locks at Bratch on the Staffs and Worcs have already been mentioned, though not shown. They remain in the memory not only because of the curious short pounds between locks, which can get you into difficulties in disposing of the water, but also because of this striking eight-sided toll-house which marks the spot. Sometimes, too, this landmark is enhanced by helpings of what looks like candy floss blowing around the waterway, but which turns out to be rather grubby detergent froth.

BELOW: Further north on the same canal is another memorable sight, which though not literally a "landmark" is certainly unusual. After a rather narrow and weedy few miles, you suddenly come on Tixall Broad, where we saw a small cruiser moored on page 65. The canal widens in a curious fashion to form a wide, deep lake which, though not measuring up to any Norfolk Broad, is a great change from the usual canal scene. It isn't easy to moor along the bank, but if you can manage it you'll have a peaceful night, with a strange architectural folly across the field to keep you company. Cannock Chase piles up above you, and shortly the canal will cross the Trent and join the Trent and Mersey.

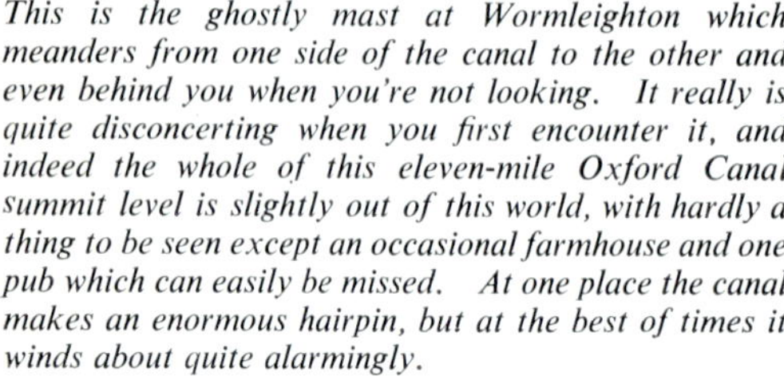

This is the ghostly mast at Wormleighton which meanders from one side of the canal to the other and even behind you when you're not looking. It really is quite disconcerting when you first encounter it, and indeed the whole of this eleven-mile Oxford Canal summit level is slightly out of this world, with hardly a thing to be seen except an occasional farmhouse and one pub which can easily be missed. At one place the canal makes an enormous hairpin, but at the best of times it winds about quite alarmingly.

And the last picture in this book, perhaps appropriately, shows Nike Three *on its way home from a late winter journey, lying at the bottom of a lock under a whole collection of landmark masts. These are those of the Post Office radio station at Hillmorton, and they can be seen for long distances from the various main roads, railways and canals in this area. This lock is in fact the same one in which* Nike Two *is sitting in the picture on page 12, but in this case seen from the other end.* Nike Three *will shortly rise up and proceed the last few miles to tie up at her regular mooring. Which is as good a way as any to end this book.*

Index of Photographs

(by canals)